INTERNATIONAL THEATRE REVIEW

Volume 10   Number 39-40

THE END OF AN ARTISTIC ERA? Julian Hilton

Executive Editor & Founder CAV. ROBERT RIETTY
Editors JOHN CALDER, DAVID ROPER
Issue Editors JULIAN HILTON, STEVE GOOCH
Production CHRIS DAVIDSON
Designer CHRISTOPHER CRESEY
SUBSCRIPTION RATES: Sterling 4 issues £9.00
USA: $15.00
Canada: $19.50

Manuscripts to be considered for publication may be submitted
but these can only be returned if a stamped addressed envelope
or sufficient postage in International Reply Coupons is enclosed.

Correspondence should be addressed to GAMBIT, 18 Brewer Street,
London W1R 4AS.

Fassbinder: Katzelmacher: © Verlag der Autoren, Frankfurt am Main
                            1970
Roth, Klavierspiele: © Verlag der Autoren, Frankfurt am Main 1981
Müller, Der Auftrag: © Henschelverlag, Berlin/DDR 1981 und ©Verlag
                        der Autoren, Frankfurt am Main 1980
Kroetz, Heimarbeit: © Franz Xaver Kroetz 1971
Turrini, Josef und Maria: © Thomas Sessler Verlag, Wien, 1980
Hacks, Jahrmarktstag: ©Aufbour Verlag, Ost Berlin/Claasen Verlag,
                        Düsseldorf 1973
Gahl, Intensivstation: ©Christoph Gahl 1980
Müller, Flotsam: ©Harald Müller 1974, rights with author.

These translations ©as follows:
Cock Artist, Home Work, Flotsam ©Steve Gooch 1982
Piano-Play ©Estella Schmid 1982
Josef and Maria: ©David Roger 1982
Market Day: ©Julian Hilton 1982
The Mission ©Stuart Hood 1982
Intensive Care © Anthony Vivis 1981, 1982

©in this edition John Calder (Publishers) Ltd., 1982

Subsidised by the
ARTS COUNCIL OF
GREAT BRITAIN

ALL RIGHTS RESERVED

ISSN 0016-4283

This double issue: ISBN 0 7145 3909 0

Photographs have been kindly loaned by Theater Heute magazine.

Typeset by Gilbert Composing Services, Leighton Buzzard, in 9 point Press Roman
Printed in Great Britain by Hillman Press, Frome.

EDITORIAL
Steve Gooch, Julian Hilton

Since the mid-60s a new generation of German-language playwrights has
grown up, highly successful on German-language stages but little known
elsewhere. The purpose of this volume is to present a selection of plays—
written in the last ten years or so—to exemplify the sort of work that is
going on. In making our selection we have had two priorities in mind: that
the works should be offered in accurate and actable translations; and that
the plays make clearer to the English audience what the current preoccupations of German theatre are. While English plays achieve continued and
lasting success in Germany, there is only a trickle of new work coming
the other way, we being seemingly content with our somewhat question-
able versions of Brecht and the set-book suitability of writers like Frisch
and Durrenmatt. Part of the difficulty German writers have in breaking
through is the traditional suspicion of the Anglo Saxon stage to political
theatre. Part is sheer ignorance.

The central aesthetic problem for the German writer is getting away
from Brecht, or at least coming out from under his shadow. The plays we
have chosen illustrate strategies for doing so. At the same time, the most
successful writers have been able to use the teachings of the Master without
being swamped by them.

Our choice has fallen on shorter plays for the most part in order to
accommodate as many authors as possible. There are many, just as challenging we have left out. In due course we hope we may be able to print some
longer works, of which there are a great many waiting to be taken up.

FOUR WALLS
Julian Hilton

Ever since John F. Kennedy told Berlin 'Ich bin ein Berliner', Berlin has
been an emblem of the Western mind, or perhaps one should say
Kennedy's sentence made this state explicit. Still a city run officially by
the 'four powers', but one which is squabbled over more than most, in its
divided nature it acts as a permanent reminder of the fragility of peace
and the stupidity of war. But Berlin has not just one wall—that which
divides East from West, the Curtain which separates, in popular mythology

at least, the free from the captives. Berlin has four walls, which symbolise the present state of German culture—and here I do not mean solely the culture of the Federal Republic. Four issues, four walls, are of particular importance: between democracy and communism; between the National Socialist past and the present; between the states and their alternatives; and between the guest- or disadvantaged native-worker and the political and financial establishment. The sense of a growing alienated group, which now includes a large section of the under 25s as well, is causing growing concern on both sides of the Wall and may turn out to be the most important wall of all.

Any wall raises the question of who is inside, who out. Hadrian's wall probably protected the barbarians from the Romans as much as the Empire from invasion. The great Wall of China was built more to keep the Chinese in, and uninfected by outside influence, than to stop any enemy invading. Yet the walled city, and even more the walled garden also has a central place in European culture, the *hortus inclusus*, where tales are told and where the outside world, be it the plague or the peasantry are forgotten. Berlin as a city, especially the Western sector, has something of the atmosphere of a walled garden, where growth takes place at unusual speed and has unusual fragility. As one comes off the East German motorway there is fun city staring at one in all its plastic splendour, capitalism at its very worst: or perhaps not quite—the souvenir kiosks on the Wall itself take that honour. But such crass contrasts are common. Only a few metres from the now collapsed concert hall of the Berlin Philharmonic are the mines and spring-guns of the East. It matters less whether the East or the West does such things than that they can be done at all.

German theatre reflects the walled garden atmosphere. More money is spent on theatre both sides of the border than in probably any comparable geographical area in the world. Theatre is taken more seriously than anywhere else, particularly by the politicians. Scandals of the sort attracted by Howard Brenton's *Romans in Britain* occur with a certain regularity, though often for political not moral reasons. Yet the atmosphere is also faintly overheated, where the competition to succeed, to make a name is so intense that genuine artistic integrity is often sacrificed in the name of novelty or shock-value. Perhaps the most obvious signs of this are the number of rewrites of classics which come to the stage, whose strategy is substantially iconoclastic, and the number of aggressively eccentric productions where the text as such has not been played with but where the direction has radically altered its emphases. The result has been a widespread drop in theatre attendance and a growing gulf between those inside the theatre and those outside; at the same time Theatre Studies in universities seem to be trapped in a crisis of confidence, aware that the paths taken over the last fifty years have not yielded as much reward as hoped, but still unable to break out of a stance which is fundamentally elitist in its perception of theatre's function.

In retrospect, 1980 may turn out to be 'Das Ende einer Kunstperiode' (the end of an artistic epoch) to use Heine's term, every bit as much as Heine saw a similar 'end' with Goethe's and Hegel's death in the early 1830's.

4

(Goethe died on March 22nd 1832 which makes the year of publication of this volume a distant part of the orgy of celebration of the 150th anniversary of this event.) The economic miracle which made West Germany's economy among the most powerful in the world, which jetted the Deutschmark to the status of world's favourite currency is now over. The living-standards are still very high when compared with those in Great Britain, but the current round of major cuts in public expenditure and the commensurate questioning of certain of the luxuries which the state has hitherto afforded indicate the start of a shift in public opinion on spending on the arts. In 1980, for example, Mainz—capital of the state of Rhein-Hessen—put 20 million marks into its main theatre alone: this for a population of 350,000 is reasonably typical of subsidy levels, and is striking by comparison with British levels not least because the Arts Council grant to the National Theatre is roughly the same size. Now such high levels of support are under question, and the theatres are not well equipped to argue the case for their own defence. Similar problems affect the universities.

At the same time, West German politics have experienced a similar swing to the right to that in Britian and America. As Chancellor Schmidt's political career must end some day, and he is none too well, the search for a new strong man is on, opening up the most complex of all West German political questions as to what sort and degree of political authority is acceptable and compatible with democratic freedoms. The spirit of Hitler, not unnaturally, stalks any such debate.

The East has also had its economic miracle, no less miraculous than the West's when one considers it had no Marshall aid, and paid vast war indemnity to its friend the Soviet Union. The East has solved the strong man problem very neatly, by replacing a 'bad' dictator with a 'good' one, that of the party and of Eric Honecker, secretary of the party. The enthusiasm for the new way of life which at least is the official line in East Germany makes even her Warsaw pact neighbours a little frightened. Prussia remains Prussia under whatever disguise, and, unleavened by a Slavonic broad-minded cynicism, the German Democratic Republic is almost manically bent on making things work. In sport it clearly succeeds with a degree of achievement which, statistically at least, looks positively suspicious for a relatively small country. But corporate spirit should not be undervalued.

Artistically things in the East are rather less happy, especially since the best artists, individualists not members of sports teams, tend to find themselves in varying degrees of opposition to the state. In the late '70s many left or were thrown out, making a large hole in the East German cultural scene. Now there are perhaps three classes of artist, those with permanent open visas to the West, those who in other words can live with both regimes, those who do well by the state but are not allowed out, and those who are in revolt and who are also not allowed out. The official tendency however, as under Stalin, is towards an orthodoxy of bland reconstitutions of the victories of the past—i.e. of Brecht and Brechtian. The events in Poland have naturally made it even more difficult for artists to achieve personal freedoms, since it is the intellectuals, the writers and the artists, who are held most responsible for Poland's surge towards new and genuine forms of democratic expression.

Writers on both sides are aware of the need for new thinking in theatre, of the need to break out of what is threatening to become a Brechtian strait-jacket. Living with the great man peering over one's shoulder is very demanding and there is a danger that Brecht's memory will as effectively undermine the capacity to experiment with the stage as Shakespeare's perhaps did during the 18th and 19th centuries in England. But where the new ideas are to come from is uncertain. One source may be the immigrant communities in cities like Berlin. What seems certain is that since 1980, and since the recent Schmidt-Honecker summit, much of the heat has gone out of the East-West competition. The aesthetic implications of what is a political acceptance of the divided nature of the German state are well caught by Günter Grass in his 1979 novel *Das Treffen in Telgte (Meeting in Telgte)* where, drawing on the metaphor of a Germany divided by the Thirty Years War (1618–1648) he suggests that the only sense in which Germany may now be said to be united is in its attitudes to art and cultures – the artist becomes therefore the bearer of the cultural heritage.

Wall 1: Democracy and communism, or the two democracies

The Wall was erected supposedly to protect the East from the infiltration of Western ideas and modes of behaviour. It also went up to stop the radical depopulation of the Eastern sector. The political debate now centres on the issue of whether the wall makes East Berlin in effect a huge prison, or whether it is indeed the 'Schützwall'–'protective rampart'–against Capitalism.

The aesthetic equivalent of this debate was expressed in the theme of an early *Experimenta* in Frankfurt, 1966, 'Brecht or Beckett?' This in effect laid out the ground for dispute between a fundamentally socialist realist aesthetic and the theatre of the absurd or the theatre of cruelty. After a longish period of the triumph of socialist realism on both sides (Kroetz, Fassbinder, Heiner Mueller, Hacks, Turrini all grew up in this tradition) the pendulum has more recently swung towards absurdism and the theatre of cruelty, with Heiner Mueller's play *Der Auftrag (The Mission)* perhaps suggesting a means by which the two may be brought into productive liaison. The most apparent difference between the East and the West however, has been in their attitudes to language, and beyond that to the classics. From early on, Hacks and Heiner Mueller, and more recently Volker Braun and Stefan Schuetz have been writing plays in verse, very much in the classic mould, a conscious attempt to work out of a tradition that sees Brecht as a logical successor to Goethe and particularly Schiller. This naturally has its political aspect, the East claiming to be in the spirit of the great days of Weimar, and operating on a higher cultural level than the West. The West has tended to respond with much simpler, documentary plays, where the problems of the working-class are discussed. At the same time, the relationship with the classical tradition has been much more negative, seeing in it one of the intellectual sources of fascist elitism.

The debate is perhaps best caught in two plays of the '60s: Hacks's *Die Sorgen und die Macht (The Problems and the Power)*, 1962, and Grass's *Die Plebeier proben den Aufstand (The Plebeians Rehearse the Revolution)*, 1966. In one sense both are untypical in that linguistically the Hacks is more 'western' and Grass's more 'eastern' than the norm I suggest above: yet the resultant linguistic proximity in itself indicates how closely the works are in debate with one another. Hacks shows what it was like to work in East German factories in the '50s, with corruption, poor production methods and low-quality products shown up for what they are. Hardly surprisingly the play met with strong disapproval on opening and was soon taken off, the particular brand of socialist realism deployed not matching official expectations of art. Grass—admittedly many years after the event—has as subject the East German workers' rebellion of June 16th–17th 1953, an event which takes on a new, immediate complexion in the light of recent events in Poland. Grass, too, had his share of problems with critics. The West did not like being told by Grass that its intellectual and political leaders had failed its working-class brothers in the East. The East was far from happy at having Hacks show the warts on the five-year plan.

The central point of comparison is the relationship between the worker and the state, and in both plays rebellion is a dominant issue. Hacks has the courage to refer to the rising in Hungary, which was going on during the period in which he sets his play, but, consistent with the optimism demanded by the socialist realist aesthetic, his characters reject revolt as being the wrong response to difficulties with the new system. Criticism is levelled at the system, but in the conviction that discussion and revised policies can help. In a key speech, and in verse, the secretary of the local party explains his position:

> We have built our Germany in a new way, we have founded a republic in which everything is tending to grow towards greatness, in which a man has room to move, room to act, a humane republic. . . . Those who are stirring up trouble in Hungary are, in my view, those who think themselves too good for the old clothes they wear.1

The official nervousness of the East seems all the more ill-considered in the light of this sympathetic and persuasive defence of the new way.

Grass is much angrier, and yet also more literary, using Shakespeare's *Coriolanus* as one vehicle for his Plebeians 'rehearsal' of the revolution, and thereby deliberately taking on Brecht, who himself wrote a version of *Coriolanus*. A company in an East Berlin theatre is in rehearsal, planning a rewrite of Shakespeare, when out in the streets the workers first strike and then start a revolution attempt. Soon the rehearsal is interrupted by the arrival of a genuine group of Plebeians (East Berlin artisans) who come to get a statement of solidarity from the 'Boss' (the Brecht figure). He refuses, concerned more with the way the 'theatre' in the streets can be brought onto the stage than with the real issue of freedom, the word the workers are shouting in the streets. Suddenly, however, a bricklayer comes in wounded, and the mood shifts to an extent that the Boss is prepared to go out onto the streets and fight. But his decision comes too late: the Russian tanks are already in position. He is left on stage to comment in a Hamlet-like soliloquy on his failure to recognise the truth of the moment:

> It was the breath of the Holy Spirit.
> But I thought it was a draught
> And called out: don't disturb! [2]

The best that can come from this failure, or so the end of the play seems to suggest, may be poems reflecting on it. Yet the judgement on Brecht, and the East German intellectuals as a group is harsh, Grass making them responsible for the failure of the cause, along, of course, with an apathetic West.

Politically, Grass suggests by the failure of communication between intellectuals and workers that the intellectuals are incapable of practising the revolution they preach; revolution is seen as intellectually chic yet ultimately an exercise in dialectic. The worker needs the intellectual to help him articulate his grievances (very much the model on which Solidarity worked in Poland) but also has a right to demand practical engagement of the intellectual. Aesthetically, the debate is perhaps more complex. The theme of the relationship with the classic—here, Shakespeare—becomes a metaphor for a debate with a political system. Yet while the political conclusion is radical change, the aesthetic is to leave Shakespeare unaltered, apparently contradictory statements. The contradiction, however, suggests that Grass is antipathetic towards socialist realist and documentary theatre, seeing in it a false attempt to bring life and art together. This is a sentiment which Kosanke, the rebel in the theatre camp comments on:

> What's the theatre supposed to do when the people, forgetting how they've been directed, act of their own accord? [3]

It is theatre's job, or so the implication, to present historical and aesthetic models for contemplation, not to try to record the revolution as it progresses—as hard-line socialist realism demands. This is made quite clear in the Chief's relationship with the tape-recorder on which he has been recording the sounds of the revolution throughout to get a 'realistic' soundtrack for the crowd scenes in *Coriolanus*.

His grotesque obsession with documentary realism is one of the reasons he is incapable of recognising the 'Holy Spirit' when it breathes. Perhaps there is another reason for Grass's harshness: the historical Chief went into exile during the Third Reich. Grass did not. Set into the text are a number of reminiscences which the Plebeians have about their fighting during the war, or their imprisonment for their beliefs, which heavily underlines the distance between the Boss's and their commitment. Grass does not seem to find it easy to accept the inconsistency of the exiled writer returning home a hero to the new state only to baulk the second chance in his life to *do* something—support the workers' revolt—instead of just writing. It is not that Grass dislikes the exile in principle: he worked hard for Willy Brandt who was one himself. But he attacks what seems to be fundamentally skin-saving exile.

Wall 2: National Socialism and the present

From a foreigner's point of view, Germany's relationship with the Nazi past is still the dominant concern. Even the nearly forty years that have passed since the end of the war do not erase that memory. And such incidents as the bomb at the 1980 Oktoberfest in Munich, though, regrettably, paid far less attention than they should be, keep alive the spectre of the extreme right once again bidding for power.

Two issues are of central concern. Firstly, the actual facts of who did what during the period 1933–45; and secondly to what extent Theodor Adorno's statement about the impossibility of poetry after Auschwitz is true. The most successful German-language plays which have made it onto English-speaking stages, or become set-texts for those learning German have tended to be either works of a parable kind, like Frisch's *Biedermann und die Brandstifter (Fire Raisers)* 1958, or *Andorra* (1961), or explosively successful iconoclasms like Rolf Hochhüth's *Der Stellvertreter (Representative)* 1963, which caused a storm in Germany, and in 1967 his *Soldaten* which made little impression in Germany but caused near riots in London. Hochhutch was also a leading figure in the internal campaign against former Nazis in West Germany, a campaign which peaked in the early '60s, as his plays came out. Nor has he lost his grip: in 1980 his work was largely instrumental in revealing the activities of the then President of the State of Baden-Würtemberg, Filbinger, as a Nazi judge, a revelation which caused Filbinger's downfall. Yet, as Joachim Kaiser acutely pointed out in 1964, this style of work was not creating a new dramaturgy, and it is very hard to write good plays about fascism and about concentration camps both because the facts themselves seem too large and demanding for the stage, and because there is limited value in simply bewailing what happened night after night in the theatre. The facts demand action.

> The so-called 'undigested past' is doubly fatal: if you write a play that is set in the present it seems untruthful, cowardly and evasive, even artificial and cramped if it takes no account, that is, of what lies behind us and the rest of the world. Auschwitz was no mere accident. Yet in that moment that a playwright takes up this issue he gets tied up in all sorts of knots. And for this reason, since when faced with such a topic there is still very little room for manouevre in what you can say.[4]

In one respect, however, Kaiser, is, I sense, wrong. He attacks a tendency to provincialism in works dealing with the Nazi past, and yet it is the provincial story which, in my experience has so far best dealt with the problem. In his two films *Rosen für den Staatsanwalt (Roses for the Public Prosecutor)* 1959 and *Kirmes (Village Fair)* 1960 Wolfgang Staudte gets at the heart of two questions which even now, twenty years later, have not lost actuality. In the earlier film an ex-Nazi has worked his way into a senior position in the public prosecutor's office (not that uncommon at the time) and is quite by chance confronted with a man he thought dead, a man who should have been executed during the war on his orders. The story comes out and the prosecutor prosecuted. The resemblances with the Filbinger affair underline the continuing accuracy of the tale since Filbinger behaved in a similar way. How carefully was de-Nazification really undertaken? Were the real culprits caught? Wasn't it rather more often the case that a defeated army was made into a criminal conspiracy while the true criminals got by?

In *Village Fair* a body is found, quite unexpectedly, which turns out to be the remains of a son of the village who deserted from the Russian front in disgust at what had been going on. In a sequence of flashbacks the village's reaction to his returning home near to the end of the war is portrayed and set against what they are all doing now. Pointedly, the mayor now was a leading Nazi then. Pointedly the decision all took and take again is to forget. Staudte's point in both films is not to attack forgetting, still less forgiving, but rather that mere forgetfulness is as bad in its way as actual complicity at the time; that each individual has a responsibility for his own internal debate with Nazism. It is a call to the German collective conscience. In both films the strength of the analysis lies in the selection of the typical rather than the oustanding. We are not shown a sort of cloak-and-dagger hunt for Martin Boorman but documentary art of the best kind, using the techniques of the *Lehrstück* to illustrate what, in essence, must have been the situation in just about every German village and town.

Staudte manages to steer a successful middle way between the dangers of over-simplification and sententiousness to which Frisch's work is prone and the shock and sensationalism, combined with perhaps undue emphasis on the big fish, which marks Hochhuth's work. What is equally important, he finds a way of presenting a case to the German audience, which still finds 'the truth' hard to hear.

Wall 3: The state and the alternatives

Since the erection of the Berlin Wall in August 1961, Berlin has physically, as it had previously politically, taken on the shape of an emblem of political reflexivity: in the West the state is democratic and the alternative, over the wall, seen as totalitarian. In the East the state is also Democratic and the alternative, over the wall, presented as decadent and capitalist. Both sides feed off each other's myths, and yet both sides are having to live with another type of opposition, growing within, an opposition which wants neutrality, an end to nuclear power, a radical change in attitudes to the environment and a radical change in the nature of politics. Here, Berlin is in the vanguard, the West's problem expressing itself through the question of squatters' rights on unoccupied houses and the East's centring on inadequate supplies of jeans, etc.—the non-fulfilment of the economic plan. In both cases, however, the real issue is the inability of the present generation of leading politicians to win even the passive support of the young.

The fact of the Wall is hard to encounter and encompass on stage. Part of the problem is technical, but part—as with British reactions to the 'troubles' in Northern Ireland—a feeling that the matter is too personal, too immediate for art. As a result the drama of the Wall still is presented in documentary fashion, typical of which was a flurry of programmes round and on August 13th 1981—its 20th anniversary—in which the history and effects of the Wall were analysed. *Closed Landscape* (ARD, 13th August) and *Bernauerstrasse 1-50* (ZDF, same day) traced the history of the building and the way in which attitudes to it have developed historically. Most pronounced is the gap in the perception of the generations, for what the 'Wall' generation has always known is a physically divided city. The result is almost total ignorance on the part of the under 20s of what goes on on the other side—whichever side you are looking from. For the older generations, the Wall has become the silent star of a continuous action theatre saga, with its own conventions and mythology. We see again the Vopo leaping the wire as the Wall went up; we see people jumping out of the windows of Bernauerstrasse 1-50 (in the East) onto the pavement (in the West) and dying on camera; we see the NBC sponsored escape route and the documentary drama of the tip-off. Richard Burton's return from the Cold, the classic fictional use of the Wall in Le Carré's thriller, looks dull by contrast.

Again it is two 'provincial' studies of the wall and the Berliners which have most recently best caught the feeling of living with an alien presence as one's neighbour. In Theodor Schürkel's televised play *Die Grenze* (ARD, 14th August 1981) the action centres on two surveying teams, one from the East, one from the West, given the task of measuring up and surveying the actual border-line between the worlds. This neat and engrossing metaphor of east-west relations managed without falling prey to sentimentality to illustrate how propagandist myths can be built and then exposed as such by real personal contact between workers well away from the political masters whom they serve. Yaak Karsunke's play *Here No Way Out – Just a Crossing Over* (ZDF, 13th August 1981) was tougher and perhaps more realistic in that it ended in conflict not accord. A West Berlin shopkeeper meets a girl in the East on a day trip, and having fallen in love, literally buys her out through a professional escape route. They hope to marry in the West, but when the girl-friend finally gets there she realises that it is so remote from anything she has hitherto experienced as to break up her relationship. The pressure she feels at having been bought, combined with a still very real suspicion by native west Germans at those who came and come out from the East are almost more than she can stand.

This image of the disturbed cross-over, with its exposure of the falseness of any view that tries to present the two Germanies as mirror images – the

11

one the reverse of the other is a fruitful one, suggesting a possible new aesthetic. The strategy which was so influential in the sixties and early seventies, that of the 'concrete utopia' drawn from Ernst Bloch's thesis *The Principle of Hope* produced a number of plays and films which on the whole quite blatantly attempted to show in concrete terms what a new socialist society might look like. The technique favoured was to show how things are in the first half, then, in a naturalistic manner, show how they should or could be. Fassbinder's film *Angst Essen Seele auf (Fear Eats the Soul)* is a good example: an immigrant worker falls in love with an elderly Munich cleaning lady who already has a grown-up family They decide to marry with the result that the family rejects them and the neighbours are disgusted. The couple go away and on their return things change radically for the better. The problem the film sets, particularly in choosing a strong and beautiful Moroccan as husband is one of implausibility, and its case is weakened by being too extreme. Yet it exemplifies the cultural problems the 'guest' worker faces, exposes the class snobberies in West German life and the violence close to the surface. More recently—and this may be the new direction—the tendency has been to leave what the new world should be like implicit in the condemnation of the present, a more persuasive tactic and one that brings the theatre of cruelty closer to the teaching play. Striking, however, about the use of film for such a purpose is the way in which many writers like Fassbinder seem to be able to move easily between film and theatre, something which could be imitated to advantage outside Germany.

Wall 4: The worker and the establishment

Although the 'guest' worker is the most obvious example of the problem of alienated labour, his difficulties are in part shared by the native German. This has become increasingly complex as an issue as more and more 'guests' actually have 'German' children—children born and educated in Germany. These children have to make difficult decisions, ones which not only provide good source-material for drama in themselves but likewise offer the chance to examine the state of German society through their eyes. Nevad Djapic's film *Peter Gombas Lehr- und Wanderjahre (Peter Gomba's Apprentice and Journeyman Years)* (ZDF, 20th August 1981) uses as narrative mode the picaresque episodic technique, drawing too on the satirical aspect of the picaresque. Gomba, a young Jugoslav, grows up in Berlin, caught between his own culture, symbolised by the folklore group to which he belongs, and the heroin and crime of Berlin. His problem is that he wants to learn a trade but cannot, because of prejudice and the recession. He will not make up his mind to become a naturalised German, as his girl-friend does and so faces bleak prospects as an illegal worker in a kitchen. A neat twist of the plot then makes him discover that in prison he is guaranteed a training in a trade, so he commits a blatant crime in order to get caught. After a lot of witty business in which he tries to persuade the police to arrest him he is finally sentenced and gets his training. But, there is a sting: as a criminal he has to be deported. The end? No. As the police send him over the border they hint that he will be back, and they do not much mind.

By contrast, Antonio Skarmeta and Christian Ziewer's film, *Aus der Ferne sehe ich dieses Land (From Afar I see This Land)* (ARD, 20th August 1981), likewise set in Berlin, is sharper in its political rhetoric, if not as persuasive as a film. The central figure is once again a young immigrant, this time the son of a family of Chilean exiles seeking asylum in the Federal Republic. Under the laws governing asylum they are not allowed to work, although they do and are caught. They need to work to raise money for their political campaign against the government back home, and to gain the release of an uncle, arrested for his politics. The boy has to negotiate his way into a new school, which he does by his intelligence and good looks, and also into a new society while under pressure from his own family not to get involved with Germans. The clash of cultures comes to a head when he seduces (or is perhaps seduced by) the school tough's girl, for which he gets beaten up. In his refusal to apologise however, he is shown as a true son of Chile and the film begins to establish a metaphoric link between Chile now and Germany in the recent past as victims of oppression and prejudice. His victory is swiftly followed by the news that the uncle is dead, a reminder that the fight against oppression touches us all. The weakness of the work is that it attempts too many problems at once. Yet it avoids the sentimental and contains powerful arguments for the need of countries to show an interest in the internal affairs of other countries.

These two examples of films about immigrants and exiles work well because they establish the metaphoric value of both exile and immigration as a central part of German experience. The seeker of asylum in his very act of seeking asylum reminds the German of his past. At the same time, the alienated worker is a growing problem now that high technology and the recession are pushing unemployment levels up in Germany to relatively high percentages of the working population. The result of what appears to be a growing feeling of alienation of a large minority of the state from the rest is a revival in the terrorist scene, a growing anti-Americanism and the rapid surge in support for the Peace Movement. Not unnaturally, writers concern themselves with these trends, with the result that some, like Grass and Heinrich Böll have been accused of actively promoting terrorism. The buck is easy to pass, but the act of doing so reflects more the short-sightedness of the passer than the chosen recipient. Politicians must soon face the fact that social disorientation is widespread, especially among the young, and sending in the police is no long-term answer.

The East takes a certain delight in exposing the Achilles heel of the West, it having no unemployment, no riots, no exploitative landlords and capitalists. Yet the West's answer, if not strictly to the point, is cogent too. It does not lock up its critics, ban demonstrations, censor its artists. In the West, writing critically about the present will not land you in official trouble. Neither side is entirely honest: there are subtle forms of censorship in the West, and even some that are not so subtle. There is disguised unemployment in the East and the failure of plan after plan hardly helps. Encouragingly however, very recently writers from East and West got together for the first time to discuss peace; and this loosening of the political frontiers seems to be being accompanied by a willingness to get away from the sterile propaganda battle into thinking about ways art may alleviate tensions. What this means is that the writers are accepting that the old German tradition of the writer as dissident is once again claiming their attention, after a brief period of general acclaim.

The walls of Berlin, said a leading socialist politician recently to an audience at the Berlin media exhibition, are manifold. I have suggested four that play a major part in the definition of the German cultural landscape. It is hard, however, to overestimate the importance of one emotion which colours the responses made to all four walls, the emotion of guilt. Writers have in fact little choice but respond to their sense of the collective guilt at the events of 1933–45. It is not that the guilt is openly displayed, but it seems ineradicable. It is the source of a complex and seemingly paradoxical relationship between the writer and society. The desire to be good, successful, respected, wise, is central to the aspirations of most senior German politicians in both East and West but central in different ways to the aspirations of most writers. All agree with the ideal of a new type of Germany and feel deeply committed to achieving it. All see culture as an essential part of the process of rehabilitation in the world which Germany is undertaking. The problem comes when commitment starts to feel like patriotism. The artist will confess allegiance to an ideal state, the politician to a real one, and the images they hold of that state are drifting slowly apart.

So the divided state of Berlin is evidence of a curious form of historical continuity. The great figures of the German theatre—Lessing, Schiller, Goethe, Lenz, Büchner, Wedekind, Brecht—were all in some sense dissidents, outcasts, personae non gratae. They found little enough, especially when young, to praise in their states. Writers now look back at this seeming tradition of dissent and are aware that the only time that Germany has been truly united in both political and ideological aspiration was during the Third Reich. Perhaps, as Grass implies, it is better for the artist to feel affinity to an imagined than a real united German culture. Perhaps the division of Berlin is the best hope of cultural unity.

Notes:

1 Peter Hacks 'Die Sorgen und die Macht' in *Fünf Stücke* (Suhrkamp) Frankfurt/Main 1965, p352.
2 Günter Grass 'Die Plebejer proben den Aufstand' in *Theaterspiele* (Luchterhand) Neuwied/Berlin 1970, p306.
3 ibid p279.
4 Joachim Kaiser 'Grenzen des modernen Dramas' in *Theater Heute 5* Heft 12, p13.

14

Cock-Artist
(Katzelmacher)

by

Rainer Werner Fassbinder

translated by Steve Gooch

Première: Anti-teater, Munich 1968, Film 1968.

Though Fassbinder is best known as a film-maker, who in recent years, together with Werner Herzog and Volker Schlöndorf, has put young West German films on the world map, his theatre background is still decisive in the way he works. *Cock-Artist* (*Katzelmacher* means literally a wop or dago) exemplifies this use of theatrical convention in film, and both the stage and screen versions of the work were produced in the same year. Fassbinder also works remarkably fast and hard. *Cock-Artist* was filmed in three days, with Fassbinder himself taking the role of the immigrant Jorgos. This type of character is, however unusual for him. He tends more towards the ugly, disturbed and violent part, such as the son in *Fear Eats the Soul* who smashes up his mother's television set in disgust at her having married a Moroccan.

Cock-Artist signalled Fassbinder's breakthrough. It was his second full-length film and, in Marieluise Fleisser's words—he dedicated the play to her—Fassbinder's 'take-off' was like an express lift: 'And then suddenly he was in the lift and shot up above all our heads, it was astonishing how he did it: Fassbinder has a pronounced talent for this sort of thing.' ('Fassbinder' in *Alle Meine Söhne*). The film also displays many of Fassbinder's central preoccupations, or even obsessions. The small-town atmosphere, the fight between the immigrant and the locals, the link between late capitalism and fascism, the sexual prowess of the hero, the disturbed link between love and sex, all are shown as inter-dependent. The link seems to be envy: capitalism means that everyone covets everyone else's goods, physical qualities etc., and the result is a Hobbesian war of all against all. Commenting on a performance in Munich in 1970, Volker Canaris wrote: 'The fabular strategy of the story of *Cock-Artist* demonstrates how everyday fascism and petit-bourgeois capitalism are mutually determining.' (*Theater Heute 11*, 1970, vol. 10, p. 116). There is no question that Fassbinder's artistic strategy is one of 'provincial' analysis, and yet, as we suggested in the introduction to the whole volume, this is—so far at least—the most effective way of showing the recent past to the present German audience.

Some indication of the potential the play still has is suggested by the effect the play had in a small studio production in, of all places, Baden-Baden. Katharina Witte writes: 'What sort of possibilities for experiment has a provincial theatre that is both politically and financially dependent (the theatre on the town, the ensemble on the theatre direction), that relies on the sale of subscriptions, since it is constantly under pressure to produce which in effect means that it cannot afford "the courage to experiment"—how can it practise WORK WITH CONSEQUENCES?' This question came in to her mind when reviewing *Cock-Artist* first on the Baden-Baden stage and then, the following night, in a pub next door. (*Theater Heute 12*, 1971 vol. 1 pp. 59–60). As the play caused a great deal of controversy in Baden-Baden its run was short. But its fabular nature suggests it would be just as effective in Great Britain in provoking thought about the role of the immigrant and coloured British worker.

16

Characters

HELGA
GUNDA
ELIZABETH
MARIE
INGRID
PAUL
JORGOS
BRUNO
ERICH
FRANZ

In fact this should have been a play about older people. But it was being done at our 'Antitheater'. At the moment they're all young.

RWF

Translator's Note

The play is set in an outlying country suburb of Munich, so the German original is written in a lower-middle class rural suburban dialect. Because of references to tractors and the general 'provincial' feel of the characters, it was necessary to try and find a fairly exact English equivalent. I've imagined the play happening in a country environment just outside London—West Essex, Hertford, Cambridge even— so it's written in the kind of strange mixture of Cockney and East Anglian you get in these places. Obviously, since any attempt at a specific geographical location in England is at odds with the characters' references to Munich, German marks and Germany in general, these things would have to be changed to their English equivalents in production—as could indeed the characters' names. But for the sake of the original I've left them as they were for the time being.

The German isn't at all caricatured, so I've played down phonetic spelling as much as possible. The characters aren't inarticulate, but only half-educated, relying finally on retrogressive moral values. That's why they sometimes speak clichés—Marie particularly.

I've laid the text out as it is in the German. There are next to no stage directions, and the sequence of 'scenes' is marked by a gap in the text. So though the script is short in pages, it will run longer when 'played out', and where the dialogue doesn't run smoothly it's because something else, an action or a pause, will presumably come between.

Cock Artist by R.W. Fassbinder, 1971
(*Photo* by Neuer Malik)

Cock-Artist

ERICH. Got a thirst on me.

MARIE. I'll get you a beer if you want. You got to give me the money, though.

FRANZ. Get me one an' all.

PAUL. An' me. Good waitress en't she. You got to give her that. You shafted her yet?

HELGA. Pauly!

ERICH. Shafted her? You'd think it was your birthday. No-one does it like her.

HELGA. You shouldn't talk like that. Always going on about it. You got no respect, none of you.

PAUL. Ever shaft anyone with your respect? Do me a favour.

MARIE. There you are. Your beer. Educated people say thank-you.

PAUL. More to education 'n sayin' thank-you, darlin'.

MARIE. What a person don't understan' he oughta shut up about.

ERICH. She's right enough there. They done cut my wages. Cos everythin's changed, they reckon. So what do you do? You keep your mouth shut.

HELGA. Just cos a girl you were at school with's got her own factory.

ERICH. Liz Plattner? One worker she's got. An' what d they make? Wonderbags!

HELGA. Wonderbags is better'n shovellin' someone else's shit.

ERICH. I don' shovel shit. I drive a tractor. An' I could own a factory like that any day.

PAUL. When's that bloody train gettin' in?

MARIE. On the dot most likely, if you must know.

FRANZ. If only they'd have a dance here once a week, things might look up a bit.

ERICH. We already had a talk to the lan'lord about that. He reckoned it were a dead an' buried loss. Him an' his fat mouth.

HELGA. Reckon yourn's any better?

ERICH. Better'n his. People'd come from all over, once it got off the groun'.

FRANZ. Band's too dear though.

PAUL. Get a juke then.

ERICH. That wouldn't bring in no-one. There's jukes everywhere.

19

FRANZ. They got one in the Crown now.

HELGA. The room's too small, though. No chance a dancin' in there.
  (JORGOS *comes in*)

ERICH. Look at him the way he's lookin'.

MARIE. What sort's that then?

PAUL. Had to have a 'tache, didn't he!

MARIE. Well, tell me then!

ERICH. How should I know!

HELGA. He's comin' over.

PAUL. You wan' somethin' then?

FRANZ. Lookin' for somethin', are you?

MARIE. What sort are you then?

ERICH. Got a tongue in your head, en't you?

PAUL. I ask you!

HELGA. You lookin for someone then? Someone in partic'lar?

PAUL. What a sight, the thick.

FRANZ. Praps he don' wan' a talk to us. Praps we're not good enough
  for him.

ERICH. Why'nt you talk then? T-a-l-k!

JORGOS. Then katalavo!

HELGA. He's foreign.

ERICH. What I tell you?

PAUL. Thought as much.

FRANZ. Italian, probably.

ERICH. Ithacan.

HELGA. What are you then, Italian?

JORGOS. Italy — no.

PAUL. Italian, that's what he is. That's all. He's Italian.

MARIE. What's he doin' here then?

FRANZ. Yeh, that's what I want to know.

ERICH. Turns up out of the blue an' won' talk to us.

HELGA. He's got to have to be goin' somewhere.

PAUL. He's Italian.

HELGA. Still got to be goin' somewhere.

ERICH. Right.

HELGA. Where you goin' then?

PAUL. Where you off to?

HELGA. Address no? . . . . . . Elizabeth Plattner an' Co.

PAUL. Elizabeth's. What I tell you!

HELGA. I'll show you the way, come on. Come on!

PAUL. That's cos she went to Italy last year. Now this's
  turned up.

MARIE. No smoke without fire.

HELGA. He's stayin' at Elizabeth's. I always said she was
  man-mad. Just look at him.

PAUL. We ain' good enough, I suppose.

FRANZ. You speak for yourself.

20

PAUL. No, you.

FRANZ. He's gotta be jokin'!

PAUL. An Italian from Italy.

HELGA. You wouldn't think she'd have the cheek. My mother always
said as much, though. Don' go mixin' with that Elizabeth, she said.
Always.

PAUL. An Italian from Italy.

MARIE. The train.

HELGA. I'd sooner stay here really. We ought to talk to someone
in the village about him.

PAUL. Come on!

ELIZABETH. Now first we got to sort out the formalities. Social
security an' the deductions. You can sleep here with us, an' that's
deducted. I had you come here cos local layabouts just won't do in
my opinion, too unruly, except Bruno, you'll be meetin' him soon.
Right now, the work. It's easy to learn, but you got to be quick
or productivity suffers. Besides, the wages they ask are scandalous.
I mean, I'd like to know just what they think they do to deserve
'em. There's that many layabouts aroun', see, refugees from the
East who've stayed on an' that. You'll be eating with me too, and
that's deducted an' all. Franz Sparr worked with me for a week,
that set 'em talkin', an' it's the same with Bruno, but we're used
to all that now. So if they start talkin', you just got to get used to
it. I asked for someone keen, cos you won't earn nothing if you're
lazy. Now you know it all.

ERICH. Who we talkin' about?

PAUL. The Italian.

ERICH. Right.

GUNDA. So what. What's the matter?

PAUL. He's Italian. That's all. (BRUNO *comes in*) Well? What's the
latest?

BRUNO. He ain't no Italian.

PAUL. No?

BRUNO. He's Greek. From Greece.

ENRICH. Really? She didn't go to Greece, Elizabeth.

BRUNO. That's got nothin' to do with him anyway. He's an
exchange labourer, see.

GUNDA. What's that?

BRUNO. Like I say. Exchange labourer.

ERICH. How come! En't we got enough workers here already?

PAUL. A Greek, from Greece.

ERICH. That won't do. That's not fair nohow.

GUNDA. Right.

ERICH. We work an' all, don't we. More'n enough.

PAUL. He carved you up with old Elizabeth yet?

GUNDA. Where's he sleep?

21

Cock Artist by R.W. Fassbinder, 1971
(*Photo* by Neuer Malik)

BRUNO. In my room.
ERICH. Your room? How come?
BRUNO. There was a bed goin', that's all.
PAUL. He talked to you yet?
BRUNO. He can't talk. Strips off for bed, though. Right down.
PAUL. No!
BRUNO. Right.
GUNDA. In front of you?
BRUNO. It's all one to him.
ERICH. What he look like?
BRUNO. Better'n us.
ERICH. What you mean, better?
BRUNO. Better built.
ERICH. Where?
BRUNO. In the cock. *(Pause)*
PAUL. They got a telly roun' the Crown now. I'm goin' roun' there.
GUNDA. I'm off now. Cheers.
ERICH. Cheers. What's on?
PAUL. Bit a pop an' that.

GUNDA. You come from Greece, do you?
JORGOS. Greece.
GUNDA. An' you like it here? Is it to your liking?
JORGOS. No understand.
GUNDA. Germany nice?
JORGOS. Much nice.
GUNDA. No much love?
JORGOS. No understand love?
GUNDA. From the heart.
JORGOS. Not.
GUNDA. No? Not girls?
JORGOS. What, girls? Fucky-fuck?
GUNDA. Yes.
JORGOS. Ah not.
GUNDA. Why not? Cos of me?
JORGOS. Yes. Not.

INGRïD. I got it from Eric and he got it from Bruno, I think. Last
   night she stripped off, got on the bed an' screamed out for the
   Greek.
HELGA. Then what?
INGRID. Then the Greek came over, an' three hours later he comes
   out lookin' all in.
GUNDA. I'm just goin' home an' the Greek's comin' the other way.
   'Hello', I says, just to be polite. An' he grabs hold of me, throws
   me in the grass an' keeps sayin' fucky-fuck. I nearly died of fright.
   Then I ran off.
FRANZ. Started foreign habits now, he has.

23

ELIZABETH. Nothin' will come of nothin'. You got to be quicker in your work, on account of your wages.

JORGOS. Work no good?

ELIZABETH. Work good, but not fast.

JORGOS. Understand. Work fast.

ELIZABETH. Right. The more you work, the more you earn.

PAUL. An' then he raped her. In this field.

ERICH. Gunda? He en't got no taste.

MARIE. I don' believe it. Not him. He always keeps his eyes to hisself.

ERICH. You got a crush on him?

MARIE. I wouldn't go gettin' a crush on him, but what a man does with his eyes has got a reason.

PAUL. Like I say. Threw her down on the grass an' raped her. An' it'll be the others next. I'm tellin' you.

HELGA. Walkin' arm in arm with him she was, through the village and laughin'.

GUNDA. They're goin' too far, them two. I'd have gone to the police. That would've been the proper thing.

HELGA. If he so much as lays a finger on me, he's had it.

GUNDA. Do him in'd be the proper thing.

HELGA. Elizabeth'd stick up for him though. An' she's got pull with the nobs in the village.

GUNDA. If I'd had an affair with the mayor, I'd have pull an' all.

HELGA. An old man like that too. An' how old was she then? Seventeen.

GUNDA. She's got no shame. I'd do 'em in, people like that, do 'em in. It'll come though, you'll see.

MARIE. I feel a love like they sing about in the songs.

JORGOS. Love much good.

MARIE. Only they all keep talkin' so. 'Bout you and Elizabeth.

JORGOS. Elizabeth no.

MARIE. I want to be the only one you go aroun' with. That's important to a girl.

JORGOS. Eyes like stars.

MARIE. Eyes like stars. That's nice.

JORGOS. Holding nice.

MARIE. Was it nice with the others too?

JORGOS. No understand.

MARIE. Girls nice in Greece?

JORGOS. Yes nice. Greece much nice. Go Greece together. Much sun an' sea.

MARIE. Will you take me with you? Really.

JORGOS. Really. Much love.

MARIE. I love you too. I can feel it, it really hurts, definite.

ELIZABETH. Is it you been puttin' it roun' I been chasin' him
an' God knows what besides?
BRUNO. I en't said a word. I wouldn't go sayin' things about you.
I mean, I couldn't.
ELIZABETH. I can tell when I go through the village, the funny
way they say hello. Too friendly by half.
BRUNO. I en't said a thing. Nothin' at all.
ELIZABETH. They never talked spiteful like that before.
BRUNO. I couldn't say things like that about you, you know that.
I put my love first.
ELIZABETH. He's gettin' better at the work now. He's learnin' now,
slowly—
BRUNO. I'm still better though.
ELIZABETH. With your hands.

PAUL. He's havin' it with your Marie now.
ERICH. She can go fuck herself for all I care. Always on about
marriage. What I want to marry that one for? She's got to be
jokin'.
PAUL. What about Ingrid?
ERICH. She's got her eye on better things. Not interested in
marriage, she says. Reckons it'll spoil her chances for the future.
There's no feelings there neither. You don't talk with her, you just
screw. An' good too.
PAUL. Helga's goin' to have a baby.
ERICH. Really?
PAUL. Like I say. Three months gone she is.
ERICH. You should a been more careful.
PAUL. She said couldn't have a kid. Some doctor in Munich told her.
Landed me right in it. My Dad'll have a heart attack when he finds
out. I thought I was goin' to do her in when she told me. She's so
bloody obvious, that Helga.

FRANZ. There's communists there, where he comes from.
INGRID. In Greece?
FRANZ. I read it in the paper. Communists all over.
INGRID. All over?
FRANZ. Right. The whole a Greece. Crawlin' with 'em.

GUNDA. Ingrid got it from Franz, then told me.
HELGA. Just goes to show, don't it.
GUNDA. You get yourself into things an' never know what'll come
of 'em. I mean, they're a menace, communists.

ERICH. He's a communist and shouldn't be allowed.

Cock Artist by R.W. Fassbinder, 1971
(*Photo* by Neuer Malik)

PAUL. I mean, it fits with what's already happened, don't it.
ERICH. An' shouldn't be allowed.
PAUL. Comes over here, one of them.
ERICH. It shouldn't be allowed an' there's them that's working on it.

FRANZ. Where d'you come from in Greece then? What town?
JORGOS. Pirea.
FRANZ. What's that like?
JORGOS. Much sun an' sea an' many come from other country.
FRANZ. An' there's no work there.
JORGOS. Work yes, but no money.
FRANZ. What you earnin' over at Old Plattner's?
JORGOS. No understand.
FRANZ. How much money? Here.
JARGOS. Two hundred twenty mark. Eat and sleep.
FRANZ. Yeh? She give me three hundred twenty with meals. I
  wouldn't stan' for it.
JORGOS. Send all home. Wife an' childs.[i]
FRANZ. Married are you?
JORGOS. Wife an' children.
FRANZ. How many kids you got then?
JORGOS. Two.

HELGA. You're goin' roun' with a married man with children.
MARIE. If that's what you wan' a believe.
GUNDA. I'd be ashamed of myself, knowin' all about him an'
  what he is an' that.
MARIE. What is he then?
GUNDA. A criminal, that's what, an' everyone knows it.
MARIE. He's no criminal with me.
HELGA. Cos you're as bad yourself.
MARIE. What I do with my love's my business.
GUNDA. Just cos the dirty pig knows what to grab for.
MARIE. Just cos he didn't want you.
GUNDA. Didn't want me! Threw me on the bloody groun',
  that's all!
MARIE. In your imagination praps. You ain't even his type.
HELGA. As if he's bothered about types an'that. All he wants
  is his end away.
MARIE. Think you're any better, do you?
HELGA. Far as I'm concerned, you're a tart. That's all.

ERICH. Look at him, lyin' there, thinkin' nothing.
PAUL. We ought to castrate him.
ERICH. Really made himself at home, en't he.

(i) Jorgos' pidgin German. 'Kinda' for 'Kinder' is here deliberately translated into
  incorrect English.

27

PAUL. Soon put that right.

ERICH. That'll be a laugh. Just cut it off. See how good he fucks then, seein' he's got nothin' else in his head.

PAUL. 'Cept he stinks like a pig.

ERICH. Bruno said he don't never wash.

PAUL. None of 'em do where he comes from.

ERICH. We ought to have a gun. Soon make him dance then. Just see him jumpin', can't you.

FRANZ. Like a young deer.

PAUL. Castrate him's better though. He wouldn't forget that in a hurry.

ERICH. We could soak it in petrol an' give it to Marie for her birthday.

PAUL. That'd be worth seein'.

FRANZ. What's Elizabeth say, now he's goin' with Marie.

ERICH. Cried, didn't she. Cos he was so good for her.

PAUL. Yeh, I bet. That's just the sort of bastard he is, after all.

INGRID. The director said I got a voice as good as Catherine Valente's an' I ought to stay in Munich for good.

GUNDA. You got to be trained, though. Anyone can sing.

INGRID. Like you, I suppose.

GUNDA. I can sing as good as you.

INGRID. Everyone to his own illusion.

GUNDA. Think you're somethin' better'n us, do you. A joke is what you are, an' if anythin's an illusion it's your director.

INGRID. I'll be a singer an' you'll see me on television an' you'll be sorry you spoke.

GUNDA. I'd be sorry I spoke if I'd got breath like yourn.

INGRID. If I got bad breath, you got one foot in the grave. If I was donkey's years old like you I'd keep my mouth shut, I'm tellin' you. (HELGA *comes in*)

HELGA. Here, have you heard? That bastard çock-artist's been an' beaten old Erich near half to death. Went mad he did. Suddenly something got into him an' he just started layin' into old Erich.

INGRID. Old Erich. What for?

HELGA. No-one knows nothin'. Paul and Franz were there, only they just stood there stunned by the madness of it.

GUNDA. Didn't they help him any then?

HELGA. Not standin' there stunned by the madness of it.

GUNDA. Somethin' like that was boun' to happen though. I always said as much. That foreigner's got to go.

INGRID. Right. I mean, foreigners are a bad lot anyway. (PAUL, ERICH *and* FRANZ *come in*)

HELGA. Here they are too.

INGRID. I can't see many bruises.

ERICH. Cos I'm a man an' know how to defen' myself, that's why. Otherwise I'd be laid out.

PAUL. Right.

ERICH. I'll get him back though. With a 'duster an' all me mates together. It's got to be beaten out of him.

FRANZ. We're goin' to get a gang on him.

PAUL. An' anyone not joinin' in's an enemy an' gets the same.

HELGA. Get things back to normal around here.

GUNDA. What about old Plattner? She's the same.

ERICH. Right. She's got to go cos she's to blame for it all. We'll soon see what's what, what they think they can do against all of us.

HELGA. She even brings him to church with her. You wouldn't credit it.

GUNDA. If you got no shame, you got no shame.

HELGA. I bet he's no Christian neither.

GUNDA. Certainly ain't no Christian

ERICH. He can drop dead.

PAUL. An' her.

ERICH. It's old Bruno I feel sorry for. He's caught up in it, of course.

PAUL. Of course.

EVERYONE. Blood of Christ, anoint me
Water from the side of Christ, wash me
Passion of Christ, strengthen me
O good Jesus, hear me
Within thy wounds hide me
Suffer me not to be separated from thee
With all they saints eternally
For ever and ever. Amen.

GUNDA. We ought to tell the vicar. Seein' as it's so shameless.

ERICH. I bought myself a knuckleduster in Munich.

PAUL. It's got to be done in secret though.

ERICH. Fuck whether it's secret or not. Just get on with it, the sooner the better.

PAUL. We got to be careful though.

FRANZ. What's she got to bring him to church with her for?

MARIE. She don' know no other way. He's got faith too.

FRANZ. Yeh, what sort though.

MARIE. Makes no difference what sort.

ELIZABETH. Just listen to 'em talkin'. They're messin' up the vicar's sermon with all that whisperin'.

BRUNO. I hadn't noticed.

EVERYONE.   The Lamb is slain, its blood outpoured
The sacrifice is made
Thy mercy and thy might, O Lord
To us have been displayed.

ERICH. We're gettin' nowhere like this. It's got to start sometime.

PAUL. Best thing'd be in leather jackets, out in the open, like they got everywhere, 'cept here.

ERICH. That's no reason to hang about.

GUNDA. I'm goin' to talk to her after.

HELGA. Me an' all.

GUNDA. Tell her once an' for all what she is.

MARIE. I'm afraid, cos no good's not comin' from no-one.

FRANZ. Things are the way they are, that's all, nothin' you can do about 'em.

EVERYONE.   Our door is marked with blood
For he is the true Paschal Lamb
Roasted for us in dearest love.

PAUL, ERICH, FRANZ. Eeny, meeny, miny, mo, catch a nigger by his toe, If he hollers, let him go, eeny, meeny, miny, mo.

ELIZABETH. You talkin' to me by any chance?

BRUNO. Don' start anythin' with them.

ELIZABETH. They can do just as they like, can they?

HELGA. You can do just as you like though, cos you were the bigwigs' doormat

ELIZABETH. Just cos they didn't want any of you lot.

GUNDA. They'd have wanted all right, only we got a bit of decency. We ain' just anyone's, you know.

ELIZABETH. Anyone's is better 'n no-one's. If I'd got your looks, I'd be ashamed to even show myself.

GUNDA. Cos of course you're so attractive, you had to get a bloody foreigner in.

ELIZABETH. Whose business is that anyway? An' he's not a foreigner, he's an exchange labourer.

HELGA. Don' make much difference in your bed, do it.

ELIZABETH. My bed's my business. You mind your own.

PAUL, ERICH, FRANZ. Eeny, meeny, miny, mo, catch a nigger by his toe.

ELIZABETH. You can see for yourself he's no nigger, an' what's more he works a sight better'n any of you lot.

ERICH. Were we talkin' to her?

PAUL. We didn't say a word to her.

JORGOS. What this not understand.

ERICH. You'll soon understan' all right, when you can' tell your toes from your fingers any more.

30

JORGOS. No understand.

GUNDA. He's turned everythin' on its head that's what, an' we wan' a bit a peace.

HELGA. We like things quiet here.

ELIZABETH. Leave me in peace then, an' things'll be quiet.

ERICH. Don't you come that now. If I'd got a communist in my house . . .

ELIZABETH. Keep your filthy han's off me.

ERICH. My han's dirty, are they? Have a look.

PAUL. They ain't a bit dirty at all.

ERICH. An' even if they were, they couldn't be as dirty as yours.

HELGA. You don't know what shame is.

GUNDA. Just take what's going.

PAUL. An' keep your criticism for other people.

ELIZABETH. I'm goin'. I can't talk to people like you.

ERICH. I ought to do for him now, bloody communist.

PAUL. Leave it now, it's too dangerous.

ERICH. I don't have to put up with talk like that.

PAUL. Another time. We'll get him on his own.

MARIE. It's all goin' to wörk out wrong again.

FRANZ. If that's the way it's got to be.

MARIE. If only there weren't this love thing.

BRUNO. If everyone's talkin' about it, there must be something in it.

ELIZABETH. No-one understands nothin' about anythin'.

BRUNO. What happened happened, though. You can't change that.

ELIZABETH. An' what did happen?

BRUNO. You had somethin' goin' with him. That's what happened.

ELIZABETH. Nothin' happend. Happened, happened! A mess is what I had with him.

MARIE. I love you so much, but I got a feelin'.

JORGOS. Got a feelin'.

MARIE. 'Bout the others. They're up to somethin' violent.

JORGOS. No understand.

MARIE. One day they go bang-bang.

JORGOS. No bang-bang.

MARIE. Cos you're so nice. You still takin' me to Greece with you?

JORGOS. Go together Greece.

MARIE. An' your wife.

JORGOS. No understan'.

MARIE. Your wife. Jorgos' wife.

JORGOS. No understan'.

MARIE. It's really got me, see. There. They all know. I don't care though.

INGRID. Another five weeks an' they're cuttin' my firs' disc. My voice is ready now, they reckon.

HELGA. Then what? How much they payin'?

INGRID. I don't know yet. He's a very nice man though. They got to do photos of me an' all.

HELGA. You'll be in the papers then.

INGRID. Right. In all the papers. All my savins 've gone into this.

HELGA. You had to pay for it yourself?

INGRID. It's for my career.

HELGA. Oh yeh.

INGRID. It is too! You're only young once, you know. You don' get a second chance. No second chances.

PAUL. I'd go for leather jackets myself. They're always best if there's bother.

ERICH. You know what they cost? Three hundred marks.

PAUL. Christ.

ERICH. There's those American jackets though. Blue. You can stick things on the back. Chicago Rockers or somethin'.

PAUL. Better'n nothin'.

ENRICH. An' everyone's got to have a duster. One of them in your pocket an' you feel a different person. Bruno's comin' in on it. He told me so.

PAUL. That's ten of us already. It'd still be better with leather jackets though.

GUNDA. An' marriage. Don' you wan' a get married?

FRANZ. I don' know.

GUNDA. That's solid, marriage is. Somethin' reg'lar like that's not to be sniffed at.

FRANZ. You never can tell though.

ELIZABETH. Have you heard what they're all saying about us?

JORGOS. Jorgos understan' all talk.

ELIZABETH. It's what they're saying that's important. You an' me, understand?

JORGOS. Understand.

ELIZABETH. I mean, they all get worked up about you. But you've been with Marie, haven't you.

JORGOS. Marie beautiful girl.

ELIZABETH. And me?

JORGOS. Much beautiful.

ELIZABETH. Well then? Aren't you interested in me?

ERICH. He chucked her in the water.

INGRID. Why in the water?

ERICH. Cos of the baby. To get rid of it.

INGRID. And?

ERICH. Nothin' happened. Give her a shock, though.

INGRID. An' Paul?

ERICH. He asked her to forgive him. Now they want to get married.

INGRID. I wouldn't want anythin' like that.

ERICH. What about love?

INGRID. That neither. It's agein'.

MARIE. He was tryin' to kill her.

GUNDA. It was probably just an accident.

MARIE. Old Ingrid's goin' off up town to sing.

GUNDA. Because she can, of course.

MARIE. Better'n we can anyway.

GUNDA. She had to pay for it all herself, you know. The photographer an' everythin'.

MARIE. Well, that's usual, en't it.

GUNDA. How d'we know what's usual?

ERICH. You happy with your foreigner then?

MARIE. Happier'n I was with you all right.

ERICH. Cos you're nothin' better'n a tart, you mean.

MARIE. What if I am? I don't care.

ERICH. How low can you sink?

GUNDA. D'you two have to argue?

ERICH. What's he got that I ain't?

MARIE. That's my business.

ERICH. You an' your mouth, I ought to knock you down.

GUNDA. You shouldn't talk like that. It gets people het up.

MARIE. I'll talk how it takes me.

PAUL. Someone do somethin' to you?

ERICH. No-one's done anythin' to me. I'm just angry, that's all.

FRANZ. Well look who's comin'.

PAUL. Yeh, look who's comin'. Whoah-hey!

BRUNO. The Greek. Just when we need him.

ERICH. Rotten bastard, what you doin' comin' along here? Think just anyone can come along here, do you.

PAUL. What you gone all quiet for?

JORGOS. No understan'.

ERICH. You understand all right, you communist. Wan' a hit me back? Just come here then.

JORGOS. Pustis malakka!

PAUL. Nice.

ERICH. Just so you don' forget, communist pig.

JORGOS. Malakka, malakka, ochi!

ERICH. Shut your noise, can't you.

JORGOS. Ochi parakalo, ochi!

33

BRUNO. There! And there!

ERICH. Just so you realise. From now on you won' be havin' it so easy.

GUNDA. It had to happen sooner or later. Runnin' round here like he owned the place.

HELGA. Lookin' at you like you were prize meat.

GUNDA. It won't stop at this either. Not till he's had enough. He's got to go.

HELGA. Right. Thing's 've got to get back to normal.

INGRID. An' you were with 'em.

FRANZ. A course.

INGRID. An' he's goin' to leave now, is he?

FRANZ. No idea. I'd go. Definite.

PAUL. We had to have our revenge, didn't we.

ERICH. Right.

HELGA. Did he get up again?

ERICH. Don' know. I cleared off.

PAUL. Makes no difference to us anyway.

ERICH. Right.

PAUL. He'll leave now all right.

ERICH. Definite.

HELGA. Now things ain't so nice any more.

ERICH. It's us who belong here, no-one else.

ELIZABETH. You didn't have to join in though. That wasn't necessary.

BRUNO. It just come over me suddenly. I didn't even realise.

ELIZABETH. If you don't want to help, all right. But joinin' in . . . . .

BRUNO. I didn't want to join in. I don't even know how it happened.

ELIZABETH. I think you're lyin'.

BRUNO. So I'm lyin'.

JORGOS. No understan' why.

MARIE. I love you, I'll never leave you.

JORGOS. I no understan' why bang-bang.

MARIE. It's all over now. Come on.

JORGOS. All me bang-bang.

MARIE. Give me a kiss, it's nice.

JORGOS. I no understan'. Greece nice, Germany much cold.

MARIE. Kiss me. I want you to.

GUNDA. Well? Is he going or what?

BRUNO. No.

PAUL. You told Elizabeth she'd get the same next time?

BRUNO. Yeh, but she don' believe it.

ERICH. She's lyin'.

HELGA. It's obvious she's better off this way.

BRUNO. She says it's better for business.

ERICH. If he stays?

BRUNO. Right, an' it's true.

GUNDA. Why's that?

BRUNO. Cos we're producin' more now, an' she's payin' him 650 marks. He sleeps in my room an' for that she takes off 150 marks.

GUNDA. 150 marks. She can do that?

BRUNO. Right. An' for food another 180. Makes 330 altogether. Means she pays him 320 marks.

ERICH. So that's it.

BRUNO. Right. It's just a trick. An' for Germany's good.

HELGA. She's got a head for business, that Elizabeth. I always said as much.

BRUNO. An' she's not gettin' rid of anyone, she says. More'n likely get another one in.

PAUL. You got to have it up here. That's the point.

GUNDA. She's had a miscarriage. Only now they wan' a get married anyway.

INGRID. Means nothin' to me, all that. Miscarriage, marriage.

GUNDA. What if nothin' comes of your career?

INGRID. I might then. For my old age. Still don't mean nothin'.

ELIZABETH. I had to talk to him for hours, persuadin' him to stay.

BRUNO. I can't help that.

ELIZABETH. If he tells them in Munich what happened here, they won't send us any more.

BRUNO. Nothin' I can do. Nothin' at all.

ELIZABETH. If it happens again, I'll throw you out.

BRUNO. I can't help that.

ELIZABETH. I'm goin' to report it too. That's no way to carry on.

BRUNO. I didn't do nothin'.

ERICH. An' I'm joinin' the army in March. That's better'n workin' here.

PAUL. I'll have to an' all.

ERICH. You got no choice. I want to get on a submarine. I mean, it's different from workin' on the land.

PAUL. You got to go where they put you.

ERICH. Don't make any difference really where they put you.

ELIZABETH. In January a colleague of yours is comin'. A Turk. Apparently he's too old for the buildin'-sites or somethin'.

JORGOS. Turkish?

ELIZABETH. A Turk's comin' here. Work like you.

JORGOS.   Turkish no good. Others no?

ELIZABETH.   No. I have to take what they send me.

JORGOS.   Turkish no good. Jorgos and Turkish no work together. Jorgos go other town.

MARIE.   He's takin' me to Greece with him in the summer.

HELGA.   What about his wife?

MARIE.   Makes no difference. Everythin's different in Greece.

HELGA.   I don' know, just goin' off like that. An' all that way.

Blackout.

Piano-Play

(Klavierspiele)

by

Friederike Roth

translated by Estella Schmid

Première: Malersaal des deutschen Schauspielhauses, Hamburg, March1981

Friederike Roth's first play, *Piano-Play* generated high feelings at its première. Benjamin Henrichs reports: 'The director punched. The theatre director smiled. Some men in the ensemble bullied the author. That's what happens when men's theatre plays women's plays.' (*Theater Heute* March 1981 p. 41). Nor was the matter as simple as that. The first director a woman, walked out on the play just before the première and a man was then put in her place. What he did to 'make the play work'—how often has that been done—made the piece unrecognisable, and Roth herself felt deeply disappointed and misrepresented.

Some of the difficulty undoubtedly lies in the play. It is a hard, tensely written work which does not yield much in terms of theatricality. Its language shows traces of the interest in linguistics (especially transformational grammar) and aesthetics which Roth has had since being a student. One of her early works *Ordnungsträume* actually used the concept of the academic footnote as a creative device and in her mixture of real and fantasy references she creates a level of discourse hung between 'academic' and 'creative' which contradicts the classical division of author and critic. *Piano-Playing* explores a similar clash of discourse levels, but adds a further element, that of the notion of a text as a musical score and of printed linguistic units as analogues of notes on staves. It will probably take time therefore for actors and directors and their audiences to learn how to make sense of this new type of structural and linguistic experiment. Nevertheless, Roth, like Hacks and Heiner Mueller, is concerned with a theatrical language which is different from socialist realist everyday speech, and she is concerned with the difference between male and female perceptions and intellects. Those who saw the first performance with a sympathetic eye found it a work of great quality, and Klaus Kolberg, surveying the theatre year for the *Allgemeine Zeitung* rated the play one of the high points of 1981. *(Allgemeine Zeitung Feuilleton,* January 2nd 1982).

Characters
SHE
HE
ERWIN
FIRST OLDER WOMAN
SECOND OLDER WOMAN
THIRD OLDER WOMAN
WAITRESS
FIRST BUYER
SECOND BUYER
INSURANCE SALESMAN
THREE MEN

Set Corn-fields flecked with poppies, a sun, a few bar tables, a bed, a piano, a small old table with two chairs or something similar, all simultaneously on stage.

Scene One

Midsummer fields, on one of those tracks through the corn which give you the feeling of being safe and at one with nature. In a sad fury she pops one poppy head after another on the back of her hands; he tries in a thoroughly engaging way to give the impression of suffering in sympathy.

SHE. Just now I find the green and the gold so serious.

HE. Stop it.

SHE. That's how nature is, isn't it. Right back there the landscape can even turn blue. But that's far away.

HE. You're overcome by nature. I'm sick with memories.

SHE. I laugh myself to death. You're killing yourself. The Maywhistle-childhood, love, has long since climbed up the tree and sailed down the stream. You've become a fine, decent human-being now. A man like that will never get sick.

HE. Stop it.

SHE. After all, I didn't invent families and houses and creeping life. They all wanted to fly to the sun once. Until they noticed that the same sun makes the beans ripen in their hobby-gardens. *(She throws stones behind her, over her head.)* Come on, let's go and find people. *(She slips her hand through his arm, friendly and familiar, and makes him walk briskly back the way they have come.)*

Scene Two

A few bar tables. At one of them sits the WAITRESS, *folding table-napkins in triangles—in piles—at the same time watching the customers. They both sit down next to the 'Stammtisch'[1], order Schnaps and then remain silent. At the 'Stammtisch' an older man—*ERWIN*— is having a good time, loud and unambiguously—with three older women. They press their corsetted breasts against his elbow with unequivocal blunt-ness. All three women have an eerie decrepit vitality.* ERWIN *talks to the* SECOND OLDER WOMAN, *who, with meticulous attention, cleans real or imagined wine stains off her high-laced breast.*

ERWIN. I'm going home with you now.

FIRST OLDER WOMAN. Forget him.

SECOND OLDER WOMAN. Why? D'you want him?

FIRST OLDER WOMAN *(piercingly).* Me? I've got grown-up kids and a grandchild on the way. I don't need a man.

THIRD OLDER WOMAN *(with a stubborn, smiling tenderness).* Cheers, Erwin.

[1] The *Stammtisch* is the table in the pub where the regulars sit. It is often round to distinguish it from the other, rectangular tables.

39

ERWIN. Forty years gnawing the same bone.

SECOND OLDER WOMAN. Then come and gnaw on my bone.

ERWIN *(without explanation, suddenly turns towards* HER*)*. You know, Miss, when they've had their menopause, women, that's when you get real pleasure.

THIRD OLDER WOMAN. Cheers, Erwin.

SECOND OLDER WOMAN. Leave that young lady alone. Here's the market.

ERWIN *(stubbornly to her)*. When they get shaggy. Then in you sail— full steam ahead. It's all over their heads.

FIRST OLDER WOMAN. Old fool.

SECOND OLDER WOMAN. You think you're better?

THIRD OLDER WOMAN. Cheers, Erwin.

ERWIN. That's enough. All of you. Now I'm going to talk to that young lady.

SECOND OLDER WOMAN. Then I'll be off home. *(She goes to the waitress.)*

THIRD OLDER WOMAN. Cheers, Erwin.

FIRST OLDER WOMAN. I'll buy another round.

ERWIN. Forty years the same bone. Drink your wine alone, you cunts. *(Shouts)* The bill.

FIRST OLDER WOMAN. But it's my turn this time.

ERWIN. Just between ourselves: they've all got cobwebs between their legs. And you won't be any better off either.

ERWIN *goes. The three older women laugh piercingly as if all of a sudden they are in agreement.* HE *and* SHE *take their money out at the same time. Both of them, but each for their own sake seem to be afraid of these women. They pay and go . . .*

Scene Three

. . . to the piano. Next to it stands a beautiful small old table. He sits down at the piano and opens the lid.

SHE *(tired and quick)*. No more.

Without comment HE *closes the piano again.* SHE *fetches wine and glasses: crabbed, silent and quarrelsome.* SHE *opens the bottle, pours the two glasses full, empties half a glass determinedly—does all that a hint too intentionally, as if* SHE *wanted to prove something but has forgotten what.*

SHE. The virtuoso jazz man with the celebrated hard touch. I can't bear it anymore.

HE. You could never get enough before.

SHE. Before.

Then one can never get enough.

Then you always want more.

Then you'll of course soon be singing the Queen of the Night.[2]

HE *(drily).* Instead, you've made a domestic pianist out of me.

SHE. Yes, am I with a voice that's far too thin to help with the backing all my life? Just imagine: one day you are sitting there and it dawns darkly on you that maybe yours is more of a small nature. *(Drawing him partly in.)* After all, your art is rather ridiculous. You have the talent of a debutante.

HE. Don't come on with the same old tales.

SHE. Your dreams are over very quickly. *(Imitating the* OLD WOMAN *in voice and gesture)* Cheers, Erwin. Oh God, when I get to that age. Black bristly hairs grow out of your face, brown spots spread all over your body. And then you start getting naturally compliant of course— Cheers, Erwin!—in old age there's no more standing on the summit— That's for sure. *(Drinks again heartily)* Hopes have long since been ploughed under ground.

HE. Stop drinking so much.

SHE. Now I'll sing myself my own lullaby. Need no piano. Need no musician. You least of all. *(Determined but at the same time not convincing at all)* The piano has got to go, as quickly as possible. *(Drinks)* It's just the melody has sunk right into me. But don't you worry, it will pass.

HE. I never promised you anything.

SHE. Because you don't even promise what you can't keep. No, you can't promise anything anymore. You can only play the piano and tend your little kiddies. Just once, one wonderful lie from you. I would've rolled in the grass, fluttering.

HE. Why lie? We are grown-up people.

SHE. It would have been a proper, sad illusion, that at least. All right, it was beautiful. But, it didn't make me happy. Lies are such fun. You enjoy them. The effect you would have had to make. Fantasies for me. That would have been the slender but highest peak.

HE. But if it's only lies.

SHE. You've got to embellish life, my dearest.

HE. My 'dearest' already . . . I'd better go now.

SHE. Get lost.

HE. See you soon.

SHE. I don't want to see you here again.

[2] The Queen of the Night has the coloratura role in Mozart's opera *The Magic Flute.* The arias are spectacularly high and difficult.

Scene Four

Night. And now SHE *is alone. In front of her, one empty bottle of wine, another nearly finished.*

SHE *(not whining but furious, ironic, with the comic self-awareness of a drunk).*
I stand on the summit. I. And a summit.
A summit and I.
That's the limit.
Alone of course. On peaks you always stand alone.
You breathe in loneliness and a superior cold air.
That makes little icicles grow in your little nose.
Lovey, better keep your hands off peaks.
Your mucous membranes are simply not made for peaks.
At first, all keen to conquer peaks, giggle and dance and sweat. Then to be afraid of the shaking ground. That's how it goes. *(It gets dark.)*

Scene Five

The bar tables. SHE *and her* GIRLFRIEND *sit at the empty 'Stammtisch' where two of the three women were sitting in scene two. The* WAITRESS *is sitting at her table again—it should look as if she's been there the whole time—piling up paper-napkins in triangles. The* GIRLFRIEND *drinks a cup of chocolate.* SHE *a glass of wine.*

SHE.   That brown wrinkled skin. How can you drink something like that?
GIRLFRIEND.   Stop making everything maggotty.
SHE.   Maggotty. That's it. Something squashed soft. And over it, something white and creeping.
GIRLFRIEND.   It was just a passing affair. Right from the start. And you know it.
SHE.   I saw an end in the beginning. Then I didn't want to see anything anymore. An end is no joke you know.
GIRLFRIEND.   Have you sold the piano yet?
SHE.   People haven't got a clue about pianos nowadays. They're surprised about broken strings. It makes me tired.
GIRLFRIEND.   Get the strings repaired and a good piano tuner. It will sound like new.
SHE.   I dreamed we got married. That was beautiful. Although the child was already dead at birth. A woman was there at the ceremony. She was a distant relative who ranted on about dark days, how she spent a few years, fixed to a stake, with a man, who in reality was neither a goat nor a buck. And he was her husband. He just sort of sprung on me. And I'd do it, and she would have all the trouble, and she wouldn't tolerate any more intercourse with her husband.

42

GIRLFRIEND. Just don't drive yourself mad.
SHE. The distant relative was his wife you know.
GIRLFRIEND. In your dream.
SHE. It was like being glassed in.
GIRLFRIEND. You're all bent and boarded up. Let's go for a walk.
SHE. Feed the swans. That's all I needed.
GIRLFRIEND. Then stick here until you're blue in the face.
SHE. You don't turn blue so quick.
Do me the favour of coming back to my place. I don't want to be alone.

The GIRLFRIEND *with her forefinger tenderly touches the bridge of* SHE'S *nose. They pay and go . . .*

Scene Six

. . . they come back again and sit at the beautiful small old table on which the ash-trays are already full of butts and there are wine-glasses for both of them. Smoke hangs over the table, as if they had been sitting there for hours.

GIRLFRIEND. It's late. Go to bed now. And tomorrow morning we're rehearsing. If you carry on drinking and smoking like this, you won't have any voice left.
SHE. In that choir my voice doesn't count. I just silently open and shut my mouth until feeding time.
GIRLFRIEND. You always loved singing motets.
SHE. Motets, motets, motets. I can't keep singing, 'ah welcome, ah welcome,' all the time. If there have to be rehearsals, why not an opera at least. Full of bewildered fantasy. That gets you away from everyday life. *(SHE lies down on the bed, in which the sun is going down, and immediately becomes more awake.)* This place smells of celery.
GIRLFRIEND. Right. Stick celery.
SHE. What will you think of next?
GIRLFRIEND. Sometimes you find operas loathsome and swear by madrigals . . .
SHE. Those were operettas. Sweep you off your feet . . . full of vervy sweetness.
GIRLFRIEND. Then for months it's got to be a requiem. You want to sing and you don't. You want to sell and you don't. You have got to decide.
SHE. I want both. A celebration where you don't celebrate anything. That would be lovely, a celebration like that. Everybody makes friendly gestures but ones which are different from ours. What a muddle: it makes you laugh. A few chic women's heads singing whining arias. With silly children's smiles lying on their faces. An important part is played

43

by a lonely lantern and an old dog. A child at play and a child asleep. A shadow and a scream from behind the wings. And masses of gorgeous creatures. They make slippery giggles and droll movements with their gentle thighs and lightly arched feet. White in white. When it's over it will be as if for a moment I had been a king. *(Pause)* It still smells of celery here. We just always sing the same old numbers. You can go, if you want to save your voice for that. Sure, you have got to live on something. And singing is not the worst. But it's no better either.

GIRLFRIEND. I'm so tired.

SHE. Yes. Well then. *(The GIRLFRIEND goes. It gets very dark.)*

Scene Seven

The stage is now dark. SHE, *alone to the audience.*

SHE. My happiness has given out. An eternity lasts too long for me. It was another of those hot summers full of sparks. The little thunder beasts are swimming in the heat. It exhumes memories of something past and special, wishes without designation. It's a devilish deception to believe we are in command of a light and easy tongue. During the day there's beautiful weather that doesn't care about us. The summer snails creep along the dry days. The blind cats scream at the sun. I staggered, like a ruffled bird that knocks its wings, into the night, where time passes immeasurably. You must know the dazzling night-shine of colours; it makes the stars slide down. Someone comes, enters; someone else comes and enters too. I don't think I'll be able to sleep ever again, not this night, not the next, none at all—Someone is sitting down beside him, so gentle and soft, a little feather, her eyes shine so bright that moths should come and settle on them. I see him kiss her, how he lets his hand move through her hair, that makes a sound anyway, just when you look at it. That was his wife of course. It seems I've stepped into the mouth of autumn.

Scene Eight

At the piano in the afternoon. The BUYER *has actually undone his shirt buttons to his trouser waistband. A heavy silver chain is tangled in his chest hair. The* BUYER *plays powerfully, with plenty of pedal, a Chopin virtuoso piece, a piece really to excel.*

SHE. Stop it for Christ's sake.

BUYER. You can see for yourself, this thing is worthless.

SHE. Sure, if one can't play it.

BUYER. I'm a piano teacher in the musicians union. . . .

SHE *(poisonously)*. One can hear that clearly enough.

44

BUYER. And I'm looking for a second-hand piano for a pupil.

SHE. Second-hand it is. I can't dispute that.

BUYER. If it were merely out of tune. But that pedal is completely useless as well.

SHE *(still hostile)*. You stepped on the accelerator pretty hard just now. One shouldn't try to mash everything together, specially not the light, pointed and sharp sounds, into some soft pudding of a tune.

BUYER *(unswervingly)*. Two strings are broken.

SHE. As a piano teacher, you can't break strings. But he could.

BUYER. Who?

SHE. And what a tone . . .

BUYER. Excuse me. Your piano has no tone.

SHE. But when the strings break and give up.

BUYER *(comically dogmatic)*. No craftsman, who really is one, will destroy his tools. Not even in revolutions. If you destroy a piano, you do not deserve a piano.

SHE *(annoyed)*. He was an unadulterated pianist. There is nothing like it. He pushed out translucent runs. He demolished pianos out of pure pleasure. Seriously. And it was. . . . .

BUYER *(formally)*. Then may I. . . .

SHE. Why don't you go now. Without formalities. Can't you even simply go?

BUYER. May I. . . .

SHE. You may nothing. You have to do what you want.

BUYER. I wanted to stay with you tonight. *(Pause.)*

SHE *(perplexed, but decides quickly)*. Then stay. *(He comes back into the room in very good spirits and sits down at the piano.)* Keep your fingers off the piano. But stay.

Scene Nine

It is now morning. The same scene as the evening before, just everything's fallen apart. The BUYER *sits tattered at the piano and* SHE, *in her bathrobe, hungover, sits beside him. Both drink beer.*

SHE *(Her hangover making her decisive and energetic)*. Right! The piano has got to go. You musn't think he gave me money for it. One just can't do it without a piano. A piano, believe me, is one of the good things which exist in spite of it. I've stopped listening to music in the morning now. That will pass. It's true. When the party's over you put the flowers in the cool. In the morning after the nightly hunt the spiders have disappeared into their holes. I've just remembered, there's one sitting on the toilet, you've got to kill it before you go. *(He hangs silently over his beer.)* If you come at closing time, they pour water over your feet and run down the shutters. It's always the same.

BUYER. Your chatter's unbearable in the early light of the morning.

SHE. This morning nothing is light. No. Honestly. Now he's romping about somewhere by the lake, with his wife and kids, and when their lips get too blue, he rubs their little bodies warm. I'm freezing. The beginning is so small and secret. But the end. Ditched shit the whole business.

BUYER. Let's get down to business, for god's sake. I'll buy your piano.

SHE. What absurd little boots you're wearing! I didn't notice them yesterday at all. *(She grasps an idea which will save her.)* No piano is meant for absurd little boots like that.

BUYER *(as if he has understood something).* You're personally attached to this instrument.

SHE *(hard and quick).* That's no instrument. That's a piano.

BUYER. Fine. Then I can go.

SHE. Don't you know someone who's sensible?

BUYER. What do you mean?

SHE. And who is looking for a piano. For himself, alone, not for a pupil, not for a woman, and not for his son. And someone who can understand sounds.

BUYER *(smiling stupidly).* I'll send someone. Count on me. But just leave me out of it. *(He goes.)*

Scene Ten

The bar tables. SHE *and her* GIRLFRIEND *sit at the 'Stammtisch'. The scene is as in scene 2 – including* WAITRESS, *chocolate and wine.*

SHE. Then, that walk through the cornfield was the end. I just didn't realise it. Just a premonition full of fears. My wings were already too clipped. I should have been gay. With flying hair and easy talk— The corn was trying to pierce the sky, I felt a tickle in my hand, as if it were caught between the corn and the sky. And everything was so quiet and didn't know where from and where to. *(She drinks a good sip of wine.)* Nature, to be precise, is one great effrontery.

GIRLFRIEND. Memories grow pale with time.

SHE. No, they don't.

GIRLFRIEND. And then they don't hurt anymore.

SHE *(annoyed).* But they do. Once he gave me a poppy as a present. Poppies had broken out all over the fields. He was dying to pee, pulls over to the edge of the lane and stands with his back turned to me. I notice for the first time that he has got bow-legs, it moved me so much I almost had a heart-attack. Just stood there forgotten by all the world. And plods into the field and fetches me a poppy. *(Embarrassing pause. The* GIRLFRIEND *looks at her incredulously.)* All right. I had shouted after him to fetch me a poppy. At least he did get me one.

GIRLFRIEND *(ironic).* The least he could do. Good boy.

SHE *(again determined).* I'll get rid of this piano once and for all.

GIRLFRIEND. You still haven't sold it?

SHE. What business is my piano to strangers. They live content and happy in their houses and they want to play a tune to that on my piano. Singing drunk 'It's a long way'. In the wide wide world. Oh well.

GIRLFRIEND. Do you want to sell or not?

SHE. Of course I want to sell. But without the charades. So you play yourself? Why do you want to sell then? Doesn't it play? Has it no tone? Do the pedals hang down? Bad wood. Too soft to the touch. Oh, you don't play the piano? Who do you have a piano then? Fulfil a childhood dream, I understand. So you haven't got a clue about pianos. Between you and me: your piano isn't worth a fig. *(Pause)* I won't let anyone touch my piano.

GIRLFRIEND. What now?

SHE. Never ever, ever— What use is the piano without him? I know. Again and again, going on and on, the same old story. Kisses, kisses. Keep repeating the whole thing from the beginning.

GIRLFRIEND. Do me a favour.

SHE. If only a wind would come at last—Do me a favour, pay for me. I've got to leave. *(She goes very quickly.)*

Scene Eleven

SHE *with the* SECOND BUYER, *at the piano.*

SECOND BUYER *(knowingly).* The issue at hand is not the piano.

SHE. The issue at hand is only the piano, what else?'

SECOND BUYER. All right then, let's play the game. How much do you want?

SHE. I've no idea what the going rates are. I'm doing this for the first time.

SECOND BUYER *(reassuring).* Sometimes you do everything for the first time. Get us a drink baby.

SHE. Since when did I become 'baby'?

SECOND BUYER. I'm sorry I didn't mean to get intimate, Madam. That's how one puts it, isn't it.

SHE. You like wine?

SECOND BUYER. Yes, always.

SHE *goes. He is alone for a few minutes—full of stupid self-confidence.* SHE *comes back. We have the usual actions of opening bottles, fetching glasses, pouring out. They drink.*

SHE. Am I correct in presuming—you are not the least bit interested in my piano?

SECOND BUYER. Let's get down to business.

SHE. I'm seeing everything lopsided and you want to get down to business. Clouds fall into my head and stupid waves and bodies of little children and the devil knows what. *(Helpless)* If you don't want the piano . . .

SECOND BUYER. Couldn't we talk about your piano later?

SHE. And now?

SECOND BUYER. You are an attractive woman. Your charms put your piano's to shame. If I may put it that way.

SHE. You'd better go.

SECOND BUYER. I'd very much like to stay with you.

SHE *(stubborn)*. So you don't really want the piano at all?

SECOND BUYER *(determined)*. Come on, baby, what do you take me for?

SHE *(suddenly)*. Well, get into bed. *(Resigned and ironic)* 'Let us sleep', said the poet and died.

SECOND BUYER. That's not exactly inviting.

SHE. You've got coins on your eyes. *(The* SECOND BUYER *lies down on the bed dressed.)* Yes, yes. *(*SHE *lies down on the bed, also remaining dressed.)* He went to sleep with his head on his arm. With his finger-tips on his lips, he listened to me for a long time. Until he just slept. He slept unobtrusively. At night I go back the way of the day. Why don't you go?

SECOND BUYER *(almost tender but at the same time threatening)*. I'm staying with you.

SHE. But it's no good. Love is kitsch. *(Pause)* Photos of fenced-in beaches . . .

SECOND BUYER *(impatient)*. What's wrong with that?

SHE. Now he tells other women how beautiful they are. Yet it's almost winter.

SECOND BUYER. Don't talk about my predecessor all the time.

SHE *(sits up enraged)*. You're not taking over. You must be mad.

SECOND BUYER. That's enough, I'm telling you.

SHE. Get out of here.

SECOND BUYER *(hits her)*. I'm no lightning conductor for your fucked-up soul-pains. *(Hits her again.)* And don't stare at me like that. Instead I'll give you some advice. Keep your hands off selling pianos. You're far too delicately strung for that, sweetheart. *(He leaves.)*

Scene Twelve

Bar tables. The same paper-napkin folding WAITRESS, *the same 'Stammtisch' table. The* GIRLFRIEND *is already there drinking a cup of cocoa.* SHE, *with a swollen blue eye, joins her; she is quite tipsy.*

GIRLFRIEND *(horrified).* What on earth!

SHE *(by-the-way and matter-of-fact).* Someone got upset.

GIRLFRIEND. Oh come on, pull yourself together. You know you're getting into something quite awful.

SHE. Believe me, it's much better than falling into your void.

GIRLFRIEND. It's not your scene.

SHE *(more and more indignant).* Where is it? Where. Everything around me is so generous and cool and never hits you. Everything runs so smooth. You're even capable of understanding those few madmen, but you'll never make them relaxed like you, no matter how hard you try. I need a Schnaps.

GIRLFRIEND *(a hint too understanding).* Corn or fruit?

SHE. Corn, of course. Corn. *(The* GIRLFRIEND *orders the Schnaps.)* It's all dry decorative thistles around me. And stale fern. One dozes away happily. *(Pause)* To think he sacrifices me so willingly. For a visit from the in-laws, just to keep his wife in a good mood. She is just as quiet and soft as you. She mustn't know anything. No, no, never shake up the well-tempered. With me, he'd hit the piano with his fists. And then he'd push me aside. To this day I can't understand it, and I don't want to understand it either.

GIRLFRIEND. That's it exactly. You don't want to get out of the state you're in.

SHE. Jesus. Don't come on psychological now. Next you'll recommend therapy. Group dynamics, if possible. *(Quoting)* In two minutes we'll really scream that pain clean out of our souls. Nobody need feel ashamed here. We all suffer. But we need not suffer, if we learn to handle our pain. So let's scream together. One, two, three, start. Thank you. Relax. *(Angry)* Until my blessed passing on I'll stick to this, share a pleasure, rue at leisure. That love sings and swings, makes unscrupulous and never puts up with forward planning, like some old, wrinkled, greedy woman.

GIRLFRIEND. For heavens sake take better care of yourself. I could sell your piano for you.

SHE. You're out of your mind. *(She starts hectically to look for money)* Have to get out of here.

GIRLFRIEND. Save your money. You just go.

SHE. As you like. Good. Well then.

When SHE *leaves, she staggers a little.*

Scene Thirteen

Between the bed and the piano a somewhat elderly INSURANCE AGENT *hesitantly comes in.*

INSURANCE AGENT. Good day. You are . . .

SHE. Just come right in, come right in. I know what it's about. It's about the piano so to speak. *(She giggles)* Don't be frightened. Come closer. *(Whispers)* You can't sell a piano standing in the doorway.

INSURANCE AGENT. Excuse me. But . . .

SHE. No need to apologize. Not being the only one. *(Examines him)* Age is not critical with pianos. *(Giggles)*

INSURANCE AGENT. I don't know anything about pianos . . .

SHE. Doesn't matter. Pianos are not that complicated.

INSURANCE AGENT. Pianos are household effects. That's not my department. For that, my colleague from the household effects insurance is . . .

SHE. Why not bring him as well.

INSURANCE AGENT. I want to make sure that you're well cared for in old age.

SHE *(perplexed)*. What? Is this a proposal?

INSURANCE AGENT. I know you're still young and you don't think of old age.

SHE. What's my age got to do with you?

INSURANCE AGENT. You definitely need better insurance. *(Starts to rummage in his brief case.)* You're in the radio choir . . .

SHE. I have sung at the State Opera too . . .

INSURANCE AGENT. . . . and you must be earning . . .

SHE. Money really doesn't come into it.

INSURANCE AGENT. . . . a tidy sum of money every month. But say, for example, you were to get laryngitis . . .

SHE. Come on, don't try that number on me.

INSURANCE AGENT *(irritated)*. . . . and you were unable to carry out your duties, you'll get on the basis of an average monthly turn-over, of, let's say . . .

SHE *(clumsily strikes an obvious pose)*. What's my average monthly turn-over rate then? I'm really on tenterhooks.

INSURANCE AGENT. Let's say, two hundred and fifty—

SHE. The month has thirty days. Two hundred and fifty divided by thirty, that would be about eight a day. Just like in Djakarta, said the seamen when the seventh woman sank exhausted to the floor.

INSURANCE AGENT. What?

SHE. Let's pack this up. Piano here we come. *(She goes to the piano and lies down on the key-board.)* You hear? *(Sprawls as good as she can on the keys.)* If that's not music, I don't know what is. *(Makes copulation movements letting her arse drop rhythmically on to the keys)* Listen to this. *(She quite spends herself)* That's music with life in it, isn't it? *(Works the piano with obvious pleasure)* God it really blows you . . . up with, with, with, with . . . *(She stops suddenly.)* Don't stand there like that.

INSURANCE AGENT. Yes. But.

SHE. But what?

INSURANCE AGENT.   Honestly, there is no need for you—
SHE *(jumps off the piano aggressively)*.   There is no need for me to what?
   Out with it. What do I not need? Exhausted old men's fictions I do
   not need. Composed music I need even less. Because I need everything,
   everything.
INSURANCE AGENT *(pompous, like a father)*.   But it's just about
   insurance. *(Business-like)* You should provide security for yourself.
   Against eventualities. They always occur. Then you look stupid.
SHE.   What's my security got to do with you. You certainly don't need
   a piano, oh no. Just security in old age. I'll tell you something, old
   chum, when you're dead and under, that piano will still be on top.
   You won't make one single inflated mark from me. Now push off
   with your security. *(He goes very quickly.* SHE *shouts after him)*
   As if you were any different. You're all the same. Wet and smart
   under the table. While hands are being shaken over the deals!

Scene Fourteen

*At the bar tables there has to be the atmosphere of a third-class bar
denoted by similar music, lights, nude photos, and indiscrimately
projected porno-films. At the table, instead of the paper-napkin
folding waitress sits a well-made up and dressed woman. Two or three
men come on during the scene with big alsatians. The* WOMAN *points
out silently where they are to go. They disappear. She then makes notes,
looking at her watch mechanically. At the 'Stammtisch' table of the
earlier scenes, sits* SHE, *in the company of loud* MEN. *One of the piano*
BUYERS *is amongst them.*

SHE *(in high spirits)*.   He was a hot one. The Helgoland bar. I must get back
   there. *(Calls)* The bill please . . . *(She notices that her purse is empty)*
   Jesus Christ, where's my money!
WAITER.   We've heard that one before. Let's not have that.
SHE.   But I had some before.
FIRST MAN.   And we'll make sure you get plenty more. *(The men
   laugh.)*
SHE.   You, didn't I lend you twenty earlier?
SECOND MAN.   Yes, and there were still plenty of notes left.
SHE.   What do you expect me to think. Look, one of you here is a
   thief.
WAITER.   Always the same. Miss, if you invited them, cough up the
   money.
SHE.   Shit bastards. I'm not loaded with it. Why take from me? Why
   don't you take it from those who heat their firesides with it? Always
   the little ones and right in the face. I sing the throat out of my neck,
   and you pinch it. *(Screams)* Who's got my money? *(General searching,
   checking over of self, reassuring and calming down.)*

51

SHE *(to the* WAITER, *attempting to be easy).* The money's gone.
It's all gone. And I won't find it again. I'll drink to that.
THIRD MAN.   Two bottles of champagne and glasses for everyone.
WAITER.   Who's going to pay?
THIRD MAN.   I'll settle it. Bring the champagne, come on. *(Slight
bewilderment at the table.)*
SHE.   No deceit. No hypocrisy. An altogether different life. I could
kill myself laughing. Nothing but scared chickens. You haven't even
got enough to be cocks. *(The first bottle is opened and poured into
glasses.)* Cheers. To all of us. *(All, except one, raise their glasses and
drink.)* Why aren't you drinking? *(He grins silently.)* That's a stupid
grin. Cheers, Erwin, or whatever your name is. I now drink to you.
(The same man goes on smiling stupidly.) Struck dumb, are we. I
understand why. A real giant joke the whole thing of course. Don't
worry. You'll survive it. Cheers now. *(He remains unchanged.)* Now
drink with me, and don't pretend you've got stones in your mouth.
FIRST MAN.   There's no stones, there's notes in it. *(Laughs.)*
SECOND MAN.   Open your mouth.
SHE.   If he doesn't want to talk, leave him.
SECOND MAN.   Open it up. *(The fall on top of him. They hold his
arms down fast and stretch him out like a crucifixion.)* Open it up.
SHE *(screaming hysterically.)*   Shut up. They'll murder you. Don't
let them. Come with me. For God's sake, will you shut up. *(In tears
while the men make his mouth bleed by forcing it open.)* . . . and
come with me . . .

*Out of the man's mouth, the other men pull the notes. They throw
the bloodstained notes over to her.*

Scene Fifteen

Stage dark. SHE, *alone, to the audience.*

SHE.   I wanted to tell you that I have broken open. No aim in mind,
I've thought right through the stories, which begin and infinitely
flow into one another. But far too long. By sitting there and inventing
stories where everything works out so well, I have created for myself,
step by step, a loneliness which you must know about as well. But
it's not the quiet calm that we dream of on the high heights, is it,
that lies down on us like the smile of a child? We remain down below
in our dreams. The little devils peep through the window; I brood
and tremble and I hear all the old wicked songs which want to make
the distance small for me. Sometimes I then see old women, how
they lift their skirts free and unashamed to show their legs with their
blue, violet veins, and intricately wrinkled old men with their quick
greedy look. All that leads to God knows where, and that's where
I want to get to. Only when I'm there will I know that my dreams

haven't come with me far enough. There'll be a summer which will make me hear the air. The little poor-sinner flowers and the old stories will have withered. Grumbling, hissing or jerking, all moaning would have dried up, and I would be happy about nothing else than the weather or how shall I put it. But maybe there will be a winter, a white in white coldness, that makes my face stand still. Then the distance comes to within a few metres and remains distant. Distant were the trees, like they are in books. A long-gone present would become clear and distinct and then disappear. Both shall be. Perhaps. You know how sinister a single hen can be in the evening, when the night is just about to come. Now you can see that I'm really broken open.

Scene Sixteen

At her small old beautiful table, HE stands there once more, and tries to pretend, happily and carelessly, despite all the time that has passed, that everything is now in the best of order. HE takes his jacket off and hangs it too matter of factly over a chair. SHE just watches him.

HE. Well, how are you? What are you up to?

SHE. I want to go away. Somewhere. I need quiet; I can't get it here.

HE. Tell me, what are you looking for?

SHE. I'll know when I have found it.

HE. North or South?

SHE *(annoyed)*. I don't know. Where there's a sun and a moon. Where the sky looks as if it were the sea.

HE. Plain or mountains?

SHE. You haven't got the faintest notion. Where it swings and clings, where it's . . .

HE. You're not looking your best. I don't think you're getting enough sleep.

SHE *(indifferent)*. Waking, sleeping. The fields will clear. Before that you dream all the time and richly of hair-pins and hawks and crows or whatever. Life is in everywhere. *(Pause. Suddenly)* I like the medieval pictures. Where it dances and drinks and sighs and lusts after it. Fat-thighed and vulgar. Right there at least hearts are being torn out and heads cut off. Breasts of women nipped right off.

HE. Oh yes, I once kissed you in front of the Barbara-altar.

SHE. Yes. And?

HE. And nothing. It's just . . .

SHE. Nothing it's just. Just nothing and nothing and nothing again. The small taste of hell, yes. But not hell, oh no. To stand in a slanting rain and wait for love and almost to despair—it blows joy away like cotton wool.

HE *(almost stalking her)*. I've heard that you've been having quite a jolly time.

SHE. Used-up men creep around my house. It upsets the
neighbours of course.
HE. I hear you spend most of your nights up town.
SHE. You've heard, have you. Well, I'm telling you, there's much worse
to come. Sure, I'll hear you scream. So small and in the midst of
blood. Anything else but not that. I can see you already designing
that sweet little gravestone. The death mask of dear, dear curly-top
in stone. How tragic that stones can't be blonde. Surely, my sweet
you can find some talented artist, who can let a curl blow out of
stone so life-like you can feel its blondness.
HE. Shut up. Right now.
SHE. I don't believe it, you're talking sensibly, well I never—
HE. Shut your fucking mouth. *(Low)* I don't want to hit you.
SHE *(screams)*. But you're hitting me all the time. The last bit
of the song. When the child sits on the horse, no music plays. Even
the stars are just spikey.
HE. I simply can't talk to you when you're like this.
SHE. Yes. I can't even make dreams anymore.

It gets dark.

Scene Seventeen

Night. SHE *sits with her* GIRLFRIEND *at her small table. Both crack
walnuts eagerly and incessantly. Their movements have something of a
bird like quality. They talk incidentally.*

SHE. So it goes on, just how I don't know. He drops by occasionally.
We actually talk in the meanwhile, like civilized people: What's new?
Does the work go well? Smart pullover you've got on. The children
all right? I am as well, thanks. Then we sleep together. When I lie
down, beside him I feel we ought to introduce ourselves—pleased to
meet you, same here. And when he leaves I smile at him, a friendly
goodbye.
GIRLFRIEND. Can you really cope with it now?
SHE *(concentrating on cracking nuts)*. You're quite right. Characters
with despair writ large on their faces and voices charged with grief
only exist in the theatre. And I've got to live.
GIRLFRIEND. Quite.
SHE. Once the devil held a fête for me. That was before.
GIRLFRIEND. Forget it.
SHE. Yes.

*While they go on cracking nuts, the sun seems to rise over the bed. But
it immediately gets dark again.* HE *has come.*

Scene Eighteen

SHE *(still welcoming him)*. It never ends. all the same, it's nice you're here.

HE. You must have known I was coming. After all, tonight is the big night, there'll be jazz, rock, classics. Plus I think there'll be some poetry, between the music, well texts anyway. I'm playing at the end. . . .

SHE. Is that right? *(Sarcastic)* We are lucky, aren't we. Combine the practical with the pleasurable, that's what they say, isn't it? *(Suddenly, for some unknown reason, she giggles)* We'll have a Pernod. Like the old days.

HE *(distractedly)*. Oh, the piano's still there.

SHE *(unconcerned)*. You've left too many traces behind you. People don't want it like that. *(She goes and fetches the Pernod and some water)* The usual? *(HE laughs. SHE mixes. They drink.)* Has peace been restored at home?

HE. You could say that. *(Pause)*

SHE. I imagine your wife to be mild and sweet smelling.

HE. That's exactly right.

SHE. She's certainly bound to wear shimmering Goddess outfits and in winter a fur with small sharp claws around her neck.

HE. What's this you're cooking up? It's always the same: pure jealousy. By the way, she really has got a fur with claws. A black fox.

SHE. Oh that's a gorgeous piece she's got there. My head's so full. In the daytime the air hums. At night it's swarming. All the time I hear piano music. You're building sandcastles with the children, some ancient Rome with underground passages. I stand aside. And I behave disgracefully. All in all.

HE. My son—you would have liked him, if you'd ever seen him. You would have understood everything.

SHE. I know, I know, he's got blond curls and is a very dreamy child. Everybody is deeply moved when they see him. *(Laughs)* The devil's brood in angels' clothes.

HE. Will you stop all this please?

SHE. Oh God, your industrious little Lieschen with the full lips. Who wants to kill herself laughing all the time but can't even do that. Yes, yes, not a word about her, no, no. Don't touch her. Convenient, isn't it? There's nothing common about you. You don't wish your old woman to go to hell. That's not how you like it. You prefer to treat yourself to a few precious blooms on the side which are delicate and discreet with their gleaming shadows and a helpless twitch round their damned tired dry eyes. No, I don't want to be a bitchy now. *(Depressed)* It all makes me so depressed. I'd just love to run as far as I can see. Where there's a morning light without cruelty. I don't want to meet love any more— *(Pause. Suddenly coming to life again for a short time)* Someone with a woman's hair-do keeps sending me roses. But they turn black in the evening.

HE.   Who's that?

SHE.   I'd so like to sleep now.

HE.   And I've got to go. So you're not coming?

SHE *(brings him to the door).* I've had enough of it. Too much of it. *(She touches his face much too tenderly.)* Play well. You've got to play well. That's the very least.

Scene Nineteen

Now SHE *is alone again. She lies down on the bed and remains there for a while. Suddenly she gets up and goes to the telephone.*

SHE *(on the phone).* Is it you—It's me. Yes. Why don't you come here—I can't sleep—Always the same: I lie here with open eyes, don't recognize anyone, stay silent and can't scream, see an open coffin with the corpse of a child. With blond curls. It acts ever so innocently and holds up flowers to the sky. The sky, I want to scream, is beautiful enough. it doesn't need your flowers. It already has the corn. It's just nobody hears it rustling—Hey, just come here very quickly.

She puts the phone down so quickly that he can't protest. It gets dark.

Scene Twenty

Dark. SHE, *alone, to the audience.*

SHE.   Insidious days and the great fear of the night. They reduce us to little moving human beings. They are ageing. We reflect upon the irridescent lives, which once should have been ours, and we open the first bottle of wine. Once it should have been like being at the beginning of the world or at its end or like a real new beginning, without similarities. A new beginning: a beautiful idea but old. The sky should have turned round and gone round the earth. But the sky had a fire dying out, and a white sun had long since come. But the white suns bring nothing else but rain. Now I don't want all that above me. Light touched, it's buzzing madly in my head. In the abyss there are such beautiful places. Who wants to know who gets kissed by the birds. They fly easy and relentless, way up there.

Her doorbell rings a few times. She does not open. Blackout.

Josef and Maria

(Josef und Maria)

by

Peter Turrini

translated by David Roger

Première: simultaneously at the Orpheum, Graz and the Trades Union Centre, Vienna as part of the 1980 'Steiermark Autumn'.

Peter Turrini's interest in and commitment to a specifically Austrian culture has been evident since his first play, *Rozzenjogd (Rat Hunt)* in 1967, which was written in a strong Viennese dialect. At the same time, the influence of his Italian father shows itself in such works as his rewrite of Goldoni's *The Landlady* (1973). The combination of this central European and Latin Catholic taste has produced work of great emotional intensity, of a certain confessional frankness and yet of a highly realistic nature. *Josef and Maria* is a Christmas story about two elderly outsiders and exploits quite consciously the names of Jesus's parents for its two protagonists. Yet these two suffer, like so many—and not just of their own generation—from a feeling of dislocation and alienation that consumerism (as represented by the pile of tawdry goods around them) engenders. Turrini is careful, however, to insist that their resultant behaviour be portrayed absolutely normally, the shock effect designed to come from the very fact that idiosyncrasy is now the rule, not the exception. This signals something of a change of direction, since the shock value of *Rat Hunt*, with its naked couple on a large rubbish dump, was achieved by much more blatant provocation.

Turrini's commitment, like Dario Fo's (as Ulf Birbaumer points out in the Turrini *Lesebuch*), is to the great majority of the population who do not go to the theatre, who see art as distant and threatening. He reads a lot to small clubs and societies, seeing in education and the expansion of the articulate working-class through education the key to a true socialist society. This has not stopped him being enormously successful. His version of Beaumarchais' *Figaro* was for several years one of the most performed plays in German-language theatres. But Turrini must be aware that for all the success, the change of heart in the bourgeoisie is slow in coming. The subtler approach he adopts in *Josef and Maria* may therefore be a sign that he is now agitating for change in what Adorno would call 'implicit' rather than 'explicit' ways, which may achieve more by seemingly saying less.

The confessional dimension to the play is historical: Josef and Maria have both been performers in the theatre. Both have suffered at the hands of fascists—Josef is a committed if disorientated socialist—of drink and of old age in a society based on energy. The result is their curiously optimistic coming together, and the reminiscences they trade invite their audiences to look back at where they too have come from and ask if they are going in the right direction. The implicit answer is that they are not.

Characters

JOSEF, nightwatchman, 68.
MARIA, cleaning woman, 65.

Set

(1)   Apron stage—piles of goods in Christmas glitter. Audience crosses
      this to reach their seats.
(2)   Proscenium stage. Non-naturalistic setting. Chaotic jumble of goods
      in a tasteless cheapening of Christmas—drink, toys, angels, meat,
      lamps, cribs, all mixed up.

Direction

The characters should not be represented as farcical types. The
ridiculous in them should not be made ridiculous. The sad and tragic
should not be played sadly or tragically. The two old people in this play
have lived so long with their singularities that these have become quite
normal to them. This normalcy and the attempt to break out of it is the
theme of the play.
The stage is glistening with coloured lights and decorations. In the background there is a door with 'Tannoy' on it. While the audience is being
seated, adverts are relayed over the speakers. The broadcast is on a
continuous tape, interspersed with a Christmas jingle.

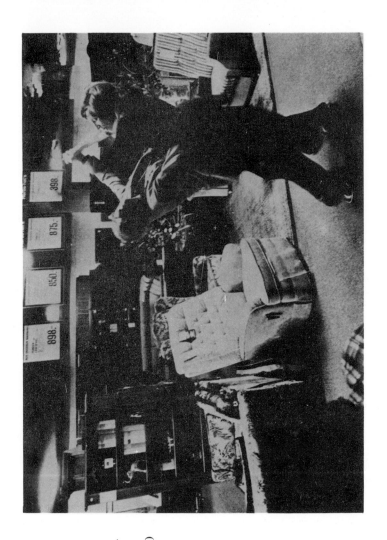

Manfred Schindler, Elisabeth Gruber
in *Josef and Maria* by Peter Turrini,
1982

(Photo by Odry)

Josef and Maria

24th December. Evening.
Hall of a large department store.

LOUDSPEAKER. May we draw your attention please to some of our
special Christmas offers starting with our finest quality ham at
36.80 a kilo and a special buy of first class Hungarian goose at only
19.80 a kilo. For decorating the Christmas table we have a beautiful
selection of non-drip candles in a wide range of colours complete
with star-shaped crystal holders at 7.90 the set. Buy a pack of 10 and
save 35 Schillings leaving you enough to put towards our own brand
electric carving knife coming complete with an interchangeable blade
set to make sure everyone gets their fair slice of the Christmas dinner.
Christmas without one is unthinkable. Available as a mains or battery
model. There's still time too to buy one of our miniature Christmas
cribs each containing the entire Holy Family: the baby Jesus, Mary,
Joseph, the Three Kings, together with three sheep and two donkeys
(all washable and unbreakable) and as an optional extra a
realistically twinkling Star of Bethlehem. The cribs come in three
sizes the 'Infant' size for the young couple with a new arrival, the
'Junior' for those with one to three older children, and finally the
'Family' size. For the older couple whose children have grown up and
left home may we recommend the 'Infant' model.

Attention please. This is a staff announcement. This is the Personnel
Manager speaking. On behalf of the management I would like to thank
all our salesmen and salesladies for their tireless service to our
customers over the festive period; to wish them and their families a
very happy Christmas Day, and as a token of our gratitude may we
take the liberty of presenting each employee with a nice little
bottle of top quality brandy which may be collected at the staff exit.
Thank you.

Christmas music. The light changes slowly from warmth and glitter to a
cold neon. Silence. An old woman enters. She has obviously been to
the hairdressers, is made up, wears an overcoat and is carrying a large
carrier bag. She goes over to a sofa and puts the bag down on it. She
takes out three Christmas presents and lays them on the sofa. She takes
off her coat, her shoes, her dress. She stands in her underwear. She
takes her overall, working shoes and a headscarf from the bag and
dresses in them. First the overall, then the shoes, then ties the scarf
round her head, thus becoming a cleaning woman. She takes a purse out
of her coat and puts it in her overall pocket. She looks at herself in a
mirror, goes up closer and studies her face, takes a tissue, spits on it and
wipes off her make-up. She goes to the sofa and looks at the three

Christmas parcels. She puts them back in the bag with her clothes and goes offstage. Silence. She returns with a scrubbing brush, a bucket and a cloth. She begins working, wiping the floor with a damp cloth. Silence.
She stands in front of some shelves, stops working, looks around as though someone might be watching her, takes a bottle of brandy off the shelf and looks at it. She puts it down near the shelves and carries on working. She wipes the floor near the Tannoy booth. She stops working, looks around, then goes into the booth.
Crackling of speakers.

MARIA'S VOICE.   All cleaning ladies not in permanent employment regrettably cannot be considered recipients of this token of our appreciation. As if the likes of us didn't do any work. That's a load of . . . . . and that's the truth of it. *(Silence)* Willi. *(Silence)* Willi? This is your mother speaking. Can you hear me? Merry Christmas! *(Silence)* And to the wife and the little boy. I wish you all a very Happy Christmas. *(Silence)* Willi! *(Almost shouting)* Willi! *(An old man in a security uniform appears. He has a bag over his shoulder and a set of keys in his hand. He hears the voice and looks around.)* Willi! Willi!
JOSEF *(loudly)*.   That's a very loud voice. I've never heard a voice like that before. *(Silence. MARIA comes out, gets her brush and starts working again.)*
MARIA.   It's nobody—I'm sorry, it's just me, Frau Maria.
JOSEF.   But it was exceedingly loud.
MARIA.   You must have misheard.
JOSEF.   As far as hearing goes, I'm a hundred per cent all there. More so than most men of my age. Are you on duty tonight?
MARIA.   Temporary help. *(He stands there rather embarrassed. Silence. MARIA working.)*
JOSEF.   Yes, well. I'll be getting along then. Goodbye.
MARIA.   Yes, all right.
JOSEF.   Oh . . . one thing—will you be here all evening?
MARIA.   Oh no—my son and his wife'll be waiting for me already.
JOSEF.   So you're spending this so-called Silent Night, Holy Night in the bosom of your family? In this respect I have been a freethinker since the year 1928.
MARIA.   My daughter-in-law's cooking a carp tonight and the lady gets very ungracious when I'm late. *(Silence. MARIA works.)*
JOSEF.   Talking about 1928, I was a lens grinder back in those days—with 'Görz Optics' down in the 10th district. Toni Sedlacek, an apprentice and a Socialist—he said, during the course of an argument, Josef! this whole Christ figure—it's completely unhistorical. There's just nothing there of him. Nothing written, nothing drawn, nothing painted, nothing sculpted—not even a scratch. *(Silence. MARIA looks at him.)*
MARIA.   She gets the fish from her own shop. It's my son's shop

actually but everything's in her name for tax reasons.

JOSEF. I could go into it further of course if you like. All the eminent historians of that time, Roman and Jewish, keep absolutely silent about him. Did Flavius ever write a single word about Christ—did Cornelius or Livy or Tacitus? I mean he writes nothing about himself and no one else writes anything about him. *(He laughs.)* The whole concept of God is nothing but a mental crutch for mental cripples. (MARIA *turns away and carries on working.* JOSEF *stands there in silence watching her. She wrings out her cloth. Suddenly* JOSEF *goes up to her, takes it and wrings it out for her.)* Permit me—if I'm not a hindrance to you.

MARIA. I'm just about through anyway. *(She continues cleaning.* JOSEF *follows her a little. He looks around the hall.)*

JOSEF. So full and yet so empty. *(He trips over the brandy bottle* MARIA *had put by the shelf. He lifts it up, looks at it and starts to lecture.)* Alcohol, you devil! I know you of old! My foster-father— started off as a butcher and then became manager of a public assistance office—a man who always laid great store by neat hand-writing. It was in 1914 when they'd just begun their great Slaughter of the Nations that he started drinking. He didn't have to join up. Managed to get himself exempted somehow. It wouldn't have been Sunday if there hadn't been a litre of beer on the table. From beer to wine—from wine to rum. Tea with rum, but it was rum with tea . . . and then just rum. Pension day was always a black day for us. He'd come back at midnight dead drunk, beat up my foster-mother; I'd run down to the police, just a child too. 'What's your father do? A civil servant? Oh well,' says the policeman, 'it can't be as bad as all that'— and sends me back home again. *(He puts the bottle back on the shelf.* MARIA *comes over, takes it off again and sets it on the floor.)*

MARIA. Don't let me interrupt you. Just the odd sip, because of the loneliness. Nothing in excess: everything within reason.

JOSEF *(returning bottle to shelf).* I wore the badge of the Workers' Temperance League right next to my Freethinkers badge and just below my Socialist Party badge. My involvement in politics wasn't just a matter of feeling, but one of understanding. Consequently I turned away form religious faith. God, who doesn't exist, and can't exist, can't be dependent on my proletarian Groschen. *(He has put the bottle back.* MARIA *takes it out again.)*

JOSEF. February the 13th, 1934. I was putting up at the police station in the 15th district and the Superintendent ripped the badge clean off me. Well, I screamed at that fascist—'So, it's already forbidden to be against alcohol, is it?' I was much better spoken than him because of my theatrical background. (JOSEF *puts the bottle back.* MARIA *takes it back. He looks at her*) However, it didn't do me much good. He still had me beaten up for causing a breach of the peace.

MARIA *(Looks at him).* We're just far too nice. Even with our own children. Sometimes I think we should just go, just get out of this world. Human beings don't care any more and that's the truth of it. *(She puts the bottle down and starts working.* JOSEF *suddenly opens his case and takes out a copy of 'The Truth'. He goes over to her.)*

JOSEF. 'The Truth' now just hasn't got nearly enough subscribers. Is it just individual ignorance or the wretched effect of capitalism? Both probably. Sometimes I have a dream, and as a free-thinker I'm not given to dreaming much but when I do, it's a dream that everybody is fighting to get a copy of this paper. The doors and windows of the council flats fly open and everyone is crying out for 'The Truth'. I have to tell them to stop pushing and in no time I've got my sales quota. (MARIA *carries on working.* JOSEF *holds up the paper to her.)* 'The Truth' is cheaper for the first three months.

MARIA. Don't let me interrupt you. In the 'Woman's Weekly' this week it says there's an 87-year-old lady. She writes that she's hungry all day long because her son and daughter-in-law don't give her any food.

JOSEF. Two-thirds of mankind is hungry and the only place you'll read that is in 'The Truth'. There's also a trial subscription.

MARIA. Dr Schöller, who always knows the answers, writes back that she should either state her case in greater detail or go into the old folks' home.

JOSEF *(Opens his paper and puts on a pair of old spectacles).* Here's just a taste of the poetic genius of our comrade Fritz Landl, murdered by the Nazi hangmen in Stein-on-the-Danube: 'Silent Night. Holy Night. All is calm. All is bright. I'm cold and I'm hungry and I'm locked up tight. So, thinking alone in my cell I lie, think of my loved ones, of life passing by. I think of my childhood, the years that were so good. I think how history shaped my life to come and how in it all the boy became man. Man's burden is heavy in life's sea of woe whose pain stretches on wherever you go. And yet I am glad I have lived at this time. It strengthens the will and sharpens the mind. The holy night of love and peace is here. It rings in my ears like a mocking jeer. Where is the love and where is the deed, where is the fairy tale of the green ripening seed. Silent Night. Holy Night. All is calm, all is bright. I'm cold and I'm hungry and I'm locked out of sight. I think, full of longing, of my loved ones at home. I think of the future, of what's been and gone.' He was spastic in the right hand so he wrote this poem on the 24th December 1940 with his left hand.

MARIA. Don't let me interrupt you. *(Dries her hands on her overalls and takes a magazine page out of her bag. Reads)*
'I must open my heart to someone although no one can do anything for me. My daughter-in-law locks the food away from me. I'm not allowed to help myself and I'm always hungry. My friends buy me a coffee now and then. She keeps my pension. I'm 87 years of age. Have I deserved this in my old age?' These are real tragedies. *(She stuffs the page back and continues working.* JOSEF *puts his paper into his bag. He looks at MARIA, takes her rag and wrings it out.)* Will your family be expecting you too?

JOSEF' I was left at the Margarethe Child Care Centre with the provision that I should belong to whoever would take me. Some people did come. A couple turned up from Breslau by the name of Datschke and they eventually became my foster-parents. Legally speaking my mother would've been allowed to visit me, but only as an aunt.

MARIA. My son, he's a good boy really but he's far too nice to her. He's very overweight and likes to lie down on his bed. 'Oh no!' she screams, 'not on the newly made bed. You go and lie on the couch.' It tears my heart out to hear her talk like that so I give him a few biscuits. She takes them away from him because they make crumbs. You can't possibly have ever come across such a nasty woman in all your life. *(She looks at him.)* Your wife must be pure gold compared to her.

JOSEF. Dr Friedmann—he was a follower of Tolstoy and gave lectures on sexuality at the Ottakringer Workers' Institute. Sex life and hygiene. He touched on love play and that sort of thing but in purely medical terms. In 1939 he fled to a place between Detroit and Chicago in the State of Michigan. Then at Christmas '46 I get a letter from him and there is one sentence I still know by heart. 'My son'—that's me, as I was logically much younger then—'my son, you must devote all your compassion and love to exploited and downtrodden humanity.'

MARIA. Don't let me interrupt; they must be sitting down together now and I bet she's overseasoned everything as usual. *(Silence. MARIA working.)*

JOSEF. So you'll have to be going soon. *(Silence. MARIA mechanically scrubs the floor, always in the same space.)* Well, that was a nice talk but if you've got to go . . . *(Silence. MARIA cleans. Suddenly she drops her brush and goes. JOSEF follows.)*

MARIA. He's got an inflamed gall bladder but don't imagine she'll give him a special diet. I smuggle the proper food into the fish shop. She'd never call me if there was something wrong with him. *(MARIA gets two glasses from a display cabinet and goes to get the brandy, JOSEF following.)* But I'm going to give her the perfume. I'm giving her the most expensive perfume and a pullover for him and a train for the little boy even if I have to leave the whole lot on the doorstep. *(She takes the bottle to the sofa. JOSEF follows.)* I'm just a simple cleaning woman as you know, but I still bought a freezer so I would have something nice in in case he calls, but she gets the dearest perfume— I have to get it for her or all hell breaks loose. *(She sits down, opens the bottle, pours and raises a glass. JOSEF watches her, horrified.)* Little Frau Maria—decent, clean, honest. You can leave all your valuables out when I'm around but if anything ever happens to him, then she'll see what I'm like. Then they'll all take notice. *(She downs her glass in one.)* Then I'll bring up Gibraltar. *(Downs a second glass.)*

JOSEF. 'No, no gentlemen, I wasn't born yesterday. My name is Thomas. Today the die will be cast and the chapter on Louis Capet will be completed.' I was an extra in the Graz Municipal Theatre at the time. The part was played by Karl Drews—another one murdered by the fascists. *(MARIA gives him the glass.)*

MARIA. Gibraltar, Dakar, Senegal, Portugal, Lisbon, Czecho. That's me. *(She holds out the glass and looks pleadingly at him. Quietly)* Do take it, sir . . .

JOSEF. You must remember my horrific childhood experience with alcohol. You ought to know that my parents used to pour alcohol down me when I was a child to stop me screaming.

MARIA. All right then, if you don't believe me. *(MARIA puts down the glass and takes an old yellowed photo from her purse and gives it to JOSEF. He sits down, takes out his spectacles and studies it meticulously. MARIA pulls up her overall above her knee and looks at JOSEF.)* Now you know everything.

JOSEF *(without looking up).* I see one half-naked woman and a zebra.

MARIA. The zebra's me. A variety act in Lisbon, 1932. The one beside me's my colleague. She was luckier than me—a consul took a fancy to her and she gave up the profession and moved into a very elegant flat. She was a bit consumptive though and was always stuffing herself. I ran into her once on the Ringstrasse in 19 . . . I don't remember exactly, 1955 or '65. She'll no doubt be dead by now. *(Drinks.)* I've acted these last forty years as though I was never on the stage and it's often been very hard. When I was working at Kapsch, the radio firm, and did more than my quota—well the boss was very nice—the other girls said they'd beat me up if I pushed up the rate any more and I thought, 'Well, what do you lot know about any of it?' And then a few days ago with my daughter-in-law. She stood right behind my son and said, 'Mother, don't come over on Christmas Eve. You'll only upset things.' I looked at her straight in her nasty, insolent face and I thought: you were never in show business, you were never in show business. *(MARIA shakes her head again.)* You can kill an old woman but an artiste never dies. *(She stretches out her uncovered leg. JOSEF stares at it.)* That is a genuine ballerina's leg. Rock firm. *(MARIA wants to take JOSEF'S hand and put it on her leg. JOSEF draws away. He puts on his glasses and rummages in his pocket.)*

JOSEF. May I bring a piece of correspondence to your attention: a farewell letter from our comrade put into first the police station, then hospital, then held in custody in the Hermanngasse, then the County Court . . . legally dealt with and beheaded: 'My dearly beloved wife: fate has determined that I must finish my young life. I have just been informed that my appeal for clemency has been rejected. So be it, I am leaving this life upright and composed for I know I have done nothing wrong. I am not ashamed of what I have done, for it was my duty to mankind to fight for the exploited. I hope you too will not feel ashamed of having had a husband who cared for oppressed

66

humanity and who stood up for his beliefs and principles. I am truly sorry that you have been put through so many trials and tribulations. Do not take it too heavily. It has not been in vain. Take for the last time my sincere thanks for everything, everything. It was always so beautiful with you.' *(While he reads he becomes more and more excited. He shakes.* MARIA *offers him a full glass.)* 'That was what gave me the strength to carry this heavy burden for these seventeen long months. Everything I own or will one day own I bequeath to you. I am sorry that I have not managed to do better for you, I hope that my wish will be respected that my body should be handed over to you. Bury me where it is easiest for you. I don't mind where. Only I beg you not to be too down-hearted for that cannot help. Just think: I have given my life to downtrodden humanity.' *(JOSEF shakes all over.* MARIA *tries to make him drink. He fends her off.)*

MARIA. Come on now, you need it, the state you're in.

JOSEF. 'Walk with pride as though I'll be coming home one day. Build yourself a new life, one just as you want it and which is worthy of you. I wish you the greatest happiness and a good companion. Greet all my friends from me one last time: all good people'—he had to write good **people** as good **comrades** was of course forbidden. 'Remain true to the mountains and to nature. Greet them from me, in spirit I'll always be with you. Do not weep, but begin again anew—be strong in spite of everything. All my best wishes, all my kisses from one who loves you so passionately—Josef.' *(JOSEF is completely beside himself.* MARIA *tries to make him drink but he avoids it. Scremaing)* The walls aren't high enough. They must be built everywhere against the threat of this fascist barbarism. *(He buries his face in his hands. Silence.* MARIA *puts her hands on his head.)*

MARIA. Don't let me interrupt you, but an old person hasn't got much to laugh about these days and that's the truth of it. *(JOSEF suddenly sits up and hectically produces an identity card which he shows her.)*

JOSEF. There! The signature. Josef Pribil. *(He holds the letter against it.)* The same signature as on the letter. *(Silence.)*

MARIA. So you wrote it yourself? *(Silence.* JOSEF *nods.)* To your dear wife. So you have got a wife. *(JOSEF looks at her.* MARIA *at him.* JOSEF *takes the glass and downs it in one.)*

JOSEF. She isn't there.

MARIA. Died so young?

JOSEF. But suppose she never lived! *(Silence.)*

MARIA. Ah so you wrote that letter to a wife that never lived! My husband was a butcher with the Field Butchery in Narvik . . . You're just very lonely too.

JOSEF. A progressive man is never alone. In 1959 at the World Youth Festival there were over 20,000 young people present. *(MARIA tops him up.)*

67

MARIA.   They don't like us at all, young people. I go into the fish-shop
with my son's special diet—he wasn't there—just her; and the
customers, she says to them so I can't help overhearing her, 'That's
the old woman. That's the old woman.' If I say anything back my poor
son's finished! So I get the shovel and mop and start cleaning up and I
feel the customers all looking at me. *(They clink their glasses and
drink.)* Herr Josef, if I may call you that, today's Christmas. (JOSEF
smiles.)

JOSEF.   I got myself put on this shift specially so it would pass quicker.

MARIA.   You know, I do believe it's the Good Lord that sent you. Oh
yes, if only my husband was still alive. I had to come straight back from
Lisbon, you see, back home to the beloved Reich. The Führer had
recalled all us artistes.

JOSEF.   Adolf the Killer! The hysterical Jack-in-the-Box! The
Schickelgruber in the service of capital!

MARIA.   In the Hitler Youth Girls' Corps we had a captain who used to
cook a goose without removing the innards. So uncultured
Frau Stadler: she went to Berchtesgaden once with the 'Strength
through Joy' and saw Hitler. 'You can't imagine it,' she said. 'That
man is a god.' I was working in the laundry in an airport in the
Bavarian Auffing and one day in he came in his smart uniform—my
future husband.

JOSEF.   Well I never. (JOSEF *laughs.*)

MARIA.   He wanted me to press his trousers for him and do you know
how often? (JOSEF *laughs.*) Three times a day. We didn't have the pill
and that sort of thing in those days and when he left for Narvik with
the Field Butchery I was pregnant. (JOSEF *drinks and giggles.*)

JOSEF.   If I want to I can be St Therses of Konnersreuth. I can bite on
my gums till the blood flows. That saved me. I put on an epileptic fit
as well and I survived. I was the only comrade who survived.

MARIA.   A lot of limbs froze up there. We didn't do too badly with him
being in the Field Butchery. He'd often send back some sausage or a
piece of bacon. But he never forgave me until his dying day for that
business with the Czech and there was absolutely nothing in it. I just
wanted to learn a little Czech because his parents were Czech and I
wanted to be able to talk to them when he introduced me to them.

JOSEF.   When they came for me I just decided I wouldn't be me—I'd be
someone else and I'd have to be strong in spirit. I hear the footsteps
of the Nazi hangmen in the corridor. They fling the cell door open. I'm
staring at them, blood pouring out of the corner of my mouth. 'Oh no,
gentlemen, I wasn't born yesterday! My name is Thomas. Today the
die will be cast. Today the chapter of Louis Capet will be completed.'
As I said, everything was play-acting— including epileptic fits—they
take me to a psychiatric clinic, called Gugelhupf. Dr Lorenzoni
interrogates me. He has me beaten up trying to get me to admit I
was simulating. Oh no, gentlemen, I wasn't born yesterday! I would
have had a big career as an actor if Reyer hadn't stopped me.

MARIA. I'd had the child and my husband was in the war. The boy just has no idea what I went through. I got myself from Bavaria to Vienna with the child in a cart, in a cattle truck, on foot, nothing to eat; God, I was so sick, when I arrived at my in-laws' flat in Vienna there's my husband in the pub playing cards.

JOSEF. Reyer wants to give an autograph and hasn't got anything to write on. I'm standing right behind him, I was already working as an extra then at the Burgtheater, I hand him a piece of paper. He signs it, turns the paper over and reads—'Down with the exploiting class. Long live international solidarity! Against war-mongering and greed for profit!' I was sacked after that even though everything had begun so well; 1928 at Laaerberg with 'Sodom and Gomorrah' under Fritz Lang. (MARIA *pours him another. They drink.*)

MARIA. My husband often hit me whenever the business with the Czech came up. Herr Josef, you're a good man. I've only got my son Willi now.

JOSEF. Since then I've dedicated myself exclusively to Party work. It's all very odd.

MARIA. Why is it human beings are so cruel, Herr Josef, please tell me.

JOSEF. Human beings and humanity . . . Long live the progressive part of mankind—it's already big and it'll grow bigger and bigger and I am just a part of it, a little grain of sand.

MARIA. Why does my son say he has to live his own life without me? Who's stopping him anyway? But I'm still his mother. Herr Josef, I was beautiful once.

JOSEF. My real mother, she never visited me, she was an actress too. A colleague of hers, a certain Gundolf Auer, he once told me that a Hungarian film he'd seen reminded him powerfully of my mother's life, 'Frau Dery' was the name of the film. Despite the most thorough investigation I could never find it on any cinema programme.

MARIA. A man came into my mother's dairy and gave me a ticket. He said he'd expect me that evening in a box at the theatre. He started me on the job in Constantinople. *(Offers him a drink)* Herr Josef, please . . .

JOSEF. It's going round, Copernicus was right; the earth is going round.

MARIA. Please look. You've seen my variety photo. At home I've got a whole biscuit-tin full of photographs from those days. You know it all. Herr Josef, I really was beautiful once, look . . . (MARIA *closes her eyes and puts her face close to* JOSEF's.) My name is Mia Ritter, changed from Maria Patzak. (JOSEF *suddenly stands up. He stumbles over to a shelf and takes a cellophane-wrapped loaf of bread.*)

JOSEF. How much does a kilo of bread cost? It's a disgrace! In '45 it was 35 Groschen a kilo. Then it went up to 60; then one

Schilling eighteen, then 1.90, up to 2.70, 3.60 and so on. Did workers' wages rise at the same speed? It all began with this disgraceful wage-price pact—or the tram fare—that was 24 Groschen. *(He staggers about. Some things fall over. MARIA goes and supports him.)*

MARIA. Come on now, Herr Josef, the two of us are going to have a bit of fun now. *(She drags him over to the Tannoy booth. He keeps stopping and lecturing.)*

JOSEF. And today it costs 10 Schillings. That's 40 times as much. Have wages gone up 40 times? A lettuce cost 7 Groschen, an egg 9 or 10 depending on the size. Bensdorp chocolate 10 Groschen a bar. I had to think it over 100 times if I could buy one. The emergency welfare if you went below the poverty level was just 9.50 and that's the honest truth. *(He gets louder and louder.)* Meat. Yes, take meat. I ate that once a year—on Good Friday. I had to of course, being a Freethinker. Otherwise it was potatoes, tripe, baked udder, elderflower pancake, all that's forgotten now. All that's forgotten. Today I have to go from Purkersdorf to Liesing, from Schechat to Grossenzersdorf just to get cheap milk. For example at the Co-op, I'm not giving them any free publicity, they're selling bread at 8.20 so I go to the Hofer where there's a special offer at 7.90. There are still people like us. You just have to listen to the appeals on the radio. How can that be allowed when we're supposed to be living in a welfare state? How many hundreds of thousands of workers are there: not the skilled, but the unskilled ones who earn 5 maybe 6,000 a month? And that's not to mention the women, the cleaners, the foreigners, the old age pensioners. But just you wait gentlemen. I wasn't born yesterday. My name is Thomas. Today the die'll be cast. (MARIA *disappears with* JOSEF *into the booth. Silence. Speaker crackles.)*

MARIA. You have to press that button. Then it works. *(Silence.)* Say something, Herr Josef. *(Silence.)*

JOSEF. Dr Lorenzoni, the one who had me beaten up, is living today in Graz.

MARIA. Whatever you want. No one will hear us.

JOSEF. On the plaque in the Mariannengasse it says Dr Egon Lorenzoni, Neurological Consultant. Underneath, Dr Peter Lorenzoni. That'll be his son.

MARIA. It doesn't matter. Whatever comes into your mind.

JOSEF. Do you know, I often stand under his window when his light's on.

MARIA. You have to speak right into it—the microphone.

JOSEF *(sings)*. Now comrades come rally, the next fight let us face. The Internationale unites the human race.

MARIA. You can talk and sing, no one can hear us. The whole floor and everything's empty. I can say Willi and it doesn't matter because he's not listening. *(Silence.)* Willi, are you thinking about your mother this Christmas Eve?

JOSEF. Silent Night. Holy Night. On the 24th December 1930, Franco bombed Madrid and Nixon did exactly the same to Hanoi on Christmas Eve 1974. Murderers! *(Silence.)*

MARIA. Merry Christmas. It sounds so loud but no one can hear. *(Silence.)*

JOSEF. Frau Maria . . .

MARIA. Yes, Herr Josef . . .

JOSEF. I did hear you the first time. *(Silence.)*

MARIA. Of course you haven't seen me looking my best. *(Silence.)*

JOSEF. What are you up to? I don't feel too good. I've got to find somewhere to sit down. *(Silence. Speaker crackles. They reappear. MARIA without her headscarf. JOSEF goes and sits on the couch and stares in front of him. MARIA picks up the fallen goods and puts them back on the shelves. She goes over to JOSEF, closes the bottle and wipes clean the glasses with a handkerchief. Silence. Staring out front)* Otto lies in the cemetery at Neustift. Fritz was sentenced at Stein. Hans is dead. Arthur too, and I got my last postcard from Professor Fried in February '53. I'm the last one of all the comrades.

MARIA. When my neighbour died they put everything she'd left on the pavement. I had a look through them in case there was anything useful. There was school reports from Knittelfeld—very good grades—and some letters from her husband written in the First World War—they didn't say much, just love and that sort of stuff. Next day the dustmen took it all away. What is left of a person if nothing is left. What I always say is, you're well out of it, you're well out of this world.

JOSEF. To try to make my insanity more convincing I decided as a pure formality to hang myself in the mental home. I get up on the stove, the plate's still warm, I put the noose round my neck and wait for the warder. Well, time passes and I take a look through the skylight into the park and see a young girl in a white dress. 'Are you mad?' the warder's suddenly shouting at me, and unfortunately I can't think of any appropriate answer.

MARIA *takes all her clothes, brushes, etc., and goes offstage. JOSEF stares in front of him. Silence. MARIA returns with a carrier bag. She puts it on the couch and looks at JOSEF.*

MARIA. It'll soon be time. (JOSEF *looks at* MARIA.)

JOSEF. Frau Maria, from my expositions you will have gained an insight into the world political situation. Will we ever live to see socialsim, what do you think?

MARIA. It's very different in the world these days. It's all much colder. *(She sits beside him.)* Who wants us? Who'd take us by the hand? *(She wrinkles up the skin of her hand and holds her hand up to him.)* Who would want to take a hand like this? (JOSEF *takes out his glasses, puts them on and studies* MARIA's *hand.*)

JOSEF. I was continually inhaling fine glass dust at the Optics Factory. They gave me the sack and wrote on my cards: 'Dismissed in good health and with all due wages paid.' All the same I'd been coughing up blood like a real consumptive. *(He opens his jacket and some buttons of his shirt and presses a finger on his chest.)* Six times I had to go into the Enzenbach Lung Clinic. It was there I developed pneumothorax—air in the pleural cavity. *(He breathes in and out deeply and taps his chest again and again.)* Today I am completely negative, completely negative. (MARIA *lifts up her overall and petticoat and shows her half-naked back to him.)*

MARIA. You have to press on the right beside the spine. That's where the pain is from my slipped disc. I had 3 stays at the Tatzmannsdorf Spa but it keeps coming back. (JOSEF *looks at her half-naked back and then his fingers. He moves his fingers.)*

JOSEF. I have a blood circulation problem in my fingers . . .

MARIA. You have to press or I won't feel any pain. *(He taps her back.)*

JOSEF. There, I've done it.

MARIA. That wasn't pressing, not properly. *(He presses.)* Harder. More to the right. Harder. That's the pain. You just can't begin to understand it unless you've had a slipped disc yourself. (JOSEF *pulls his shirt up.)*

JOSEF. There was one other time I coughed—in the opera when I was attempting a second career. (MARIA *presses her finger on his chest. He breathes deeply in and out. It turns into a gentle stroking.)* They'd promised me the part of a lion in 'The Magic Flute'. The assistant director was going at me to roar loudly. 'Yes, yes' I say. It wasn't exactly the hardest of tasks to perform after all. They gave me a lion suit and I put the head on me but unfortunately I hadn't reckoned on all the dust in the mask. When I was supposed to roar I got this terrible coughing fit. It wasn't on to be a coughing lion in 'The Magic Flute'.

MARIA. Yes, the music . . .

JOSEF. Maria Cebotari, a wonderful singer—cancer. Oggl, his second name escapes me, baritone. Rucicka—she was from Yugoslavia, Otto Langer, Jan Kiepura with his wife, Martha Eggert, and Helga Rosswaenge in 'Boheme' . . .

MARIA. I've only been to the opera once—with the gentleman who got me on the job in Constantinople. I'd always believed God was protecting me but when that gentleman started to take liberties in the box I just thought 'His will be done'. One was so young and stupid at that age.

JOSEF. Listen, I'm just a poet and my job's writing. How do I live? Well, I live somehow. 'From my heart stream forth such lovely songs'—as an extra you're so close to it all, you pick it up. I could have done any of the great leading roles.

MARIA. Carlos Gardel.

JOSEF. Who?

MARIA. Carlos Gardel. Every child in Casablanca knows him. A tango singer. D'you know how to tango?

JOSEF. With my foster-father spending all our money on drink, the thought of dancing lessons was . . .

MARIA. It's quite simple—just keep watching my legs. *(She gets up and performs some tango steps.)* Watch now, one and two and tango and one and two and tango. You've got to bend forward over me everytime I say 'and'. Wait, I'll put on some music and it'll be easier. (MARIA *goes over to the record section, selects a record. JOSEF suddenly and very fast does up his shirt and uniform, puts on his spectacles, takes out his 'The Truth' and buries himself in it. MARIA puts on a tango record, turns the record-player up full and goes back to him.)* Herr Josef, tango!

JOSEF. There's a very interesting article. If I might be allowed to draw your attention to it. In the Soviet Union the production of wheat went up by over 30% in ten years whereas the production of soya beans on the other hand . . .

MARIA. Come over here, Herr Josef. Today's the day the die will be cast. You said it yourself. *(She pulls him up, holds him tight and drags him across the stage.)* It's not difficult. One and two and tango and one and two and tango. Now hold me round the middle, firmly, when I bend back you bend forward over me.

JOSEF. I'm sorry, I can't do it.

MARIA. Yes, but you're getting there. You've got to bend forward and not backwards. One and two and tango.

JOSEF. When I reached the age for dancing I was at the Workers' High School in the Mollardgasse. Physics—there was something that interested me. Light, the speed of light. I'd get up at 5 in the morning, there was no heating in the room I had rented, then off to the factory and back to study till two in the morning. Latin vocabulary, Austria Romanum and that sort of thing . . . I didn't manage it. One thing I did learn—you don't need higher education and you certainly don't need Latin and the Punic Wars.

MARIA. But you're getting there, Herr Josef! One and two and tango. You've got a natural talent.

JOSEF. Me?

MARIA. Yes, you. Believe me, I can draw a parallel or two.

JOSEF. You mean I can dance?

MARIA. Don't forget the forward bend. (JOSEF *bends low over her.)* But the way you did that! Elegant is the only word! *(Both tango. JOSEF is completely changed. He takes over the lead. The record ends. JOSEF lets MARIA go and put on the record again. He goes back to MARIA and takes her round the waist.)*

JOSEF. Frau Maria! Tango! *(They dance wildly.)*

MARIA *(laughing).* Herr Josef! I don't know you any longer.

JOSEF *(loud).* No one can know me. For years—what am I saying?—

all my life, I was illegal, I was someone else. *(He laughs)* Today the die is cast. *(He holds MARIA tighter and dances more wildly.)*

MARIA. Herr Josef, you seem just like Rudolf Valentino.

JOSEF. Who was that gentleman?

MARIA. The Sheik. King of the Desert. Hero of the New World. He had his hair combed back so smooth and shining! Such a terribly good-looking man!

JOSEF *lets her go, looks round, takes a bottle of mineral water, opens it, pours a little onto his hands and rubs some into his hair—then combs it flat with a broken comb. MARIA looks at him and laughs. JOSEF grabs her round the waist and stares penetratingly at her.*

JOSEF. Like this?

MARIA *(laughing)*. Oh you're a one!

JOSEF. I'm Valentine or whatever the gentleman's name is. Don't you notice my theatrical background now?

MARIA. Valentino. Rudolf Valentino. The most elegant man of his epoch. Always in tails even in the desert.

JOSEF. Whatever you want. *(He runs to the clothes racks, dives in and searches out a dinner jacket. He takes off his uniform jacket and puts on the dinner jacket. It's at least 3 sizes too big. He runs back to MARIA, shouting)* Tango! *(He grabs her. The record finishes. He goes over to the record player.)* No, no, gentlemen! *(Laughing)* I wasn't born yesterday. *(He sets the record going, seizes MARIA and they tango, wilder than before.)* Am I Valentino now? Am I or am I not?

MARIA *(laughing)*. There's just one thing.

JOSEF. Tell me. I can play anything.

MARIA *(laughing)*. He seduced women, by the dozen. No one could resist him.

JOSEF *(laughing)*. Would you resist me if I made a proposition of that nature to you? (MARIA *laughs.*) Yes or no? *(Silence. They dance on. Suddenly MARIA lets go and stares at him.)*

MARIA *(seriously, with a mixture of tragedy and resignation)*. Yes, I wouldn't resist you. (JOSEF *stares at her. MARIA goes quite naturally to a large bed and pulls back the covers. JOSEF takes off his spectacles, cleans them and puts them back on. Record ends. Silence. MARIA undoes her overall. JOSEF watches her helplessly. Suddenly she stops and smiles at him.)* The lighting here's a little too bright for me, if you know what I mean, Herr Josef. Perhaps you could find the mains switch . . .

JOSEF. Yes, yes. It's part of my duties to be fully conversant with the electrical installations. (JOSEF *goes offstage. Blackout. JOSEF returns, knocks over some things.*)

MARIA *(calling)*. That's fine.

JOSEF. No, no, it's all too much of a risk. *(Goes offstage. Lights on. Goes to Maria. She's in bed, the covers up high, smiling.)*

MARIA.   Like an artiste in a magazine. Mia Ritter, Queen of the
Oriental Ballet. *(She laughs, kicking her feet under the blankets.)*
JOSEF.   Magazines are bad for you! *(While he talks,* JOSEF *takes off
the jacket and painstakingly folds it, laying it near the bed, then
similarly with his shoes, shirt and long-johns.)* The way they're turned
out in their millions those magazines are poisoning people's
consciousness; and progressive people too, if you think that according
to the statistics everyone reads a magazine twice a week and that must
include progressive people, and what's the result: 'The Truth' loses
ground and old subscriptions aren't renewed. *(JOSEF finishes undressing.
He's only wearing underpants and socks with garters. He gets into bed as
though it was no different from his nightly ritual at home. He lies about
a metre apart from MARIA. Both pull the blankets up to their chins
and look straight ahead. Silence . . . MARIA moves closer and lays her
head on his shoulder.)* Frau Maria?
MARIA.   Yes, Herr Josef?
JOSEF.   I think in this situation a less formal mode of address is
indicated.
MARIA.   I'm Maria. *(JOSEF shakes her hand.)*
JOSEF.   Josef. One moment. *(He jumps out of bed.)*
MARIA.   What are you doing now?

JOSEF *takes the brandy bottle, gets two glasses and comes back to the
bed. They toast glasses. He stands there in his underthings, glass raised.*

JOSEF.   My dear Maria. There are moments in life when the level of
attraction between two people reaches such a degree that a sexual
union is only a question of time. We need no holy man, no wedding
ceremony, none of all that superstition; we want to encounter this,
the most beautiful experience man has to offer, with clear minds and
a free will. It is in this spirit that I would ask you to address me as
Josef. *(He downs his drink in one.)*
MARIA.   Not like that—we must drink a proper toast together.
JOSEF.   Pardon me.

*He refills his glass. Both drink brotherhood interlocking their arms.
They empty their glasses.* MARIA *closes her eyes and puts her face
close to* JOSEF'S. *He refills his glass and looks at her.*

MARIA *(eyes closed).*   Before a man kissed me for the first time I was so
terribly excited. One had read so much about the kiss that seals it all.
(JOSEF kisses MARIA and spills his drink. MARIA lets go of him.)
Funny, it's getting very damp. *(MARIA sees the spill and gets out. She's
still got her combinations on.)* For God's sake—the linen! *(JOSEF looks
at the wet patch on the sheet then drinks out of the bottle.)*
JOSEF.   Please forgive me, gentlemen, O great owners of this store who
grow fat on the money you suck out of us, fogive me please for making
this tiny little mess on your precious sheet—but no, this is the moment
of the great reckoning, the die has been cast and I'm saying enough is

enough! I, Josef Pribil, hereby declare that this storehouse of capitalism be passed into the hands of the people and therefore I . . . go and get a clean sheet, Maria.

MARIA. But we'll have to pay for it, Josef!

JOSEF. Pay? We're not paying anything, Maria. Remember we're the ones who are mad and they want to commit. In the Party they always say—oh, Josef, he can sell papers all right, but don't let him have his say, he's mad you know. And when the young people see me on my bike in my shorts and garters I hear them all saying, 'Look at the old loony.' They never consider that socks without garters could get caught in the chain. The fascists stuck me in the madhouse, had me committed, and now they're trying to do it again. Maria—tango! *(He grasps her, pulls her round in a circle.)*

MARIA. They're always telling me I'm getting so senile I'll have to be committed.

JOSEF lets MARIA go and goes to the shelf. With great matter-of-factness he removes and chucks away all the things he doesn't like. MARIA goes and gets another sheet.

JOSEF. Asparagus, too much lead—not healthy. Salmon—that's alright. Caviar, Russian of course, I'll take that certainly. Salt biscuits just make you thirsty. Dried fruit coated in chocolate, that sounds more like it . . . *(JOSEF gets more and more confident and cheekier. He scrutinises, chucks away or selects something. MARIA meanwhile changes the sheets. JOSEF, hands full of goods, goes up to MARIA and lays them out in front of her.)*

MARIA. I knew a car salesman once in Albania. He was so generous too! Wait there a moment, Josef. *(She goes to her carrier-bag and takes out three Xmas presents. She puts them in front of JOSEF.)* That's for you. *(JOSEF looks at her.)* Go on, open it. *(JOSEF opens the largest packet.)* That was for my son.

He takes out a pullover, puts it on. It's far too big for him. He opens the next one—perfume. He opens it and puts some on his wrists. And behind his ears. He opens the third packet—an electric train. Holding it in his hand he kneels before MARIA.

JOSEF. 'My dearly beloved wife: fate has determined that I must finish my young life. I have just been informed that my appeal for clemency has been rejected. So be it, I am leaving this life upright and composed for I know I have done nothing wrong. I am not ashamed of what I have done, for it was my duty to mankind to fight for the exploited people. I hope you too will not feel ashamed of having had a husband who cared for oppressed humanity and who stood up for his beliefs and principles. I am truly sorry that you have been put through so many trials and tribulations. Do not take it too heavily. It has not been in vain. Take for the last time my sincere thanks for everything, everything. It was always so beautiful with you.'

MARIA. You really are crazy but you're a poet. *(She holds his head against her breasts.* JOSEF *sobs.* MARIA *takes him to bed like a child. She lies beside him. Silence.)* Are you ticklish Josef?

JOSEF. Really I don't know—I've never tickled myself. *(*MARIA *tickles him.)*

MARIA. Is my little boy ticklish, is my little boy ticklish? *(*JOSEF *jumps about yelling and almost falls out of bed.)* My God, you are ticklish!

JOSEF. Yes, it's incredible! *(Silence. Both snuggle up together.* MARIA *puts her head under his arm.)*

MARIA. My husband was very ill in his last years and there was naturally nothing doing in that direction. And of course since his death, ten years ago now, there hasn't been anyone else. I'm sure I've quite forgotten what to do.

JOSEF. My last experience of this nature was in the train between Moscow and Leningrad—the night of the 15th to 16th May 1956. I'd sold the highest number of subscriptions for 'The Truth' and as a result won a trip to the Soviet Union. I'm lying in the sleeping car and just above there's a very pretty comrade. Being in the land of free love, where with the decline of religion one is much less inhibited, and under cover of the dark I reached up to her. She screamed blue murder—in Russian. Really, even in socialism everything isn't all that it should be. But you've got such fine skin, Maria. *(Silence.)*

MARIA. You should've known me 40 years ago, Josef.

JOSEF. I was starving then, out of work, had tuberculosis and was always down at the police station. You wouldn't have given me a second glance, Maria, no woman ever looked at me!

MARIA. Let me think back 40 years ago. I sent a parcel to my mother from Casablanca—she wouldn't accept it—said she couldn't take anything from a daughter who paraded herself naked in front of men. *(Silence.)* Sometimes I wish that everything could begin again from the start. Life as white as snow. D'you know the game we all played as kids, Josef?

JOSEF. Yes. No. You know the tragedy of my childhood in that respect.

MARIA. It was called 'Make the world disappear'.

JOSEF. How does it go?

MARIA. Listen. You count to three. One . . . two . . . three . . .

JOSEF. One . . . two . . . three . . .

MARIA. Now close your eyes and hold your breath. Tight.

JOSEF. Tight. *(Both have their eyes closed and hold their breath.* JOSEF *opens his eyes.)* And what happens when you open your eyes again?

MARIA *(eyes closed).* Whatever you've wished to happen, Josef, happens.

JOSEF. I've already finished the game.

Blackout.

Market Day at Plundersweilern
(Das Jahrmarktsfest zu Plundersweilern)

by

Peter Hacks

after J.W. von Goethe

translated by Julian Hilton and Hanne Boenisch

Peter Hacks has been criticised for retreating into the past for fear of offending the East German government with his views. The criticism is naive and unjust. Hacks made a conscious decision to leave the West and the reasons for his doing so have probably remained unaltered. But having attracted official displeasure in 1962 with his relatively tame criticisms of the way communism was in practice functioning, he has had to find other ways of commenting. *Plundersweilern* is a good illustration of what he has done. For his source, Hacks uses Goethe's play of the same name (in fact the second version, 1778) in which Goethe both links German theatre with the Carnival tradition of Hans Sachs's plays and at the same time parodies, in classical hexameters, the story of Queen Esther. Hacks' verbal debt to Goethe is chiefly in the Esther section, though Hacks takes the story to a conclusion while Goethe leaves it open. But the spirit of the piece is much more deeply in Goethe's debt, not least for a major practical reason: when the second version was first performed at Ettersburg in 1778, Goethe played the market trader, Haman and Mordechai. Hacks turns this use of multiple role—in itself an implicit comment on types of character—into a governing principle and in so doing gives the lie to his darker purpose; by using a 'classic' source Hacks covers himself against official anger— how can one criticise the god Goethe? But in the way he varies the piece, especially by adding a good deal of new material on the relationship between the poet and authority, Hacks indicates plainly enough where he stands.

Plundersweilern is a Lehrstück in the Horatian sense of the word— a play which instructs by pleasing: Goethe uses Horace on the title-page. It suggests historical perspectives to German culture which go back well beyond 1945, 1933, 1870 or even 1848. Yet it also shows how, in dealing with the shadow Goethe casts across German literature, a way may be found to deal with Brecht. Its success with German audiences (being three years in succession one of the most performed plays in German houses) suggests Hacks's mixture of satire and entertainment may be an important corrective to more explicit pieces of social comment. After all, as Brecht said, theatre that is no fun is not worth threepence.

Roles
Mr. A as AHASVERUS, PRINCIPAL, FIRST FOOTPAD, SILHOUETTE MAKER, MRS SHOWER.
Mr. B. as HAMAN, MORDECHAI, SECOND FOOTPAD, LACKEY, COSTERMONGER, AUNT, ACTOR, TEACHER SCHIEVELBUSCH.
Ms. C as ESTHER, ACTRESS, MARMOTTE, POLICEMAN, MISS SCHIEVELBUSCH.

Set
An acting booth on an empty stage.

Note

The play must under no circumstances be performed by more than three actors.

The existing melodies to *Marmotte, Marlbrough* and *Rochelle* are to be used. The other songs should be sung to graceful and jaunty melodies written in the style of the late 18th century.

Seneca's Death (Senecas Tod) by Peter Hacks
(Photo by Ilse Buhs/Jürgen Remmler)

Act One

1ST FOOTPAD *(drunk).* When,
  When,
  When,
  When,
  When, oh when will the music start?
  The bitter hours we've slogged away,
  Night on night, day on day,
  And all because we thought to start might
  Surely bring an end in sight.
  When, when, when, when,
  When, when, when, when,
  When, oh when will the music start?
  Musicians standing at the ready
  Lots to play on round the room
  Here's the timpani all steady
  For God's sake someone hit it soon.
  (Goes behind the booth, still singing.)
  When, oh when will the music start?
PRINCIPAL *(enters from the booth).*
  Christian, heathen? Who's the raver?
  Here we're on our best behaviour.
  For here is played a comedy,
  In fact the famous history
  Of Esther fair, and so tis said,
  Sharer of Shah of Persia's bed.
  The Persians—who knows this today?—
  Were wondrous people, by the way,
  Who somewhere, sometime were very great
  Or so the Bible doth relate.
  —Has he gone, the rogue?
  (Looks round the corner)
  No, he hasn't, as I see:
  Can't bear the thought of leaving me.
  —Hey, you there. You don't belong here,
  It's over there the tent with beer.
  This circle here is sacred ground,
  Where only more aesthetic souls are found,
  Natures that discriminate twixt good and bad.
  And get yourself a haircut, my good lad.
  —Just look at him! How pig-headed can you be?
  He even poked his tongue out at me.
  O wicked youth! We were young like you,
  Boisterous and lazy too;
  The devilish pranks that we have played,
  The stuff of which our memory's made.
  But young folk nowadays won't work:

82

They drop out, soul search, lay around and shirk,
As if the end of the world were near:
I think I'll call a policeman here. *(Exit)*
2ND FOOTPAD *(drunk)*.   When, when, when, when,
When, oh when will the music start?
It's nothing like as fun to sit 'ere
As some of 'em would like to kid yer.
The only reason I kept quiet
Was cos the music was going to start.
(FIRST FOOTPAD returns)
BOTH.   When, when, when, when,
When, when, when, when,
When, oh when will the music start?
Will they cheat us of their playing
When we paid so much for staying,
Play musicians, tinkle a tone,
Or one of us might chuck a stone.
When, oh when . . .
(ACTRESS pokes her head out between the curtains of the booth.)
ACTRESS.   Quiet now boys, that's quite enough.
1ST FOOTPAD.   Georgie, look, what a fine bit of stuff.
ACTRESS.   Are you trying to hassle me before I start?
How am I supposed to sink into my part,
With all its foreign ways and notions,
Play Queen Esther, by such loud commotions?
2ND FOOTPAD.   Not seen many birds like her before,
The blondest head I ever saw.
ACTRESS.   More respect please, and no violence,
Apollo's service starts with silence. *(Exit)*
1ST FOOTPAD.   Funny accent, thinks real mean,
The lady speaks just like a queen.
We may marvel, but not comprehend:
Let's go and pinch her lovely end.
(They push behind the curtains. Commotion.)
ACTRESS *(off)*.   Still liking it, still?

*(MARMOTTE. The commotion grows louder, the FOOTPADS tumble
one after the other out of the booth.)*

1ST FOOTPAD.   What a hateful loathsome slut,
Wearing her necklace round her nut.
It'd make me retch to sleep with her,
Her weight in gold wouldn't get me there. *(Exeunt)*
MARMOTTE.   Through many a land I've made my way,
Avecque la marmotte,
And food I found 'most every day,
Avecque la marmotte,
Avecque si, avecque la,
Avecque la marmotte.

83

And many a man that I have seen
Avecque la marmotte,
Has lusted after a virgin,
Avecque la marmotte,
Avecque si, avecque la,
Avecque la marmotte.

And I have seen a maiden fair
Avecque la marmotte
That turned my way and then did stare
Avecque la marmotte,
Avecque si, avecque la,
Avecque la marmotte. *(Exit)*

*(*TOWNCRIER *with a bell.)*
CRIER.   Good news I bring,
   Ring a ring ding
   It's clear as can be, clear as sunlight,
   The fair at Plundersweilern has just begun, like.
   And if I hadn't cried it out,
   You'd all ask what's the fuss about.
   Trade's the thing
   Good news I bring.
   The morning of a great feast day
   For our renowned and ancient town,
   That puts its cares and woes away,
   And gladly lets its hair down.
   When cookies crunch and gin is free,
   When woodwind pipes for dance and glee,
   When trade and traveller hear the call
   Of home and of their own four walls,
   Then's the time for close attention,
   Lest things be done we dare not mention.
   And so my public duty's to declare
   This instant all the bye-laws of the fair.
   Hear ye, ye mighty and ye mean.
   Ring a ring ding.
   Up there beside the town hall
   The guildsmen have their stalls,
   And there along the furrier's street
   Are barrelled beer and things to eat.
   And by the cathedral's west facade
   You'll find the worthy home of art.
   Gypsies, wrestlers, tight-rope dancers,
   Doctors who have all the answers,
   Stiltmen, dancing bears and tumblers,
   Wit and wealth for deft or fumbler,
   And there's a man, admired by all,

84

Can reckon things political,
How Plundersweil made friends with Russia,
And why that friendship's growing lusher.
And since the square has got four sides
There's the rabble's booths besides,
Whose bellies else would go unfilled,
If they weren't members of a self-styled guild.
They swear and chatter, grunt and groan
You'd wish you'd left your ears at home.
And that's the audience, on its feet,
Gawping up and down the street,
Wond'ring if this stupid rubbish
Has an opening, middle or a finish.
What's up? Why that loud and crazy shout?
It's dinner time they're on about.
Some don't like it — to that the law is wise
These chaps' talk is full of lies.
Hand out sacks of golden pistols,
But shoes they've none to fit new soles.
And this mild crisis of liquidity
Has often bred indecency
— Or should I put it plain and blunt
You know an old sow by its grunt.
But then, they can't help their faces
And by the way, we've kept you places.
And if things look a little queer
It only happens once a year.
Good news I bring,
Ring a ling ling.

SILHOUETTE MAKER. Hey, brother.
CRIER.   That I am not, you liar.
SILHOUETTE. Sorry friend. I meant Mister Crier.
    Where's the booth that I have left?
CRIER. What's that you do?
SILHOUETTE.   Cut silhouettes.
CRIER. The demon cutter who before you know it
    Has knocked you out a little portrait.
SILHOUETTE. The silhouette I'd dare to call
    The fine arts' queen, the peak of all.
    If you're a man of high estate,
    Of known importance, influence great,
    But sadly to your consternation
    Your face is harmful to your reputation,
    That little wit you own infertile,
    Come to me and get a fresh profile.
CRIER. Sounds not bad, from man to man,
    But you're not, I hope, a charlatan.

85

SILHOUETTE. Mister Crier! Modern art
  Is science for the better part;
  Not like the art of days gone by
  When brush would o'er the canvas fly,
  Calling every alteration
  From the truth creation.
  Breathes there the man who'd now be so free?
  God's is the light, the shadows we.
CRIER. I like a man who knows what's what.
  By St. Luke's hospice, that's your spot.
  Perhaps I'll have myself done later,
  Squashed a beetle on my bedroom wallpaper. *(Exit)*
SILHOUETTE. See people how you can interpret
  A man's behaviour from his silhouette.
  An inventory: first the chin,
  There sit will and determination,
  And so when we must fill in forms
  To hold it back becomes the norm.
  And next the mouth, which like a glass
  Doth mirror all the moods that pass
  Across two lips which soft as feathers
  Calm the roughest of emotional weathers.
  For man and woman next the nose,
  Suggesting joys now hid by clothes;
  For courting couples still unsure
  What that means, say! I'll tell you more.
  And last, the temple of the soul, the forehead,
  Which sometimes holds a brain, Lavater said:
  And in the confines of a single picture
  Are all four elements in conjuncture.
  Sensibility and will,
  Logic cool and rational:
  From moral states like ours we've banned
  Primitive behaviour out of hand.
  That this is so you best can tell
  From looking at a noble's pigtail
  Jove up front, a tail behind
  So the German head is rhymed. *(Exit)*
  (COSTERMONGER crosses the stage.)
COSTERMONGER. Rinaldo bold turned balladeer
  To sing his life-song as he'd penn'd it;
  Your money guarantees long life and cheer:
  Who's the poet, who's the bandit? *(Exit)*
PRINCIPAL. Thank God he's gone, the drunken lout:
  I've told the magistrate to sort him out.
  *(COSTERMONGER returns and erects his stand with his picture
  on it.)*

It's true the police seem in no hurry,
In fact they're ogling with that scurry
Of lechers at the naked mermaid.
They told me I was prude and staid.
To take art lightly, trifling, nought,
I'd die for shame at such a thought.
(Turns round and sees the balladeer.)
No!
(With an expression of the utmost anguish exits into his booth.)
COSTERMONGER.   The ballad of the robber captain Rinaldo Rinaldini,
by Master Christian August von Vulpius.

Down in darkest reach of forest
Hidden in a cavern deep
Of robbers bold there slept the boldest
Until his Rosa broke his sleep
(POLICEMAN enters.)
Mankind sleeps in the lap of sin
Until its conscience wakes it.
(POLICEMAN makes to exit.)
And with a smile he opens his eyes
To greet the early morning sun
And round she coils him in her thighs . . .
(POLICEMAN turns round.)
And knees him smartly on his chin.
(POLICEMAN exit.)
Outside the cave the dogs are barking
All is bustle, on the run,
Now the battle hour's advancing,
Each man double loads his gun.
The captain's ready for the fray
And walks amid his fellows burly,
'Lads, I wish you all good-day.
Say, why are ye up so early?'

'Over there the troops are lined,
Closing in on our retreat.'
'Let them come if they're inclined
To fence the robber with his nimble feet.'

'Death or victory' they cry,
Victory and death are nigh,
Hurrah, how they . . .
(POLICEMAN appears.)
. . . tremble how they fly,
The powers that be are on the march.

Rinaldini, son of hell,
(POLICEMAN exit.)
Cuts his way through rank on rank
Till he reaches, on a hill,
A rocky castle, cold and dank.

And there between those high dark towers
Love favours him with happy chance
Gone from mind are those sad hours
In the magic of Diana's glance.

Darling Rinaldini bold,
Robber of hearts and women's rest,
In battle how your heart is cold,
How warm your love for this fortress.
(POLICEMAN again.)
And that's how sin and vice are punished,
Go not that way to the fire.
(COSTERMONGER exit. PRINCIPAL looks out between the curtains.)
PRINCIPAL.   Can I open up at last?
POLICEMAN *signals.*
What's the point of good men's protests
If the law won't intervene
To stop the filthiest show there's been.
I thought, at least until this minute,
At sland'rous dirt they'd draw the limit.
POLICEMAN.   We do not wholly share your view,
And having listened carefully to
The singer, he is I am convinced a man
Of morals and an Anglican. *(Exeunt.)*
(HAMAN opens the curtains.)
HAMAN.   Oh! thou whose darkly glowing soul doth light my every way,
Whose thoughts fill out my nights and guide my steps each day,
O vengeance! turn not thy hand from me in this late hour,
From me thy servant, for this very day I try my power.
What boots me all the pomp that round my head doth gleam,
What good that my regard is every person's dream,
What helps it that a kingdom 'fore my feet doth crawl
When one bold individual will not lick my boots at all?
I parade in state, with all my pomp and train
Enter through the king's own gate, but all in vain.
I wait for his bold gaze to tremble, in vain for recognition too.
He thinks he's clever, good and worthy, but he's just a Jew.
Ha! just like Jerusalem in fire and ash must fall
So too this people and Mordechai above all.
If only I could stir to boiling Ahasverus' blood.
The trouble is with kings, they're oft too good.

88

AHASVERUS. Hey, Haman. Are you there?

HAMAN.   Yes, I've waited here quite long.

AHASVERUS. You never seem to sleep enough, I fear there's something
wrong.

HAMAN. Noblest monarch, since thou, as is fitting, choose,
To pass majestic over down and rose
Thy servant's happy lot, for which I thank the stars
Is rendering thanks that thou mayst wear the crown with so few cares.
Such stubborn people ruled with such great ease,
The power you have's divine, from God come gifts like these.
Although, of course, a mortal man would hardly dare
To spend his whole time smiling at the air.

AHASVERUS. You're right indeed, the Gods are bang on course:
This is what we've always done, the members of my house.
None of them has sweated hard to win what he has won,
And care and tribulation has been the death of none.

HAMAN. How vexed I therefore am oh noblest lord to curb
And much against my will thy serenity disturb.

AHASVERUS. Your duty bids you, in few words, to speak.

HAMAN. The dire news I have to tell makes any words seem weak.

AHASVERUS. In that case, let it pass.

HAMAN.   The Jews I think thou knowst?

AHASVERUS. The people I remember, one of mine, is that not so?

HAMAN. Thou gavest them leave to multiply and spread
To work the way that they are wont, and see their numbers fed:
Thou even tookst the name of God from one who left them cold,
And through his evil trickery as slaves he had them sold.
But nonetheless they seldom thank their saviour as they should,
Ignore thy laws entirely and go back to their own God.
So that these your subjects now heed his command,
And pass by thy dread altar which sacred once they found.
Remind them of their duty, master, this I do implore
And, if they chance to disapprove, then issue them a law.

AHASVERUS. My friend, I praise you. Most loyally you speak.
But while lieutenants one way tread, another kings do seek.
They may sing their psalms to whom they choose—I do not care:
As long as they perform their tasks and pay their taxes' share.
Whether this man feels a Persian, or like a Persian prays
Is doubtful at the best of times and not worth anxious days.
Saint or sinner when they seek their wives by night
Is one to me. Just let them bear me children who can fight.

HAMAN. Oh mighty lord, divinely blessed, with ease of manner clad,
This people, I assure thee, lord, are just plain mad.
They couldn't care two farthings about thy laws and will,
They do exactly what they want and go their own way still.

AHASVERUS. My good man, you must be so wrong, this is not true.
How can it be that any man to my will is untrue.

HAMAN. But that's just what I'm trying to say,
  That they just go their own sweet way.
  You've only got to watch them sitting bearded black and curly,
  To know there's pride in every glance and manner highly surly.
  Their God is surely Ahriman, a devil half at least:
  A God should be a cow, or like a calf, or beast.
  You can watch our God in motion, see just how he feeds,
  In a word then you can see just how our God proceeds.
  Their God he is invisible, no kidneys and no heart,
  It makes it very difficult to have him up in court.
  They alone can see him, far too pale for us,
  But for all that they like to think themselves quite wondrous.
AHASVERUS. But still they're pretty quiet?
HAMAN.   But if they get the bright idea
  Of giving those fomenting thoughts of theirs a little try-out here?
  There's no place for light within those breasts so black,
  No place for Ahasverus or for Uramack.
AHASVERUS. They tell me, mind, that some of them can rhyme.
HAMAN. If thou believest all that, my lord, then certainly 'twas time
  To warn thee, for the poet spins from nothing his fantastic dreams
  And people who are made like that aren't worthy of esteem.
AHASVERUS. Don't worry man, my kingdom's safe and ordersome.
HAMAN. That's just the reason why a single stone
  If loosed from out this splendid work, where every piece
  Doth hang from one another or support at least,
  Where not a part doth not accord to plan,
  Would be enough to crack the whole bright span.
  A well-planned state can better cope with war and debts
  Than whiffs of art and products of the poets.
AHASVERUS. This is all quite true, and yet, as ever, wrong
  For that which is most fixed is often not that strong.
  You are sore concerned, but sore are my ears too,
  And, by the way, let's not forget my tolerance towards you.
HAMAN. Who dares contradict when mighty kings command?
  Yet this people, spoiled and murmuring is heard throughout the land;
  As long as there is law and order, it cannot hope for much
  And knows the way of noise yields little joy as such.
  But secretly it feeds a fire that smokes away unfanned
  A puff of wind, and then there'll be a burning 'cross the land.
  This is the first time that there's been such trouble,
  Yet for any power they have, we have double.
  We'll send the army marching, our victory we'll cheer
  And all the time we'll sit quiet here as if there were no war.
  (MARMOTTE enters and watches.)
HAMAN. Revolt which in an instant flares,
  Must be quickly smothered by hard measures.
  Wit and counsel are the seeds of treason,
  And if they fight together they may storm the throne.

AHASVERUS. The throne sits fast enough as long as I am on it:
They all know how I flash my bolts down upon them from it.
Its steps are golden and its pillars marble,
Eternities will pass before they find its equal.
HAMAN. But why, oh master, dost thou force me to speak plain?
AHASVERUS. Come you've tried me long enough, this talk's a pain,
I've better ways to spend my time than such a chat.
HAMAN. But master, it's your life they're maybe aiming at.
AHASVERUS. How? What?!
HAMAN.   I have said. Thus runs their plan.
Who here is strong enough not to fear, is there such a man?
Deep in fiery hell their horrid deed was born,
And thou who art so like the sun may see no further dawn.
To no avail that throne and crown and sceptre guard thee,
Thou then claimst no more Mede or Persian duty,
In fearful darkness treason's evil hand
With patricidal purpose shall cut life's sacred band.
Thy blood, for which the blood of many men has flown
Will over bed and pillow pitiably be strewn.
Pity cries within the palace, pity cries in Susan's streets,
Pity those who in thy service gave themselves complete.
Thy noble corpse shall gather scorn like offal flies
And all thy closest servants feel the butcher's knives.
AHASVERUS. Oh! Oh! What awful thoughts are these! I feel quite green
I think I'm dying here and now. Pray go and tell the Queen.
My teeth are chattering, my knees as well:
I feel a cold sweat coming, I see blood and hell.
HAMAN. Be a man.
AHASVERUS.   Oh! Oh!
HAMAN.   Keep calm.
AHASVERUS. They're killing me; but why? It's you who's done
the harm.
HAMAN. Now mayst thou recognise a man who speaks out straight.
AHASVERUS. Go burn them instantly! Wherefore do you wait?
HAMAN. Careful is the watchword now. For now there's no direct
concern.
AHASVERUS. And in the meantime twenty men will stab me turn
by turn.
HAMAN. Our weapons will prevent such deeds.
AHASVERUS. I lived till now as carefree as among my kids.
They wish me dead. That causes me great pain.
HAMAN. Oh master, he who dies shall never eat or drink again!
AHASVERUS. Now I feel myself again, be still. The globe shall shake.
Go bid them thousand, nay ten thousand gallows make.
HAMAN. Oh irrepressible master, hear me please.
That would be such a waste of people and of trees.

AHASVERUS.   Arise. No man has ever bettered you for heart!
   Your noble soul doth teach you to take the enemy's part.
   Arise, what do you mean by this?
HAMAN.   There are some scum indeed
   Among this people, but all are not so made.
   Thy sword must wary be of spilling spotless blood.
   A prince must princely, not raven as a tiger would.
   The monster with its thousand claws
   Is helpless if you lop its head and jaws.
AHASVERUS.   Well said. So lop the head and do not hang about.
   The emperor has uttered, the law has spoken out.
   Who is the villain who finds me too vital?
HAMAN.   It is old Mordechai, the good Queen's uncle.
AHASVERUS.   Oh bother me, I'll never hear the end of this!
HAMAN.   Oh, once he's dead thou'lt sure be left in peace.
AHASVERUS.   So string him up right quick, and from me keep her far.
HAMAN.   If thou dost not summon, no man may enter, where thou art.
AHASVERUS.   We've got no gallows. I have always been too lenient.
HAMAN.   In thoughtful expectation, I've got one that's convenient.
AHASVERUS.   Don't ask me any more. Enough I've done forsooth.
   I've ordered thee to do the deed and I shall stand aloof. *(Exit)*
HAMAN.   When next the sun climbs in the sky, slaughtered shall be
   Mordechai.
   The more that he's despised the brighter so shine I.

He draws the curtain. After the applause—MARMOTTE *applauds.*
HAMAN *bows, and exit.* MARMOTTE *applauds.* HAMAN *re-enters,*
bows, threatens him and exit. MARMOTTE *applauds.* HAMAN *does*
not return.

Act Two

MARMOTTE. *Enter* MISTRESS SHOWER

SHOWER.   He's there, the darling little chappie,
   Finding him again makes me so very happy,
   His daring nose, his cheeks so tanned,
   Curls so long and raven black and
   Eyelashes like silken strands o'er naughty eyes,
   To learn that he might be a she would sure be no surprise.
   From the ice-mountain high he comes,
   Down to our little valley home,
   With narrow waist and naked feet
   Will no one welcome him, none greet?
   —Hey, boy.
MARMOTTE.   At your service.

SHOWER.   How to start?
    Oh, how swiftly, trembling beats my heart.
    Is there no mother to look after you?
MARMOTTE. No mother nor no father too.
SHOWER. The best of fathers is only a man:
    But see how soothe and care a mother can.
    You're an orphan boy.
MARMOTTE. This marmot is my only toy.
SHOWER *(embraces him).*
    How deeply I do pity you. *(Enter* AUNT*)*
AUNT. Well, Mrs Shower, there's a do!
SHOWER. You, boy, run along and play
    We'll meet up later in the day.
    (Gives him money and he exits rear.)
    —Madame Aunt, so she too takes the air
    The old traditional merriment of the fair.
    Give me your arm and let us go
    Examine all the pleasure of the show.
AUNT. Saints preserve us, I will not be prickly
    But better she should go, and quickly.
    I lead a quiet and blameless life for sure
    Curtain my windows, lock my door,
    I give a wide berth in my piety
    To lust and impropriety.
    There can be no thought that I willingly
    Display myself so publicly.
SHOWER. What causes you to venture hither?
AUNT. My love of science and of nature.
    Let me explain. Upon this very spot
    They discovered a most marvellous marmot.
    This rarest of all alpine cats,
    Upon the sloping glacial flats
    Clips a pine nut in its claws,
    Lifts its nose and shows its jaws
    Turns a circle, whistles fierce
    So loud you have to close your ears.
    The news of this I've just now had.
SHOWER *(aside).* She says the cat but means the lad.
AUNT. Its little face would give me joy
SHOWER *(aside).* That lovely youngster from Savoy
AUNT. Is that not it! It is I'll bet.
    Hey boy, where's your marmoset?
MARMOTTE. At the fire-station Madame. Madame must know
    It bit a counsellor on his toe.
    It won't be released until tomorrow.
SHOWER. She understood? Let her come again tomorrow.
AUNT. What? Tomorrow?

93

SHOWER.   Not got it, still, still?
   Today no tunes, nor whistles shrill.
AUNT.   And shall the little lad be starving?
   Sing me a song *(Gives him money.)*
SHOWER *(gives him money)*.   No, for us both you'll sing.
MARMOTTE.   Too generous always, too fine,
   'Marlbrough s'en va-t-en guerre' is my rhyme.
   It tells what grave distress the Briton bore,
   What loss he suffered in the war.
   Marlbrough he went to war-a
   Tarum tee tum te tara
   Marlbrough he went to war-a
   With steely helm and shoe
   Lady Marlbrough Adieu
   I'll soon be back to you.

   For Easter I'll take Brussels,
   Tarum tee tum te tussels,
   For Easter I'll take Brussels,
   For Whitsun I'll have Brest
   I swear I do not jest,
   At least, I'll do my best.

   Then off he went to battle
   Tarum tee tum te tattle
   Then off he went to battle
   And she began to wait
   Six months went by in spate
   Who did not come? Her mate.

   Here comes a tired rider
   Tarum tee tum tee tider
   Here comes a tired rider
   To her at eventide:
   'My husband has he died?'
   'Why no, Madame' he replied.

   'The French they fired a land mine
   Tarum tee tum tee tand mine
   The French they fired a landmine
   I saw the shot with shock
   The Duke's whole frame did rock—
   The blast blew off his cock.'
SHOWER.   His cock! my heaven, what a naughty name!
   His cock! dear aunt let's quickly home.

AUNT *exit.* SHOWER *shuts her ears but stays with an expressionless
face where she is.* ACTOR *puts his head out between the curtains.*

94

ACTOR.   Peace out there. We're of a mind to
    Proceed smoothly towards act two. *(Exit)*
MARMOTTE.   Peace yourself. Quiet in there,
    Or all of us will disappear.

    Lost oh lost in war-a
    Tarum tee tum tee tora
    Lost oh lost in war-a
    My comfort in the night.
    And where was my delight
    After Churchill's fight?

    His cock I saw being buried
    Tarum tee tum tee teried
    His cock I saw being buried
    Or what was left of it
    The army beat retreat
    And gave the cock salute.

    It lay on England's standard
    Tarum tee tum tee tandard
    It lay on England's standard
    A wreath around its head
    Four soldiers pale they led
    Poor Churchill's cock to bed.

    And muted drums were rolling
    Teerum tee tum ta tolling
    And muted drums were rolling
    A solemn funeral hymn
    And peace and rest attend him
    House Marlbrough's fallen limb.'
SHOWER.   Too lovely. But quickly home with me
    Where we can sit more comfortably
MARMOTTE.   But shall I trouble the Monsieur?
SHOWER.   He'd love to hear you, that I'm sure.
    *(*AUNT, *at the edge of the stage.)*
AUNT.   The old sow's pulled a fast one there,
    How she strokes his virgin hair.
    Probably make him sign a proposal
    To put his Marmot at her disposal.
SHOWER.   First I'll cook a soup for you.
AUNT.   The heart may wander, but the gut stays true.
SHOWER.   With meat and bones, as it should be,
    And stirred with love, as much as could be,
    As if dear Cupid blessed the feast.
AUNT.   He'll be spooning hard at least.

SHOWER.   And all the while your mouth salivers
   I'll patch those holes there in your trousers.
AUNT *(goes over to them)*.   Oh too, too kind you are madame:
   Already shorn the little lamb?
SHOWER.   You here, where the songs are wild?
AUNT.   A naughty song, but well beyond his ken poor child.
   Such dirt, in fact, when sung by him,
   Can match the music of the cherubim.
   He lacks little but a virtuous guide.
SHOWER.   A role for which she's fully qualified.
AUNT.   Why not?
SHOWER.   And will she quicken his mind too?
AUNT.   In this town there is no one who
   Could do so better than an upright dame
   Who all her life untouched by shame
   Has stood by virtue of her age and rank,
   For law and order, church and bank.
SHOWER.   Such moving words, they edify.
AUNT.   How quick he trusts me, sweetie pie!
   Poor little soul, though you lie
   In darkness, heaven's sweets you soon shall try.
   (Gives him money.)
   Aren't you tired of running about?
MARMOTTE.   Can think of worse holes to hang out.
SHOWER *(gives him money)*.   Don't you want a steak and beer?
MARMOTTE.   Cold nights in August, so they say round here.
AUNT *(gives him money)*.   Rather sleep in a Christian bed
   Than have hay or moss beneath your head?
MARMOTTE.   Bed is bed, and one would do now:
   Moss and hay make no good pillow.
SHOWER *(gives him money)*.   You sometimes like a woman's touch?
MARMOTTE.   The ladies understand so much.
   Once I saw a maiden selling milk,
   Her breasts and calves were smooth as silk,
   She said: if I on following the way
   Reached the mile of village road
   —Go past the larger farms I should—
   I'd see, set deep amid the meadows gay
   A little house, I'd recognise for sure
   By the windows, so she said,
   Open just the teeniest bit,
   And the roses blooming round the door.
   And there there'd be a winter cot
   For me and for my fluffy marmot.
AUNT.   Naughty boy.
SHOWER.   Little devil!

MARMOTTE.   I earn my money on the level.
Another song, another glee.
BOTH.   Shame! Shame! *(Both cover their ears.)*
MARMOTTE.   Dear ladies, I entreat ye.
If ye will not hear my song
Then help the chorus bit along.

He sings. The women cover their ears and remain expressionless, but sing the chorus nevertheless.

Fifty maids from La Rochelle
Went aboard a man o'war
Thighs so white and quick as hell
Hardly a hair on their skin they bore.
Ah, la feuille, s'en vole, s'en vole,
Ah, la feuille, s'en vole au vent.
And as the tide ebbed from the harbour
Off to sea sailed the motley crew,
They chose a captain from their number
Just fifteen and the oldest too.

'We are, or so they said, 'content
To live out lives away from men.'
But only seven weeks were spent
When itchy arse got hold of them.
Ah, la feuille, s'en vole, s'en vole,
Ah, la feuille, s'en vole au vent.
At last a caravelle was sighted
Bearing down across the sea
With gorgeous pirates richly freighted,
The best a man could hope to see.

On the Rochelle battle-cruiser
All for boarding stood to station
And every virgin looked to choose her
Captive sweet for celebration.
Ah, la feuille, s'en vole, s'en vole,
Ah, la feuille s'en vole au vent.
By the silvery moonshine full
Young and naked on the deck
Back and forth the rowers pull
Thighs wide open, heads laid back.

That night there were no sails set,
That night there were no nets cast down,
That night the loving bodies met,
Girls and boys were joined as one.
Ah, la feuille, s'en vole, s'en vole,
Ah, la feuille, s'en vole au vent.

By break of day the caravelle
Set course across the foam again,
Anu the girls from la Rochelle
Fresh as daisies sang this refrain:

Somewhere on the world's wide sea
I lost my virginity.
Turn oh wind, oh turn for shore!
And shall I see my friend once more?

All exeunt. MISTRESS SHOWER *returns.*

SHOWER.   If you thought that this sketch was weak
    It's not as silly as you think.
    Women my age don't get men:
    Wait until it's your turn then. *(Exit)*

ESTHER *and* MORDECHAI *open the curtains.*

MORDECHAI.   O dire destiny! O what an awful fate!
    O tragedy that I these tidings must relate.
    A raven am I as I fly to you and night attends my coming.
ESTHER.   Come spit the news out and please stop your groaning.
MORDECHAI.   Boo hoo! My heart, boo hoo, it cannot stand the strain!
ESTHER.   Just have a good sob and then try again.
MORDECHAI.   Boo hoo! it will it will, boo hoo, my heart will break!
ESTHER.   What's up?
MORDECHAI.   Boo hoo! Tomorrow I shall be hung by the neck!
ESTHER.   What's that you say my friend, is this certain beyond doubt?
MORDECHAI.   Sure as sure, boo hoo, I've just found out!
    All is ordered, that is sure, but whether I be shot
    Or hung, that they have decided not.
ESTHER.   That's pretty stupid pal.
MORDECHAI.   You said it queen.
    I thought with your protection I'd be screened
    From tyrant's wrath.
ESTHER.   No word against my lord.
MORDECHAI.   Tis fate I blame, the king deserves no bitter word.
    Never trust, oh happy man, the day that seems most clear:
    You might as well build on the sand as on the rocks, I fear.
ESTHER.   Who drove the king to such a bate, huh?
MORDECHAI.   Who else? Twas Haman, nasty agitator.
    He tarred my name with pitch because he scribbles verses too
    Which everyone finds ludicrous, a just and reasoned view.
ESTHER.   What cause?
MORDECHAI.   I saw him riding through the city gate
    And did not salute, I didn't know him till it was too late,
    My eyes you know, dear child, oh boo! for years
    Have slowly worsened and to blindness I am near:
    Boo hoo! to wish to hang a man for failing sight.

98

ESTHER. You did not want to bow. If you're minded you can see all
  right.
MORDECHAI. Shall I in grey-haired eminence salute that punk?
ESTHER. He's the strongest after Ahasver.
MORDECHAI.   Oh bunk!
  My head is much too full to make it strain for art.
  What does the devil want from me? Is he so smart?
ESTHER. He can hang you.
MORDECHAI.   Good, so what?
ESTHER.   So what? Then why the shouting?
MORDECHAI. Some people think the only way to show you're there is
  clouting.
  I know what he is up to on his mighty throne,
  Lechery is his god-head and sin his education.
  By canopies o'er ceilinged that on a scarlet band
  Are sown with cottons blue and white, with rings of silver spanned.
  He sits with cretinous expression, round about him fawns his party
  And yawns and feels in such a garden feast inutterably hearty.
  No, no. The man's a nono, stuffing, fucking, getting pissed—
ESTHER. But while you live you're on his list.
MORDECHAI. Boo hoo, he'll kill me. I only wish I had the wit
  To think of rhymes still worse than his, then God damn it
  I'd hang him; but I never manage. So unless you run
  And ask the king for mercy, I am done.
ESTHER. But this, poor dear, I cannot do.
  One can't go to the king. He comes to you.
  The man who goes unasked to court
  Is dead for sure. You can't have thought—
MORDECHAI. Oh peerless one, for you there is but little risk.
  For who, when faced with beauty, can resist?
  And anyway those laws were just a measure
  To stop the masses messing the king's leisure.
  Go on, and quick, or otherwise they'll have my head.
ESTHER. But there's no point! We'll both be dead.
MORDECHAI. You love your uncle?
ESTHER.   Him I love for sure.
  But I confess, I fear Ahasver more.
MORDECHAI. Save my worth and honour for the world.
ESTHER. I'd love to do it, were I bold.
MORDECHAI. You need more guts, then you'd have a bash.
ESTHER. But uncle you're so old and I so blooming fresh.
MORDECHAI. Who may you thank for being alive at all?
  Shall you waver as my saver, when I brought you up from small?
  I gave my knowledge freely, for that there is no charge,
  But expenditure on patience was inordinately large:
  Even in the best born children evil's lurking in the gut,
  The slightest whiff of smut and in a trice the girl's a slut.

You thank nature that you're bright, disarming,
But as a child you found crime quite charming.
You should remember how I shielded you,
And don't forget to thank me for your husband too.
The king required a wife, so on the instant princely pleasure
Brought together all the virgins left in Persia.
The chamberlain inspects the group, and sends some home at once,
The rest left trembling at the turn of chance.
They bathe a whole year—quite a few were scurvy—
And then he looks them through again, those that were not dirty.
But how, if not through me, did you carry off the prize?
There were so many beauties. You alone were wise.
And wisdom in a woman, it draws the men up close
They like to think it there, so long it never shows.

ESTHER.   In deepest thanks I will enjoy my happy hours,
I'll keep your grave clean and water all the flowers.

MORDECHAI.   Shame, shame! Such horror and such dire need.
Shame, shame, it's no fun living when you're soon to be dead.
You see your head before you, there in the rain it's hung
Or in the white snow, or the scorching sun,
And there's a Crow and Mrs Crow engrossed upon their dinners
Lucky to be alive they are, guzzling my fat and innards.
And last of all, clicking together, my bones so white and dry,
Rattling ever back and forth as in the breeze they fly.

ESTHER.   Does a just man make such moan before his death?

MORDECHAI.   They're hounding me. Must I take it with oblige
noblesse?

ESTHER.   Well then, how I wish—

MORDECHAI.   You'll do it? My tears shall fall.
What do you wish?

ESTHER.   I wish this were not happening at all.

MORDECHAI.   In that case, I depart, lest my pain should pain you.
(Aside) A strong heart must alone decide what it should do.
(Exit. Re-enters.) It's true, you're going?

ESTHER.   I must first consider everything.

MORDECHAI.   I go then. Farewell.
(Exit. Re-enters.) You will not let me swing? *(Exit.)*

ESTHER.   Best thing I go and see what calls me in the dusk,
And get it over with.

MORDECHAI *(returns)*.   What? Go like that? No musk?
To go unperfumed would be wanton, almost worse than flight,
To go so naked and unarmed to fight the holy fight.
No. Adorn your body with the scent of spice and myrrh.
The night is yours and darkness still not o'er.
Your thighs, your breasts, and all your lovely skin
You must anoint with balsam and perfume.

ESTHER.   How do you know?

MORDECHAI.   I know a lot.
ESTHER.   But then, how taught?
     Your God's no wife, or so at least I thought.
MORDECHAI.   Believe me, if you go a mess I fear you blunder,
     Fare well.
ESTHER.   How I wish you were six feet under. *(Exit* MORDECHAI*)*
     The old and kindly man who changed my nappies daily,
     With whose grey beard I used to frolic gaily,
     That ever was to me as father, mother kind,
     Who nurtured me with wisdom, (not that apparent now mind
     You) I was too hard on him. He's had his fill or irritation.
     But yet why can't we hate those whom we show compassion.
     I whose life has never been a vexing bore to any
     The horrid twists of chance puts in a nasty quandary.
     Blessed in fortune, with a life so splendid,
     A freak of fate and the whole lot's shit.
     I make the man I love go hopping mad
     To save the one I care for just as bad.
     Is that what good means? It's certainly not clever.
     Commandment of humanity, or call to mad endeavour.

She draws the curtains closed.

Act Three

Schoolmaster SCHIEVELBUSCH *with his daughter* DOTTY *and the*
PRINCIPAL.

PRINCIPAL.   Oh final straw of this most painful day.
     The man whom I see coming this way
     Is the schoolman Schievelbusch
     Whose ghastly scribblings, dunce's mush,
     Are bywords here for virtue and thereby
     Represent the muse of poetry.
     What should I do? I'd like to run
     But that I may not. He's a well-regarded man.
     —The worthy schoolman!
SCHIEVELBUSCH *(with a speech impediment).*   The worthy principal,
     You honour me. It's not an everyday event
     That such a recognised talent
     Will greet a muse like mine so menial.
     You saw my lute I dare surmise,
PRINCIPAL *(aside).*   I saw it, then I closed my eyes.
SCHIEVELBUSCH.   In returning such a compliment
     A little gem I shall with pleasure now present
     The sort of flash of the moment inspiration,
     That in those moments of recreation
     Crackles through my brain.

PRINCIPAL.   Such comfort to the ear, I do proclaim.
SCHIEVELBUSCH.   I should, of course, not wish to tire.
PRINCIPAL.   I beg you, sound the note of your lyre.
SCHIEVELBUSCH.   I am a minor village poet.
PRINCIPAL.   Yet in such fields stands great Parnassus' feet.
SCHIEVELBUSCH.   Oh sir, do not despise me yet
   My winged steed is drab, thick-set
   And not unlike a plough-horse made.
PRINCIPAL.   I look not in the mouth of a gift-jade.
SCHIEVELBUSCH.   No leniency I pray. We are all
   Equal in the kingdom poetical.
   We would all like, great and small,
   To shock the public, like Catull.
PRINCIPAL *(aside)*.   Sure I'll praise you, stupid git,
   Honey-tongue you arse to tit.
   If you choose to flatter fools
   Your job is marred by having scruples.
   —The poet I attend, and on the singer's lips I hang.
SCHIEVELBUSCH.   Enough torturous suspense, 'tis time I sang:
   Outing with Aphrodite, or, Heartwarming Morning,
   Afternoon and Evening Hours.

   The oriole chirps his ditty
   And I walk with pretty
   Aphrodite, her hand
   In mine, across the land.
   Morning light on path and hedge
   And there, upon the field's edge
   Quivers a quail, invisble
   To us although it's audible.

   The mist dissolves above the meadow
   In the fiery sun's first shadow.
   For me as well, blest amatory,
   And so I start to tell my story,
   Someone beyond the far horizon
   Sighs for me and has her eyes on
   Me, and then she nods and smiles low,
   As if such things she did not know.

   'Tis pleasing so far, think you not?
PRINCIPAL.   So soft and happy.
   I do so hope there's more, dear chappie.
SCHIEVELBUSCH.   Harvest cart, loaded high,
   Purple cockle, red poppy,
   Wears the ryefield in her hair.
   And she picks a pair.

Celsius' pillar's now reached thirty points,
Fellow, don't be harsh on those old joints.
Come, oh come into my arm,
Kiss me fellow Arcadian!

With pleasure how the breast doth swell,
If I were silent now a lie I'd tell.
And right beside a rosy hedge
Sweet secrets to my love I pledge,
And dream in frenzy of a longing true—
Such heaven when you deserve it too.
And then she nods and smiles low
As if such things she did not know.

Good that last bit think you not?
PRINCIPAL.   Öpen I speak,
    You've written better than a Greek.
SCHIEVELBUSCH. No small hurdle that I trow.
PRINCIPAL *(aside)*.   God I wish the day would end right now.
SCHIEVELBUSCH. Hesperos' candle raised its flame
    Over wood and dark mountain,
    And just behind them there's a flimmer
    To herald Selen's coming shimmer.
    Night torches. And I'm made aware
    Of the so-longed-for cooling air.
    A sudden pleasure doth me steep
    And I must take a breath right deep.

Happy say I is the man
Whose leather death doth not yet tan,
And who with every legal power
In effort spends the Rhadamantine hour.
Yet only he doth know the world a place
Of pleasure who doth lighten up your face.
So shall I never walk alone,
But evermore with you shall roam.

    Well?
PRINCIPAL.   Speechless I am; pity, pity!
    Let me embrace you, speechless, for your ditty.
    No word's enough, enough I feel to capture
    The full extent of this my rapture.
    (Aside) Words to curse him I'd have sure enough!
SCHIEVELBUSCH.   Come on, think of ways to do it, poet say your stuff.
PRINCIPAL.   Fine morals and such graces sweet
    'gainst expectation, here we meet,
    Amid the provinces such ditties.
SCHIEVELBUSCH.   Provinces—
PRINCIPAL.   I mean far from cities.

103

SCHIEVELBUSCH. Province . . . that word's no bane to me.
  Some hear, it's true, the term unwillingly:
  Plundersweil was often written down
  As the world's most boring little town.
  So says Herr Braun, and so Herr Heym
  And even the Herr Brecht—it's an old rhyme.
  It is as if these great men, all and one
  Of world-experience had none.
  Since was not every town on earth
  Blessed with equal dullness at its birth?
  It's such a tedium, a bore,
  And naturally I've seen *(He names the place they are acting.)* before.
  And yet I know no faster riser
  Than the town of Plundersweiler
  Seventeen-twelve when I was young
  This our town was widely sung,
  For having two great breweries,
  And, see today, she shines with three.
  Enough. I do not wish to lose
  Your interest. But put on my shoes.
  Haven't had the benefactions
  Enjoyed for years by certain factions
  Who trumpet in each almanac
  The stable birth of every cat.
  I lack support to make my way.
  They can shut me up any day.
PRINCIPAL. My word on it, I'll spread your name,
  In every court shall course your fame.
  (Makes to exit.)
SCHIEVELBUSCH. Not so hasty, by your leave?
PRINCIPAL.   Is there no pity?
SCHIEVELBUSCH. You've still not heard dear Dotty's ditty.
PRINCIPAL *(aside)*. Good God! Her too. Pray make me deaf.
  —The Demoiselle, I do believe
  Has drunk from the Katalian spring?
SCHIEVELBUSCH. What? My little Dotty darling?
  You say she is no longer pure?
PRINCIPAL. I swear she is.
SCHIEVELBUSCH.   Then pray, touch not her honour!
PRINCIPAL. Let the maiden speak her rhyme.
  (Aside) Apollo help! You didn't last time.
DOTTY. Most reasonable pleasures of the garden by Dotty Schievelbusch
PRINCIPAL. What?
DOTTY. Most reasonable pleasures of the garden by Dotty Schievelbusch.
PRINCIPAL. What?
DOTTY. Most reasonable pleasures of the garden by Dotty Schievelbusch.

SCHIEVELBUSCH. The little dear has, when she utters,
    The teeniest touch of troublesome stutters.
    Where this fault came from and in what way
    Or what caused it, none can say.
    I beg you pay it no attention.
PRINCIPAL. Upon my honour, not worth a mention.
DOTTY *(sings.* SCHIEVELBUSCH *accompanies her on the lyre).*
    The potato is a flower you know,
    The maize doth bloom with feathers yellow.
    And doth it not suffice the tender dill
    To know that it bears fruit so beautiful?
    With all your glamour and your scent
    Roses proud and lilies bent,
    Our hunger you in no way feed:
    The wondrous things are those we need.
PRINCIPAL. How good! how beauteously unique!
    Present and future both here speak.
    With pleasure one beholds this apple now
    Fall'n direct beneath the blooming bough.
    By the way, how do you like the plays?
SCHIEVELBUSCH. Dreadful! They're a gross disgrace.
PRINCIPAL. Oh!
SCHIEVELBUSCH. The question is important, must be raised:
    I wonder only at the time and place.
    The Good Lord's word is our behest.
    But the bits we add are liked the best.
    I don't think that worthy classics old
    Should be changed one jot, let alone retold.
    Amazed I am that out of truth and taste
    Can come such rubbish, such worthless waste.
    The hero Ahasverus cries and groans
    Because he feels the death knell in his bones,
    And listens to the counsel of the devil:
    No king would ever be so evil.
    And how on earth did Mordechai in fact
    Get inside the harem, balls intact?
    One such cock-up follows hard the next.
PRINCIPAL. On life, that would be a suited text:
    Yet when folly finds a place in art,
    There is a reason for the foolish part.
SCHIEVELBUSCH. The poet's powers linguistic
    Are dissolute and frantic,
    What have you done to mother German
    Writing so in verse inhuman?
    Always regular this drivel
    Neatly parted down the middle.
    Can hardly walk for so much twisting:
    Who can speak such stuff, who listen?

PRINCIPAL. A rhythmophobic are you not?

SCHIEVELBUSCH. An enemy of rules is my proud lot,
Straight from the heart and never turning
Speaks the honest, upright German.

PRINCIPAL *(aside)*. My lungs are bursting, but I shall not speak.
We're still performing all next week.
(Goes to the booth and speaks to the actors through the curtain.)
All round the house a good reaction,
The audience is spellbound by the action.
No darling, the women are just green with envy,
Their silence is just raptured frenzy.

DOTTY. There's not much they can do to save this play,
But decent acting may improve its chance today.

PRINCIPAL. The young miss understands a lot.

DOTTY. And now the most absurd point in the plot.
This Esther is supposed to be a queen
And by this vast assembled audience seen—
And still her hair has not been done.

PRINCIPAL. The action plays before the dawn.

DOTTY. The globe would have to crack or drown
To catch me at cornflakes in my dressing-gown.

SCHIEVELBUSCH. We're no way trying to denigrate,
We wish to teach when we berate.
Yet hark when innocence doth speak its mind.
My daughter's breakfast's most refined.

PRINCIPAL. You judge as if you knew your business.

SCHIEVELBUSCH. Everything we judge like this,
Since everything as we conjecture
Is judged by how it fits our picture.

PRINCIPAL. You're God incarnate I suppose.

SCHIEVELBUSCH. A man who God's intentions surely knows.
An enlightened man of honour
No mortal can be more.

PRINCIPAL. Enlightenment, if so remark I may,
Is not quite as ready as you say.
Another century we'll spend
Before this foolish bickering will end
And all we know to be so true and good
Is everywhere accepted, understood.
Truth's a pretty boring meat
If there's nothing else to eat.
And yet I yield, with humble spirit;
Our course, young lady, is already set.
Just as a mist that veils the moon
Hails a sunny afternoon.
For this I think for certain,
Soon will come free verse's turn.

That is if not just bookish learning
But life itself t'enlightenment were turning,
And you who serve the present hour
Should shut your gobs, best thing by far.
And even in these times I see
Through the mists of coming days
A golden temple, on whose walls shall be
A motto: to art, from the people praise. *(Exit)*
DOTTY.   Nice one daddy, you really did that man.
SCHIEVELBUSCH.   The fellow's just a thorough sham.
   (AHASVERUS opens the curtain.)
AHASVERUS.   The genius who grants me ever slumber even
   Last night did dim his candle quite unbidden.
   I had to stand a night in deepest fear
   Partly sighing, partly trying to think things clear.
   This sort of thing's quite new to me, the morning's all in tatters,
   I'll have to find the guilty one and have his guts for garters.
   What was Haman, beastly spoilsport, up to when
   He asked that Mordechai's poor neck should hang?
   The Jew has had a book of proverbs brought to press.
   Hating such a man is stupid, not seeing him is best.
   And now throughout the world I hear the cry
   'The sun of Persia's strangling Mordechai.'
   And even if they're stupid, what else does ruling mean
   Than reckoning for folly within one's mighty scheme?
   I'm sick to death of all the fuss.
   You out there, be glad you're not the boss.
   I've wavered long enough. My word stands firm.
MORDECHAI *(Off)*   Boo hoo!
AHASVERUS.   Who witters here
HAMAN *(enters)*.   My Prince.
AHASVERUS.   Who knocked? The worm.
   The sun has only just gone up o'er streets of Susan.
   How did you sleep?
HAMAN.   Well, indeed.
AHASVERUS.   Cheekier every day, this man.
HAMAN.   Empire's father, grant thy son
   That he with happy mien may now approach the throne.
AHASVERUS.   Lovely to see you. Uah! *(Aside)* I'd find him much more
   funny.
   If in the morning he were not as frisky as Bugs Bunny.
HAMAN.   Thy word is godlike, thy glance hath magic power,
   Thy wish is spoken and fulfilled within the hour.
   The man thou blessest blossoms, but arguing with thee
   Means little better than for one's own death to plea.
   And so the crafty devil, thy assassin and thy foe
   Whence light doth shine no more, prepared is to go.

107

To Ahriman's dread kingdom the rope will draw him through:
A spectacle for kings. O come and see it, do!
And so I do invite thee, to thy delight, I trust:
It's just the sort of joke for kings whose tyrant is a must.
For has the world a pleasure greater than to see
That man struggling for life who is our enemy.

AHASVERUS. No mercy do you grant him then, poor man.

HAMAN. My Prince, where Mordechai doth stand, stands not Haman.

AHASVERUS *(aside)*. There of course he's right. One of the pair
Must down old Orkus' throat, we've got no actor spare.

ESTHER *(off)*. Stop! Stop!

AHASVERUS.   The Queen—

HAMAN.   Has left the harem royal.
She dares to leave her place before thou call.
(ESTHER enters).

ESTHER. Stop! Stop! Oh master, how happy would I be
Were it not this monster by thy side I see.

AHASVERUS. What do you mean by coming here?

ESTHER.   Justice I implore.

AHASVERUS. Justice is just what's going on, I'll hear no more.

ESTHER. My uncle's spotless.

AHASVERUS.   That has not been shown.

ESTHER. Here, this man. Here's the guilty one.

AHASVERUS.   Don't care. I'm hanging that one.

ESTHER. My princely husband, pride and pleasure
My lovely strong man, darling Ahasver,
I know no other fortune than to bow to thee.

AHASVERUS. Then be a dear and go.

ESTHER.   Thy order shall my pleasure be.
A servant will obey his king, because he knows his place.
But I delight in doing things just as my husband says.
His well-being is my joy, his smile is my cheer.
And I revel in his glance.

AHASVERUS.   Stop talking that way, dear.

ESTHER. Yet as I know how dear I am to thee
I come to thee to beg, not fearing, on my knee.
And love not mercy should rather grant my plea
That givingly receives, and giving shall rewarded be.

AHASVERUS. I don't want to.

ESTHER.   But darling mine.

AHASVERUS.   How prettily you smell.

ESTHER. Yes, for thee.

AHASVERUS.   Oh crafty devil, how you charm my heart as well.

ESTHER. Give me my Mordechai. What? Do I find you cold?

HAMAN. Is this still Persia's court? Oh rottenness most bold!

ESTHER. The rotter here is you; and where my master's might
Is infinte, 'tis hard to keep the rotters out of sight.

Yet my lord Ahasverus has always stayed a man.
I thank the Gods for this, that I thus love him can.
And so my duty's to prevent your net of rot
By spreading mine more sweetly, with all the power I've got.
The man who keeps himself but clean lets in the raving devil
And even the most noble soul must sometimes grapple evil.
HAMAN. The woman deserves death.
AHASVERUS.   What for?
HAMAN   Thou didst not call.
AHASVERUS. But now she's here. So hark, her voice is beautiful.
HAMAN. Who would rather not be good? Who not hand out honour?
    But laws of state must always be the state's most trusty pillar.
    Thy kingdom, broadly cast, and populous, it shivers
    Whenever law, that binds it up together, quivers.
    Whoever's crazed enough to break it dies the death.
AHASVERUS. Ah, my dear Haman, did you come at my request?
HAMAN. Of course, we all know that the law is far from faultless.
    Sometimes it may even be upset by those most spotless.
    The word is then that if by law the law itself lose face
    The case goes upwards to the king's own grace.
    But then again there is another aspect,
    That he who enters the presence—a tradition I respect
    Has only to be touched by thee, or by the sceptre's rod,
    In friendly welcome and the sentence is made void.
AHASVERUS. That's true.
HAMAN.   Tradition stands above the law, 'tis wiser.
ESTHER. So grant the rod thy wife.
HAMAN.   Nay, me. That'd be much nicer.
    Oh, go on, do us both: why dost thou keep us waiting?
AHASVERUS. But one of you I'll save, the other's for beheading.
HAMAN. I'm your right arm.
ESTHER.   I'm your soft body.
HAMAN. I'm your clever counsellor.
ESTHER.   I'm your dalliance lady.
HAMAN. So, so.
ESTHER.   Think it over, great grandson of King Cyrus.
    What was it that thou saidst to me just recently as
    You first discovered where my thighs and buttocks join.
HAMAN. I serve Persia.
ESTHER.   And I thee, as do my loins.
HAMAN. I sit on thy chair.
ESTHER.   I lie in thy bed.
HAMAN. Mark not her words, or like a chained bear be led,
    As any man who takes a whore's word for true coin.
AHASVERUS. Dear Haman, look, it's your fault that I'm not enjoying
    This: and he who says he'd rather have his wife speaks true
    To touch his rod up than have it touched by you.

So to the courtyard run along, send Mordechai to me:
And then there'll be all set for you an empty gallows free.
There you'll be quite comfortable: just hang yourself at leisure.
HAMAN.   Quarrelling with a stupid fool will never bring you pleasure.
You'll be seeing long enough what your weakness's done. *(Exit)*
ESTHER.   He'll be seeing short enough: now leave us both alone.
(MORDECHAI returns.)
AHASVERUS.   Oh no! Not another troubler trying out my law.
MORDECHAI.   Nephew by marriage, lovely boy, you're radiant I am sure
Haman's swinging now, so clever, glad you had him topped.
Clev'rer still though that his power to my lot has dropped.
AHASVERUS.   It has?
MORDECHAI.   What? Not? She did not weep, implore?
AHASVERUS.   For that, I think not.
MORDECHAI.   Well, that we must ignore.
She's a young slip, and sometimes leaves the odd thing out.
But she would have?
AHASVERUS.   Had she, I'd have given you his clout.
MORDECHAI.   I'm sure you would. And sure you're feeling heavenly
delight.
I'm off into your kingdom to pull the reins in tight.
AHASVERUS.   That too. The last—
ESTHER.   Peace!
MORDECHAI.   Weakness of the court
Is cured. Folly reigns in palaces where no thought
Is ruler: but happy is that land where power dissolves itself.
Where love may sing it lullabies, whose guide is wisdom's self.

Blackout.

The Mission
or
Memory of a Revolution

(Der Auftrag)
(oder Erinnerung einer Revolution)

by

Heiner Mueller

translated by Stuart Hood   ·

The play uses motifs from a story entitled 'Light on the Gallows' by Anna Seghers.

Première: in the small theatre on the third floor of the East Berlin Volksbühne, Jan 1981. Directed by the author.

Heiner Mueller has never been a comfortable member of East German society, his plays frequently coming into conflict with the Party. Mueller's early dramatic strategy was an honest form of socialist realism, as expressed in such works as *The Correction* and *The Wage Cutter;* but this gradually gave way to a concern for a more classical and symbolic mode of representation, Mueller plundering Graeco-Roman mythology for analogues of contemporary cultural issues. Most recently, he seems to be exploring ways of bringing both strategies into harmony. *The Mission* shares the linguistic richness of the classical imitations, and shows a similar concern for the way in which language may heighten and intensify both feeling and dialectical reasoning: yet it goes further than the previous material in the breadth of its subject matter. The mission itself, its almost mystical purpose, generates an atmosphere of searching for a meaning to history in the context of a deterministic repetition of the theme of disorientation and frustrated hope. The Mission, it appears, is given by the revolutionary powers in Paris in 1794 and the task is the liberation of the West Indian slaves. But by the time the task can be carried out the government in Paris has passed to Napoleon and the Mission is cancelled. Suddenly, however, the mission and the time change, and the new environment is modern day New York. Trapped in a lift in a skyscraper the destined agent finds himself transported to the deserts of Peru . . . In suggesting through such temporal shifts an affinity between a relativistic view of time and the relativism of revolution, Mueller seems to argue the case for considering Marxist-Leninism as more a state of mind than a materialist belief, and this state of mind may include the Peruvian desert dweller as much as the Haitian slave or the man in the New York lift.

Two antecedents stand out: Büchner's *Dantons Tod (Danton's Death)* which Mueller quotes and parodies; and Brecht's Lehrstück *Die Maßnahme (The Measures Taken).* From Büchner comes the connection between sexuality, death and revolution which Mueller develops to include imperialism: and the submerged didacticism of the play shows how—building on the Lehrstück as a means of narration—it is possible to teach without appearing to do so. As Andrzej Wirth commented on seeing the première: 'A product of Mueller's intensive debate with the Lehrstücken, *The Mission* is itself no Lehrstück, or perhaps may be understood as the internalisation and subjectivisation of a Lehrstück.' (*Theater Heute,* February 1981, p. 6) On the surface, Mueller's early collaboration with Hacks—which then came to an end in the mid 60s—seems incomprehensible if *The Mission* is compared to *Market Day at Plundersweilern:* yet the appearance is a little deceptive. Mueller, like Hacks, doubles many of the roles—Antoine, Debuisson and the Man in the Lift are played by one man; Antoine's wife, First Love and Angel of Despair by the same woman. The episodic technique, again similar to Hacks's, suggests affinities where none is made explicit, affinities not least between the slaves of Haiti and the population of certain towns like Plundersweil. As Wirth commented: 'Role-play in this instance does not serve the exploration of modes of behaviour but the demonstration of certain collocations of consciousness.' It is not, in other words, the facts of a situation in their literal and specific manifestation which count, but the spirit which they embody.

Characters
GALLOUDEC
SAILOR
ANTOINE
WOMAN
ANGEL OF DESPAIR
SASPORTAS
DEBUISSON
NEGRO
FIRST LOVE
MOTHER
FATHER
SLAVES

Memoir of a Revolution

Galloudec to Antoine: I am writing this letter on my death-bed. I
am writing it in my own name and in the name of Citizen Sasportas
who was hanged at Port Royal. I wish to inform you that we must
return the assignment which the Convention gave us through your
person because we could not fulfil it. Perhaps others will achieve more.
You will not hear anything more of Debuisson—things are going well
for him. It seems traitors have a good time when the peoples walk
through blood. That is how the world is and it is not good that it is so.
Forgive my hand-writing—they have taken off one of my legs and I am
writing with fever. I hope this letter finds you well and remain with
republican greetings.

SAILOR, ANTOINE, WOMAN

SAILOR.   Are you Citizen Antoine? For this here is a letter for you.
From someone called Galloudec. It isn't my fault if the letter is
old already and maybe the whole matter has been dealt with. The
Spaniards kept us prisoners in Cuba, then the English on Trinidad,
until your consul, Bonaparte, made peace with England. Then I
was robbed clean in the street in London because I was drunk, but
they didn't find the letter. About this Galloudec—he's had it. He
croaked in a hospital in Cuba—half prison, half hospital. He lay
there with gangrene—I had fever. **Take the letter, it has to get there
even if it is the last thing you do, you must do that for me**, was
the last thing he said to me. And the address of an office and your
name—if you are this Antoine. But there's no office there any longer,
and no one where the office was knows anything about you if that's
your name—Antoine. Someone who lives behind the builders'
scaffolding in a cellar sent me to a school where someone called
Antoine is supposed to have worked as a teacher. But they knew
nothing about him. Then a charwoman told me her nephew had seen
you here. He's a waggoner. And he described you to me—if you're
the one.
ANTOINE.   I don't know anyone called Galloudec.
SAILOR.   I don't know what was so important about the letter to him.
Something to do with a mission. With an assignment he had to give
back so that others could go on with his work. Whatever kind of
work it was. Towards the end he talked about nothing else. Except
when he screamed and that was his wound hurting him. It came in
waves. And it lasted a good long time till he was through with dying.
The doctor said his heart is too strong—he should have been dead ten
times over by now. Life is a bastard. The other one he writes about in
his letter—a nigger—had a quicker death. He read me the letter.
Galloudec, so I would know it by heart in case it got lost. And if you
don't know who he is yet I'll tell you what they did to him and how

114

he died. You weren't there. First of all they cut off one leg at the knee and then the rest of it. It was the left one. Then. . .

ANTOINE.   I know nothing about a mission. I don't hand out assignments. I'm not a person of authority. I earn my money by tutoring. It isn't much. And I've seen enough slaughter. I know all about the human anatomy. Galloudec.

WOMAN *with wine, bread, cheese.*

WOMAN.   You have a visitor. I sold a medal. The one for the Vendée campaign when you killed off the peasants for the Republic.

ANTOINE.   Yes.

SAILOR.   As far as I can see you still have everything. Not like this Galloudec whom you don't know and who's as dead as a door-nail. The other one was called Sasportas. They hanged him—if you want to know—because of the mission the one you don't know about—at Port Royal in Jamaica. The gallows are on a cliff. When they're dead they're cut down and fall into the sea. The sharks do the rest. Thanks for the wine.

ANTOINE.   Sasportas. I'm the Antoine you've been looking for. I have to be careful. France isn't a republic any more. Our Consul has become Emperor and is conquering Russia. If your belly's full it's easier to talk about a lost revolution. Blood that's congealed into tin for medals. The peasants didn't know any better either, did they? Trade's flourishing. These people in Haiti—we feed them their own dirt these days. That used to be the negro republic. Freedom brings people out on to the barricades and when the dead awake she's wearing a uniform. I'm going to let you in on a secret—she's only a whore after all. And I get a laugh out of it. Ha ha ha. But there's something empty that was once full of life. I was there when the people stormed the Bastille, I was there when the head of the last Bourbon fell into the basket. We reaped the heads of the aristocrats. We reaped the heads of the traitors.

WOMAN.   A fine harvest. You're drunk again, Antoine.

ANTOINE.   She doesn't like it when I talk about my great days. The Gironde trembled before me. Look at her, my France. Her breasts sucked dry. Between her thighs the desert. A ship without a rudder in the surf of the new century. Look how she founders. France needs a blood-bath and that day will come. (ANTOINE *pours red wine over his head.*)

SAILOR.   I don't understand all that. I'm a sailor. I don't believe in politics. The world isn't the same all over. Here's the letter. *(He leaves.)*

ANTOINE *(shouts).*   Take care, sailor, when you are leaving my house. The police of our Minister of the Interior, Fouché, don't ask if you believe in politics. Galloudec. Sasportas. Where's you leg, Galloudec? Why's your tongue sticking out of your mouth, Sasportas? What do you want of me? What's your stump of a leg got to do with me? Or your halter? Am I supposed to cut off a leg? Do you want me to hang myself beside you? Ask your Emperor about your leg, Galloudec. Show the Emperor your tongue, Sasportas. He's winning in Russia — I can show you the way there.

What do you want from me? Go on—go away. Get away with you.
You. Tell them, wife. Tell them to go away—I don't want to see them
any more. Are you still there? Your letter's arrived. Galloudec. That's
it. At any rate you've got it all behind you now. Long live the
Republic *(Laughs.)* You think I'm doing all right, don't you? Are
you hungry? There. *(Throws bread onto the dead bodies.)*
WOMAN.   Come to bed, Antoine.
ANTOINE. That's the way to heaven on the cheap
                So long as my ribs hold out and keep
                My heart sound in my breast—the damned beast.

While they make love the ANGEL OF DESPAIR *enters.*

ANTOINE'S VOICE.   Who are you?
WOMAN'S VOICE.   I am the angel of despair. With my hands I
    distribute ecstasy, numbness, oblivion, the pleasure and torment
    of our bodies. My speech is silence, my song a scream. Fear lives
    in the shadow of my wings. My hope is the last dying breath. My
    hope is the first battle. I am the knife with which the dead man
    breaks open his coffin. I am the one who will be. My flight is revolt.
    My heaven the abyss of tomorrow.

We had arrived in Jamaica—three emissaries of the French People's
Convention—our names Debuisson, Galloudec, Sasportas. Our mission—a
slave revolt against the sovereignty of the British crown in the name of the
French Republic. Which is the motherland of revolution, the terror
of thrones, the hope of the poor. In which all men are equal under the
axe of justice. Which has no bread for the hunger of its suburbs but
enough hands to carry the torch of liberty, equality and fraternity to
every land. We stood in the harbour square. In the middle of the square
a cage had been set up. We heard the wind from the sea, the hard rustling
of the palm-leaves, the sound of the palm-brushes with which the negro
women swept the dust from the square, the groans of the slave in the
cage, the surf. We saw the breasts of the negro women, the bloodily
scourged body of the slave in the cage, the governor's palace. We said:
This is Jamaica, shame of the Antilles, the slave-ship of the Caribbean sea.

SASPORTAS.   By the time we have finished our work.
GALLOUDEC.   You can start right away. Didn't you come here to free
    the slaves. That's a slave in the cage. Unless he's freed today,
    tomorrow he won't be one any more.
DEBUISSON.   They expose them in cages if they have tried to run away
    or for other crimes—as an awful warning—till the sun shrivels them
    up. It was like that before when I left Jamaica—ten years ago. Don't
    look, Sasportas, that's one we can't help.
SASPORTAS.   It's always only one that dies. It's the dead that are
    counted.
DEBUISSON.   Death is the mask of the revolution.

SASPORTAS. When I leave here others will be hanging in the cages
with white skins till the sun burns them black. Then a lot of people will
have been helped.

GALLOUDEC. Perhaps we should put up a guillotine instead. It's
cleaner. The red widow is the best charwoman.

DEBUISSON. The darling of the faubourgs.

SASPORTAS. I still maintain that a cage is just right for a white skin
when the sun is high enough.

GALLOUDEC. We aren't here to squabble about the colour of our
skins.

SASPORTAS. We aren't equal till we've flayed each other.

DEBUISSON. That was a bad beginning. Let's put on our masks.
I am who I was: Debuisson, son of slave-owners in Jamaica, with
an inheritance of a plantation with four hundred slaves. Come back
to the bosom of his family to take over his inheritance from the lowering
skies of Europe, dark with the smoke of the fires and the bloody fog of
the new philosophy, back to the clean air of the Caribbean after the
terror of the revolution had opened his eyes to the eternal truth that
everything old is better than anything new. Besides, I'm a doctor,
one who helps humanity without respect for persons, master or slave,
I heal the one for the other so that everything stays as it is as long as
it lasts, my face the pink face of the slave-owner, who has nothing to
fear on this earth except death.

SASPORTAS. And his slaves.

DEBUISSON. Who are you, Galloudec?

GALLOUDEC. A peasant from Brittany who learned to hate the
Revolution in the bloody rain of the guillotine—I wish the rain had
fallen thicker and not only on France—true servant of his worship,
Monsieur Debuisson, and I believe in the sacred hierarchy of the
monarchy and the church—I hope I shan't have to pray for them
too often.

DEBUISSON. You stepped out of your role twice, Galloudec, who are you?

GALLOUDEC. A peasant from Brittany who learned to hate the revolution
in the rain of blood from the guillotine, I believe in the sacred hierarchy
of the monarchy and the church.

DEBUISSON. Sasportas. Your mask.

GALLOUDEC. You shouldn't find it difficult to play the slave,
Sasportas, with your black skin.

SASPORTAS. Fleeing from the victorious black revolution on Haiti, I
joined Monsieur Debuisson because God created me for slavery. I am
his slave. Is that enough? (GALLOUDEC applauds.) Next time I'll
answer you with a knife, Citizen Galloudec.

GALLOUDEC. I know you've the hardest part to play, Sasportas. It is
written all over your body.

SASPORTAS. By whips which will write another alphabet on other
bodies in our hands.

DEBUISSON. Victorious revolution—that's not good. You don't say

117

that sort of thing in front of masters. Black revolution isn't good either. Blacks riot when it gets that far—but no revolution.

SASPORTAS. Didn't the revolution win in Haiti? The black revolution.

DEBUISSON. It was the scum that won. In Haiti the scum rules. (SASPORTAS *spits.*) You're spitting in the wrong direction. I'm your master. Say it.

SASPORTAS. Fleeing from the scum that has turned Haiti into a sewer.

GALLOUDEC. Sewer is good. You learn quickly, Sasportas.

DEBUISSON. Take your hand from your face and look at the flesh that is dying in that cage. You too, Galloudec. It's your flesh and your flesh and my flesh. His organs are the Marseillaise of the bodies on which the new world will be built. Learn the tune. We are going to hear it for a long time. Whether we want to or not. It is the tune of the revolution, our work. Many people will die in this cage because we do our work. That is what we do for people like ourselves with our work—and perhaps only that. Our place is in the cage if our masks tear too soon. The revolution is the mask of death. Death is the mask of the revolution. *(A huge* NEGRO *appears.)* That is my family's oldest slave. He is deaf and dumb—something between a human being and a dog. He will spit into the cage. Maybe you should do the same, Sasportas, so that you learn to hate your black skin for as long as we need it. Then he will kiss my shoes—he's licking his lips already; can you see—and he'll carry me, his old and new master, on his back into the house of my fathers, grunting with delight. The family opens its lap—tomorrow our work begins.

The huge NEGRO *spits into the cage, looks at* SASPORTAS, *bows to* GAULLOUDEC, *kisses* DEBUISSON's *shoes, carries him off.* GALLOUDEC *and* SASPORTAS *follow one behind the other.*
The revolution is the mask of death. Death is the mask of the revolution. The revolution is the mask of death. Death is the mask of the revolution etc. The return of the prodigal son. FATHER *and* MOTHER *in an open cupboard. On a throne* FIRST LOVE. DEBUISSON, GAULLOUDEC, SASPORTAS *are undressed and dressed by* SLAVES. DEBUISSON *as a slave-owner*—GALLOUDEC *as an overseer with whip*—SASPORTAS *as a slave.*

FIRST LOVE. Little Victor has been playing at revolutions. Now he's come back to the bosom of his family. Home to papa with the worm-eaten brain-pan. Back to Mama with her smell of rotting flowers. Did you hurt yourself, little Victor? Come closer and show me your wounds. Don't you know me any more? You don't need to be frightened, little Victor, not of me. Not of your first love. Whom you deceived with the revolution, your blood-stained second love. Whom you rolled with in the gutter for ten long years in competition with the rabble. Or in the mortuaries where she counts her loot. I can smell her perfume of horse-shit. Tears, little Victor? Did you love her so much? Ah Debuisson, I told you she was a whore. The snake with

118

sex that sucks blood. Slavery is a natural law as old as human kind.
Why should it come to an end, before humanity does? Why should it
not last as long? Look at my slaves—and yours—our property. All
their lives they have been animals. Why should they be human beings
because it says so on a piece of paper in France? Which is hardly
legible because of so much more blood than has flowed here in your
beautiful Jamaica and mine because of slavery. I'll tell you a story. In
Barbados a plantation-owner was killed two months after the
abolition of slavery. They came to him—his freed slaves. They came on
their knees like in church. And do you know what they wanted? To get
back to the security of slavery. That's what people are like—their
first home is their mother, a prison. (SLAVES *lift the* MOTHER's
skirt over her head) Here it is gaping, their home, here it is wide open,
the family lap. Say the word if you want to return and she'll stuff you
in, the idiot, the eternal mother. The poor man on Barbados wasn't
so lucky. They beat him to death with clubs, his no-longer slaves, like
a mad dog because he didn't take them back out of the cold spring air
of freedom under the beloved whip. Do you like the story, Citizen
Debuisson? Freedom lives on the backs of slaves, equality under the
headsman's axe. Do you want to be a slave, little Victor? Do you love
me? These are the lips you kissed. *(A* SLAVE *paints a huge mouth on
her)* They remember your skin, Debuisson. These are the breasts that
warmed you, little Victor. (FEMALE SLAVE *puts make-up on her
nipples*) They haven't forgotten your hands and your mouth. This is
the skin that drank your sweat. This is the sex that received your seed
that burns my heart. (SLAVE *paints a blue heart*) Do you see the
blue flame? Do you know how they catch the runaway slaves in Cuba?
They hunt them with bloodhounds. And so I will take back, Citizen
Debuisson, what your whore the revolution stole from me—my
property. (SLAVES *as dogs accompanied by* GALLOUDEC *with a
whip and with tally ho's from the* FATHER'S GHOST *chase*
DEBUISSON) With my dogs' teeth I shall bite the traces of my tears,
my sweat, my cries of pleasure, out of your sullied flesh. With the
knives of their claws I shall cut my wedding dress from your skin.
Translate your breath, which tastes of the dead bodies of kings, into
the speech of suffering which is the speech of slaves. I will eat your
sex and give birth to a tiger which will swallow time that makes the
clocks chime in my empty heart through which the rains of the
tropics pass. (SLAVE *puts a tiger mask on her*) **Yesterday I began to
kill you my heart/Now I love your corpse/When I am dead/My dust
will cry out for you.** I shall give you this bitch as a present, little
Victor, so that you can fill her with your blighted seed. But first of all
I shall have her whipped so that your blood mingles. Do you love me,
Debuisson? A woman shouldn't be left on her own.

SLAVES *take the whip from* GALLOUDEC, *shut the cupboard, take off*
FIRST LOVE's *make-up, put* DEBUISSON *on the throne with* FIRST

LOVE *as his footstool, dress* GALLOUDEC *and* SASPORTAS *up as*
Danton and Robespierre. The theatre of the revolution opens. While the
two players and the public take their places the conversation of the parents
can be heard from the cupboard.

FATHER. That is the resurrection of the flesh. For the worm gnaws eternally
and the fire is never quenched.

MOTHER. Is he whoring around again? Crick-crack—look—my heart's
broken.

FATHER. I give her to you, my son. I give you them both, black—
and, or else, white.

MOTHER. Take the knife out of my belly, you painted whores.

FATHER. On your knees, scum, and ask your mother's pardon.

MOTHER. High on the mountains
the wind blows wild
and Mary is killing
her Christ child
Back to Greenland. Come children. The sun shines every day
there.

FATHER. Make the idiot shut up.

SASPORTAS-ROBESPIERRE. Take your place, Danton, in the pillory
of history. Citizens, look at the sponger who devours the bread of
the hungry. The debauchee who violates the daughters of the people.
The traitor who wrinkles his nose at the smell of the blood with
which the revolution washes the body of the new society. Shall I
tell you why you can't look at blood any more, Danton? Did you
say 'revolution'? Your hand in the flesh-pots was your revolution.
A free ticket to the brothel. That was what you swaggered for on
platforms to the applause of the rabble. The lion that licks the boots
of the aristocrats. Do you like the taste of the Bourbon's spittle?
Are you warm up the monarchy's arse? Did you say courage? Just
shake your powdered mane. When your head falls under the axe of
justice that will be the end of your taunting of virtue. You can't say
I didn't warn you, Danton. Now the guillotine will speak to you,
the glorious invention of the new era which will march over you as it
does over all traitors. You'll understand what it is saying—you spoke
its language once—you spoke it well in September. (SLAVES *knock
off* GALLOUDEC-DANTON's *head and throw it to each other.*
GALLOUDEC *manages to catch it. He sticks it under his arm*)
Why don't you stick your fine head between your legs, Danton,
where your intelligence sits with the lice of your debauches and the
chancreas of your vice.

SASPORTAS-ROBESPIERRE *knocks the Danton head out from under*
GALLOUDEC's *arm. He crawls after it and puts it on.*

GALLOUDEC-DANTON. Now it's my turn. Look at the monkey with
the broken jaw. The blood-sucker who can't stop drooling. Is your

120

mouth too full? Incorruptible—drumming up virtue. That's the
fatherland's thanks—a gendarme's fist. (SLAVES *tear the bandage from*
SASPORTAS-ROBESPIEBRE's *head; his jaw drops. While* SASPORTAS
is looking for the bandage and the jawbone:) Have you dropped
something? Lost something? Property is theft. Do you feel the wind
on your neck? That is freedom. (SASPORTAS *has found the bandage
and the jawbone and puts the Robespierre head together*) Watch out
that you don't lose your sly head altogether, Robespierre, out of love
for the people. Did you say revolution? The axe of justice, is that it?
The guillotine is no bread factory. Thrift, thrift, Horatio. *(The*
SLAVE *knocks the Robespierre head off* SASPORTAS *and uses it
as a football)* That is equality. **Long live the Republic.** Didn't I tell
you, you're next. *(Joins in the* SLAVES' *game of football)* That is
fraternity. (SASPORTAS-ROBESPIERRE *weeps*). What have you
got against football. Entre nous—shall I tell you why you were on
about my fine head? I bet if you drop your trousers there's nothing
but a puff of dust. Ladies and gentlemen, the theatre of the revolution
is open. Attraction—the man without loins. Maximilian the Great.
Max the good boy. The man who sits and farts. The Arras wanker.
The bloody Robespierre.
SASPORTAS-ROBESPIERRE *(puts his head on again).*   My name stands
    in the Pantheon of history.
GALLOUDEC-DANTON. A little man stands in the wood
                with not a word
                he wears a great big purple robe
                and a great big sword.
SASPORTAS-ROBESPIERRE.   Parasite syphillitic tool of the aristocrats.
GALLOUDEC-DANTON.   Sycophant eunuch lackey of Wall Street.
SASPORTAS-ROBESPIERRE.   Swine.
GALLOUDEC-DANTON.   Hyena.

They knock each other's heads off. DEBUISSON *applauds.*
SLAVES *tear him from the throne and put* SASPORTAS *in his place
with* GALLOUDEC *as footstool. The coronation of* SASPORTAS.

SASPORTAS.   The theatre of the white revolution is over. We
    condemn you to death, Victor Debuisson. Because your skin is white.
    Because your thoughts are white under your white skin. Because your
    eyes have seen the beauty of our sisters. Because your hands have
    touched the nakedness of our sisters. Because your thoughts have
    eaten their breasts their bodies their cunts. Because you are a
    property-owner, a gentleman. Therefore we condemn you to death,
    Victor Debuisson. The snakes will eat your shit, crocodiles your
    arse, the piranhas your balls. (DEBUISSON *screams*) The terrible
    thing about you is that you can't die. So you kill everything around
    you. For your dead social orders in which ecstasy has no place. For
    your revolutions without sex. Do you love this woman? We are
    taking her so that you can die more easily. It's easier to die if you

don't own anything. What do you own still? Tell us—quick—time is our school—it doesn't come back and there's no breathing-space for didactics. If you don't learn you die too. Your skin. Why did you take it off? Your flesh our hunger. Your blood empties our veins. Your thoughts—what about them? Who sweats for your philosophy? Even your piss and your shit are exploitation and slavery. Not to speak of your sperm. A distillation of dead bodies. Now you don't own anything anymore. Now you are nothing. Now you can die. Bury him.

DEBUISSON.   I am standing between two men whom I don't know in an old lift with metal beams that clatter as it goes up. I am dressed like an office worker or a worker on his day off. I have even put on a tie—the collar is rubbing my neck. I am sweating. If I move my head the collar catches my neck in a noose. I have an appointment with the boss. (In my thoughts I call him Number One.) His office is on the fourth floor or was it the twentieth? I've only got to think about it not to be sure any more. The news of my appointment with the boss (whom I call Number One in my thoughts) reached me in the basement—a huge space with empty concrete chambers and signposts to the bomb shelter. I imagine it's about a mission I'm to be assigned. I check that my tie is sitting properly and tighten the knot. I wish I had a mirror so that I could actually see the tie is sitting properly. You can't possibly ask a stranger if your tie is sitting properly. The ties of the other people in the lift are impeccable. Some of them seem to know each other. They are talking quietly about something I don't understand. But their conversation must have distracted me. At the next stop I read with alarm on the indicator above the door the number eight. I have come too far—or else I still have half-way to go. The time factor is decisive. Better five minutes early than five minutes late, they say. When last I looked at my watch it said ten. I remember my feeling of relief. Still fifteen minutes till my appointment with the boss. But now when I look at my watch again between the eighth and ninth floors it says exactly 14 minutes and 45 seconds past ten. So I am going to be late—time is not on my side. I think over my situation quickly—I can get out at the next stop and run down the stairs three steps at a time to the fourth floor. If it is the wrong floor that naturally means a loss of time that I perhaps can't make up for. I can go on to the 20th floor and if the boss's office isn't there go back to the fourth floor provided the lift isn't held up or run down the steps (three at a time) maybe breaking my neck or a leg because I'm in a hurry. I can see myself lying on a stretcher which at my wish is carried into the boss's office and put down in front of his desk—always ready and present but not quite fit. Meantime the name of the game is the question—which can't be answered in advance because of my carelessness—what office is the boss in (whom I always call Number One in my thoughts) waiting for me with a mission?

122

(It must be an important mission or why would he not get someone
lower down on the scale to hand it to me?) A quick glance at my
watch makes it incontrovertibly clear to me that it is far too late
even for normal punctuality although our lift—as a second glance
shows—has not yet reached the 12th floor. The hour hand points to
ten, the minute hand to fifty—seconds are of no interest any more.
Something seems to be wrong with my watch but there's not time to
check it—I am alone in the lift without having seen where the other
gentlemen got out. With terror that tugs my hair by the roots I see
the hands of my watch, from which I can no longer tear my eyes away,
racing round the face with increasing speed so that between one blink
of the eyes and the next more and more hours go past. It becomes
clear to me that something has been wrong for a long time—with my
watch, with this lift, with time. I give way to wild speculations:
gravity loses its grip, a disturbance, a kind of stutter in the rotation
of the earth like cramp in the thigh at football. I'm sorry I know too
little about physics to be able to resolve the shrieking contradiction
between the speed of the lift and the passage of time indicated by my
watch. Why didn't I pay attention at school? Or read the wrong books.
Poetry instead of physics. The times are out of joint and somewhere on
the fourth or twentieth floor (that 'or' cuts like a knife into my careless
brain) the chief waits in a room which is no doubt extensive and
furnished with a carpet behind his desk which presumably stands at
the narrow end of the room opposite the door—waits for me—for a
failure—with my mission. Perhaps the world has gone haywire and my
mission, which was so important, that the boss wanted to give it to me
personally has already become meaningless through my negligence.
INVALID as it says in the language of the bureaucracies which I have
learnt so well—a useless science—REGISTRY—where no one will look
at it again because it had to do with the last possible measure to
prevent the catastrophe whose beginning I have lived through shut-up
in this lift that has gone mad along with my wrist-watch. A desperate
dream within a dream—I have the capacity merely by rolling myself up
to turn my body into a projectile that will burst through the roof of
the lift and catch up with time. Cold awakening in the slow lift looking
at the racing watch. I imagine the desperation of Number One. His
suicide. His head whose portrait decorates all the offices on the desk.
Blood from a black-rimmed hole in (presumably) the right temple. I
heard no shot but that doesn't mean anything—the walls of his office
are naturally soundproof, incidents were allowed for during the building
of it and what happens in the Boss's office is no concern of the
populace, power is lonely. I get out of the lift at the next stand—with
no mission—with the tie (it's unnecessary now) still comically tied under
my chin and stand in a village street in Peru. Dry mud with wheel-
tracks. On both sides of the street a cold plain with rare scabs of grass
and patches of grey shrub reaches vaguely for the horizon over which
a mountain swims in the haze. Left of the street a barracks building—

123

it seems deserted—the windows black holes with broken glass. In front
of a hoarding with advertisements of a strange civilisation stand two
huge natives. Their backs are a threat. I ponder whether to turn back—
I still haven't been seen. I had never thought during my desperate
ascent to the Boss's office that I could feel homesick for the lift that
was my prison. How am I to explain my presence in this no-man's land.
I can produce no parachute, no wreckage of plane or car. Who will
believe that I have landed in Peru from a lift—the road before me and
behind me, flanked by the plain that reaches out for the horizon.
How can understanding be possible—I don't know the language of this
country—I might as well be deaf and dumb. It would be better if I were
deaf and dumb—perhaps there is pity in Peru. All that remains for me
is flight into what I hope is uninhabited territory, perhaps flight from one
death into another, but I prefer hunger to the murderer's knife. I have
not the means in any case to buy myself free with the little cash I have
in this foreign currency. Fate does not even grant me this—to die doing
my duty—my cause is hopeless. Employee of a dead boss that I am—my
mission locked away in his brain which will not release anything until
the treasure-house of eternity is opened—the wise men of this world
wrestle with its combinations this side of death. I hope I am not too
late to loosen the knot of my tie which it cost me so much sweat to
adjust correctly on my way to the boss and to make that conspicuous
article of dress disappear into my jacket. I had nearly thrown it away—a
clue. Turning round I see the village for the first time—mud and
straw—a hammock can be seen through an open door. Cold sweat
at the thought that I might have been observed from it but I can make
out no sign of life—the only moving thing a dog rolling in a steaming
midden. I have hesitated too long. The men detach themselves from
the hoarding and come diagonally across the street towards me at
first without looking at me. I see their faces looming over me—one
a kind of black with white eyes—there's no way to catch his glance,
the eyes have no pupils. The head of the other is grey silver. A long
calm look from eyes whose colour I can't make out—there's a shimmer
of something red in them. Through the fingers of his right hand which
hangs down heavily there runs a spasm—the veins gleam out of the
metal. The silver one passes behind me in the footsteps of the black.
My fear lifts and gives way to a feeling of disappointment—am I not
even worthy of a knife or the strangling grip of metal hands. Was there
not something akin to contempt in the calm gaze that was turned
on me for the duration of five steps? What is my crime? The world
hasn't come to an end—provided this isn't another world. How does
one carry out an unknown mission? What can my mission be in this
desert spot at the back of beyond? How is an employee to know what
goes on in the head of the boss? No science in the world will tear
my lost mission out of the brain tissues of the deceased. It is buried
with him—the state funeral which is perhaps already underway—is no
guarantee of resurrection. Something akin to mirth runs through

me—I put my jacket over my arm and button my shirt—this walk is
a walk I am taking. The dog runs across the street in front of me with
a hand slanting between its jaws—the fingers are towards me—they
look burnt. Young men cross my path with a threat that is not aimed
at me. Where the road peters out into the plain a woman is standing
in a pose that suggests she has been waiting for me. I reach my arms
out towards her—it is so long since they touched a woman—hear a male
voice say "This woman is a man's wife". The tone of the voice is
final so I walk on. When I look round the woman stretches her arms
out to me and bares her breasts. On a grass-grown embankment two
boys are tinkering with a cross between a steam engine and a loco-
motive which stands on a broken piece of railway-track. As a
European I see at first glance that they are wasting their time—this
engine will never move from the spot but I do not tell the children—
work is hope—and walk on into the landscape which has no other task
than to wait for human beings to disappear. Now I know my destination.
I throw off my clothes—externals are no longer important. Some time
THE OTHER will come towards me—my antipodes, my ghostly double
with a face like snow. One of us will survive.

DEBUISSON, GALLOUDEC, SASPORTAS.
DEBUISSON *gives* GALLOUDEC *a piece of paper.* GALLOUDEC *and*
SASPORTAS *read it.*

The government which gave us the mission to organise a slave revolt
is no longer in office. General Bonaparte has dissolved the Directorate
with the bayonets of his grenadiers. France is called Napoleon. The
world becomes as it was—a haven for masters and slaves. (GALLOUDEC
crumples the paper) What are you staring at? Our firm has been struck
off the register. It is bankrupt. The goods we have to sell—payable in
the currency of tears, sweat and blood—are no longer trade in this
world. *(Tears the paper)* I relieve you of your mission. You Galloudec
from Brittany, you Sasportas the son of slavery. Myself, Debuisson.
SASPORTAS *(softly)*. The son of a slave-owner.
DEBUISSON. Everyone has his own freedom or slavery. Our play is
at an end, Sasportas. Take care when you take off your make-up.
Maybe your skin will come off too. Your mask, Sasportas, is your
face. My face is my mask. *(Hides his face in his hands.)*
GALLOUDEC. You're going too fast for me, Debuisson. I'm a
peasant. I can't think so quickly. I've risked my neck for a year or
more—worn my throat to shreds preaching at secret meetings,
smuggled weapons through cordons of bloodhounds, sharks and
informers, played the fool at the tables for the English cut-throats
like your dog, burnt by the sun and shaken by fever in this damned
corner of the globe where there is no snow—all for this lazy mass of
black flesh that doesn't want to move except under the boot and
what has slavery in Jamaica to do with me, if you think about it, I'm
French—wait, Sasportas—but I will turn black on the spot when I

125

understand why none of this is true any more—because in Paris some general has got above himself. He isn't even French. But to hear you, Debuisson, you'd think that this General Bonaparte is just what you've been waiting for.

DEBUISSON.   Maybe I really have been waiting for General Bonaparte. Just as half of France has waited for him. Revolution is tiring, Galloudec. During the people's sleep the generals rise up and break the yoke of freedom which is so heavy to bear. Do you see how it buckles your shoulders, Galloudec?

SASPORTAS.   I don't think I understand you either, Debuisson. Not any longer. The world a haven for masters and slaves. Slaves have no homeland, Citizen Debuisson. And so long as there are masters and slaves we are not relieved of our mission. What has a general's coup to do with the liberation of the slaves in Jamaica, which is our task? Ten thousand men wait for our order— for yours, if you like. But it doesn't have to be your voice that gives that order. They aren't sleeping. They aren't waiting for a general. They are ready to kill and to die for that yoke of freedom of yours that they have been dreaming about all their lives—which are a daily death—as if it were an unknown lover. They don't ask about the shape of her breasts or the virginity of her sex. What is Paris to these men—a far-away heap of stones which for a short time was the metropolis of their hopes, was France, a land in which the sun can't kill, where blood is the colour of the dawn for a little while, on a pale continent beyond the grave of Atlantis. Your general—I've forgotten his name already—there will be no more talk of him when the name of the man who freed Haiti is in all the school books. (DEBUISSON *laughs*) You're laughing.

DEBUISSON.   I'm laughing, Sasportas. Ask me why.

SASPORTAS.   Maybe I haven't understood you again. I don't know whether to kill you or ask your pardon.

DEBUISSON.   Do as you like, Sasportas.

SASPORTAS *(laughs)*.   Ah Debuisson. For a second I thought you believed what you were saying. I should have known. I should have known it was a test. I have failed the test, haven't I? Each of us must be as cold as a knife when the signal is given and the fight begins. It isn't fear that makes my nerves twitch but joy at the prospect of the dance. I hear the drums before they are beaten. I hear through my pores. My skin is black. But I doubted in you and that is not good. Forgive me, Debuisson. You bathed your hands in blood for our cause. I saw that it wasn't easy for you. I love you for both these things—for the one that had to be killed was a man like me and he needed his death before the next bout of torture that you were supposed to heal him and make him better for—cure him of the results of the first bout as a doctor and helper of humanity; but he said—'Kill me so that I can't turn traitor' and you killed him for our cause as a doctor and a revolutionary. (SASPORTAS *embraces* DEBUISSON.)

126

DEBUISSON. There is no need to apologise, Sasportas, it was not a
test. Our names will not be in the school-books and your liberator
of Haiti where the freed negroes are attacking the freed mulattoes
or the other way round will have to wait a long time for its place
in the book of history. Meantime Napoleon will turn France into
a barracks and Europe perhaps into a battlefield—in any case, trade
will thrive and peace with England will come too—business is what
unites people. The revolution has no homeland any more—that is
nothing new under this sun of ours which will perhaps never shine
on a new earth—slavery has many faces, we haven't seen its last one—
you haven't, Sasportas, and we haven't Galloudec, and perhaps what
we took for the dawn of freedom was only the mask of a new and
more terrible slavery compared to which the rule of the whip on the
islands of the Caribbean and elsewhere was a friendly foretaste of the
delights of paradise and perhaps your unknown love, freedom, has no
other face than treachery when her masks are worn out—what you
don't betray today will kill you tomorrow. From the standpoint of
human medicine the revolution is still-born—from the Bastille to the
Conciergerie the liberator becomes a prison-warder. Death to the
liberators is the last truth of the revolution. And as for my murder in
the service of our cause—the doctor as murderer is not a new role in
the theatre of society. Death is not so important for those who help
humanity—another chemical state—until the desert triumphs every
ruin is a place to build against the fangs of time. Maybe I was only
washing my hands, Sasportas, when I bathed them in blood for our
cause—poetry has always been the language of uselessness, my black
friend. We have other corpses on our backs now and they will be the
death of us if we don't throw them off before the grave. Your death
means freedom, Sasportas, your death means equality. It was good
to ride on them when they were still our mounts, the wind of tomorrow
on our temples. Now the wind of yesterday is blowing. We are the
mounts. Our masters have luggage—the corpses of the terror, pyramids
of dead. Do you feel the weight? With every doubt that goes through
the convolutions of our brains they weigh more. A revolution has no
time to count its dead. And we need time now to call off the black
revolution which we have prepared so thoroughly in the cause of a
future which is already the past like all the other futures before it.
Why is the future only singular in our language, Galloudec? Perhaps
it is different with the dead—if dust has a voice. Think it over before
you risk your neck for the freeing of slaves in an abyss which is
bottomless since this news which I shall now take into my body so that
no trace is left of our work. Do you want a scrap too? That was our
mission — now it only tastes of paper. Tomorrow it will have gone the
way of all flesh, every ascent to heaven has a goal and perhaps the star
is already on its way out of the cold wastes of the universe, a lump of
ice or metal, which will knock the bottom out of the facts on which we

constantly replant our fragile hopes. Or the cold itself which freezes our yesterdays and tomorrows into an eternal today. Why are we not born as trees, Sasportas, to whom all this means nothing. Or would you rather be a mountain? Or a desert. What do you say? Why do your eyes stare at me like two stones. Why are we not simply here waiting for the war of the landscapes? What do you want of me? Die your own deaths if you don't like life. I won't help you into the grave—I don't like it either. Yesterday I dreamed I was walking in New York. The district was decayed and no whites lived there. A golden snake rose up on the sidewalk in front of me and when I crossed the street—or rather the jungle of molten metal—there was another snake on the other sidewalk. It was gleaming blue. I knew in my dream—the golden snake is Asia, the blue snake that is Africa. When I woke I forgot it again. We are three worlds. Why do I know that now? And I heard a voice say: **And behold there was a great earthquake: for the Angel of the Lord descended from Heaven and came and rolled back the stone from the door and sat upon it. His countenance was like lightning and his raiment white as snow.** I don't wish to know about any of that any more. For a thousand years people have laughed at our three loves. They have rolled in all the gutters, they have swum down all the sewers of the world, and dragged themselves through all the brothels, our whores of fraternity. Now I want to sit among those who do the laughing. Free to do what I want, my own equal, my own man and no man's brother. Your skin stays black, Sasportas. You, Galloudec, remain a peasant. They will laugh at you. My place is where you are laughed at. I laugh at you. I laugh at the negro. I laugh at the peasant. I laugh at the negro who wants to wash himself white with freedom. I laugh at the peasant who walks about with the mask of equality. I laugh at the stupidity of fraternity which has made me, Debuisson, master of four hundred slaves who needs only to say Yes Yes and Yes to the hallowed system of slavery, blind to your filthy slave's hide, Sasportas, and to your four-legged peasant's gait, Galloudec, with on your shoulders the yoke your oxen carry in your field which doesn't belong to you. I want my share of the cake of the world. I will cut my piece out of the hunger of the world. You others have no knife.

SASPORTAS.   You have torn up a flag for me. I will cut a new one out of my black skin. *(He cuts a cross in the palm of his hand)* That is farewell, Citizen Debuisson. *(He presses his bleeding hand to* DEBUISSON's *face)* Do you like the taste of my blood? I said that slaves have no homeland. That is not true. The slaves' homeland is revolt. I am going to battle armed with the humiliations of my life. You have put a new weapon into my hand and I thank you for that. Maybe my place is on the gallows and maybe the halter is already growing round my neck as I talk to you instead of killing you—you to whom I owe nothing but my knife. But death is unimportant and on the gallows I shall know that the negroes of all races are my accomplices and that their number is growing every minute you spend at your slave-owner's trough or between the thighs of your white whores. If the living cannot fight any more the dead will fight. With each heartbeat of the revolution the flesh grows back on their bones, blood to their veins, life in their death. The revolt of the dead will be the war of landscapes, our weapons the woods, the mountains, the seas, the deserts of the world. I shall be wood mountain sea desert. I—that is Africa. I—that is Asia. I am the two Americas.

GALLOUDEC. I will go with you, Sasportas. We must all die. And that is all we have in common. After the massacre in Gaudaloupe in the middle of a pile of bodies, all black, they found a white man who was just as dead. That at least can't happen to you any more, Debuisson. You are out of it.

DEBUISSON. Stay. I am afraid, Galloudec, of the beauty of the world. I know perfectly well that it is the mask of treachery, which is already growing into my flesh and doesn't hurt any more. Kill me before I betray you. I am afraid, Sasportas, of the shame of being happy in this world.

Said, whispered, screamed Debuisson. But Galloudec and Sasportas went off together, left Debuisson alone with treachery who had come up to him like the snake from the stone. Debuisson shut his eyes against the temptation to look his first love, who was teachery, in the face. Treachery danced. Debuisson pressed his hands to his eyes. He heard his heart beat to the rhythm of the dance-steps. They grew quicker with the heart-beat. Debuisson felt his eyelids twitch against the palms of his hands. Perhaps the dance had stopped already and it was only his heart that thudded while treachery, her arms folded over her breasts or her hands on her hips or clutched in her lap, looked at Debuisson with brimming eyes—her sex perhaps already quivering with desire while Debuisson was pressing his eyes into their sockets with his fists out of fear at his hunger for the shame of happiness. Perhaps treachery had already left him. His own hungry hands refused to obey him. Debuisson opened his eyes. Treachery displayed her breasts with a smile, silently opened her thighs, her beauty struck Debuisson like an executioner's axe. He forgot the storming of the Bastille, the hunger-march of the 80 thousand, the end of the Gironde, their last supper, a dead man at the table, Saint Just; the black angel, Danton; the voice of the revolution, Marat, crouched over the dagger; the broken jaw of Robespierre, his scream as the executioner tore away the bandage, his last compassionate glance at the jubilation of the throng. Debuisson groped for the last memory that had not yet deserted him—a sand-storm off Las Palmas, crickets came on board along with the sand and accompanied the voyage over the Atlantic. Debuisson ducked his head before the sand-storm, rubbed the sand out of his eyes, and stopped his ears against the song of the crickets. Then treachery threw herself on him like a heaven, the joy of the lips of her sex a red dawn.

Blackout

Performance Studies. A new field that's expanding the concept of theatre and dance.

New York University's School of the Arts is defining a new area of scholarship — performance studies. Research in this new field is expanding the very concept of theatre and dance. It is bringing the social sciences and the arts together.

Performance studies goes beyond dramatic literature, beyond theatre and dance history, beyond familiar forms. It encompasses non-Western, indigenous, folk, and postmodern performance; explores all aspects of performance — from everyday interactions to shamanism, from Broadway to Kabuki, from ballet to burlesque.

Students learn how to document and analyze performances, undertake cross-cultural studies of rituals and festivals, and examine theories of performance. They also investigate the nature and role of critical writing, intern as dramaturges, work at the Shubert Archives, and help edit *The Drama Review.*

Graduates are teaching and working professionally — in universities, theatres, museums, archives, and publishing.

Areas of concentration include: performance theory, dance, contemporary performance, performance writing and dramaturgy, folk performance, and performing arts archives. The faculty is composed of highly respected scholars: Brooks McNamara, Richard Schechner, Theodore Hoffman, Michael Kirby, Barbara Kirshenblatt-Gimblett, and Suzanne Youngerman. Guest faculty includes Victor Turner, Herbert Blau, and Deborah Jowitt.

For information about the M.A. or Ph.D. program, return the attached coupon or telephone (212) 598-2596.

NEW YORK UNIVERSITY
A PRIVATE UNIVERSITY IN THE PUBLIC SERVICE

School of the Arts Admissions
New York University
P.O. Box 909, Cooper Station
New York, N.Y. 10276

I would like to apply for ☐ fall
☐ spring ☐ summer admission.

Name

Address

City/State/Zip

Telephone

New York University is an affirmative action/equal opportunity institution.

ATA
12/81

Intensive Care
or
An Endless Vegetable-like Existence
(Intensivstation)

by

Christoph Gahl

translated by Anthony Vivis

First broadcast: 22nd September, 1980, Hessischer Rundfunk

Originally broadcast as a radio play by the Hessian Radio network, and subsequently winner of the major prize for radio plays in Europe, the Prix Italia 1981, Christoph Gahl's *Intensive Care* is still an eminently stageable play. Although non-localised sound and dream-like sequences of dialogue exploit the particular advantages of radio as a dramatic medium most effectively, there is no reason why non-naturalistic acting and split-staging should not enable a successful transfer to the stage. This is perhaps not surprising in view of the fact that Gahl works in both television and theatre and displays a strong talent for imagery and image-making.

The central issue in the work is the right of the patient in intensive care to decide whether he should live or die, a question as hotly debated in West Germany recently as in Great Britain (in Brian Clark's *Whose Life Is It Anyway?*). Gahl does not however, stay on a naturalistic plane, bringing into the story the character of Hypnos, the god of release and sleep with whom both the moral and the poetical aspect of dying are discussed. The result of the debate is not, as one might expect, that the individual should be allowed to die in peace so much as a plea that dying should be regarded as in some sense a communal act, in which those who live should help those who die to die well. The special place of death—intensive care—denies in its insistence on technology and life at any price the right of dignified death: so extreme does the technology become that Lorenz, the dying man, sees himself finishing as a brain-stem without a body, being preserved indefinitely.

The bulk of the work—the dialogue—is exactly as performed on radio. We have however, altered the stage directions with a view to stage performance. That this meant very little change supports, so we hope, our contention that it could easily be staged.

'It is not the loneliness of the Intensive Care Unit, nor is it cannulas and tubes which help someone die a dignified death, but a continuance of love and the nearness of fellow human beings. What a person needs when alive he needs all the more when dying. We, however, leave people to die alone in Intensive Care Units.' *Christoph Gahl.*

Characters

LORENZ, a patient
HYPNOS, a man not wearing a white coat
EVE, the Ward staff-nurse
OTHILDE, Lorenz's wife
FLEURETTE, Lorenz's daughter
SEVERIN, consultant
PAVEL, a young patient
JUDGE
FATHER
CHAPLAIN

A note on staging

The stage directions we have introduced are the minimum necessary to make the piece function on stage. The main location is the intensive-care unit of a clinic. The bed should be centre stage, with the machines around it. It should also have screens. The corridor should be reached by the exit right, and left is a door leading to a wash room.

The change of mood between the naturalistic scenes and those with Hypnos are probably best achieved by a move from naturalistic to non-naturalistic lighting. It would probably be appropriate for Hypnos to stay on stage, except for the courtroom scene.

It would be advantageous to use short musical sequences to help underline the shifts and ambiguities of mood, the ironic quality of certain scenes and relationships between certain characters and events.

Scene One

LORENZ *is in bed in the intensive care unit hooked up to all manner of machinery. He is breathing heavily. Enter* HYPNOS.

HYPNOS. Lorenz? *(No response).* Why don't you answer, Lorenz? *(No response)* In your dreams you don't have to lie there like a corpse.

LORENZ. Who are you?

HYPNOS. In your dreams you can even get out of bed. In your dreams you can move around without cannulas and tubes.

LORENZ. Who are you?

HYPNOS. I don't wear a white coat. *(Silence)* Can you hear me?

LORENZ. Leave me alone.

HYPNOS. You don't want to?

LORENZ. I can't.

HYPNOS. Do you think you're dead? *(Silence)* You're-dreaming, Lorenz. *(No response)*

LORENZ. It must be nearly morning.

HYPNOS. Yes, Lorenz. The night nurse has just been relieved. *(Long silence)*

LORENZ. Are you still there?

HYPNOS. I'm listening.

LORENZ. Last night my heart stopped beating. I felt my pulse give out. So I pressed the call button. Why, I don't know. Then my heart stopped beating. *(Pause)* I slowly hoisted myself up—very slowly and contentedly. I stepped out of my own body. I looked down at myself lying motionless in the bed . . .

HYPNOS. You were dreaming, Lorenz.

LORENZ. The night nurse came rushing in, took my pulse, pulled back an eye-lid, ran out again and sounded the alarm . . .

HYPNOS. It isn't the first time your heart's stopped.

LORENZ. I was hastily wheeled out of the room. Then somebody jammed an oxygen-mask over my face. *(Pause)* A complete waste of time.

HYPNOS. It isn't the first time you've collapsed.

LORENZ. A blinding light was switched on. Then the cannulas were inserted, the tubes connected and my respiration and circulation artificially restored . . .

HYPNOS. And how many times has that happened, Lorenz?

LORENZ. I stood there watching and I realised how pointless it all was. I'd finally done it. Escaped the doctor's clutches. I was dead. At long last I was dead.

HYPNOS. You had stopped living.

LORENZ. It's the same thing.

HYPNOS. Your heart had stopped functioning. But you had not died, Lorenz.

LORENZ. I tell you I was dead.

134

HYPNOS. You survived your death. The doctors brought you
   back. And how many times have they done that, Lorenz? *(A nurse
   enters and walks around the room attending the machines.)* They
   won't let you off the hook. You're not dead just because you close
   your eyes to your surroundings. Listen, the day's starting. You can
   make out sounds. Someone is walking across the room. You feel a
   hand on your pulse. Now you feel a damp cloth on your face. The
   tubes you're connected to, the monitors all around you—they're still
   there just as usual. Every sign of life the machines coax out of you is
   registered as evidence against your being dead.
LORENZ. Who are you? *(No answer)* Who are you?
HYPNOS. You can call me what you like. *(The nurse exits.)*
LORENZ. You say you don't wear a white coat.
HYPNOS. Don't you believe me?
LORENZ. Why should I? You don't believe I'm dead.
HYPNOS. You're fooling yourself, Lorenz.
LORENZ. I want you to respect the fact that I'm dead.
HYPNOS *(amused)*. Really?
LORENZ. Leave me alone. *(Silence)*
HYPNOS. Don't you understand, Lorenz? You're fooling yourself.
   However much you want me to be, I can't be Thanatos.
LORENZ. Tell me who you are then.
HYPNOS. I open your eyes once they are shut.
LORENZ *(astonished)*. Hypnos?
HYPNOS *(amused)*. You could call me that.
LORENZ. Hypnos with the little wings.
HYPNOS. That's what they taught you at school.
LORENZ. Yes . . . In those days I liked him. I knew everything there was
   to know about him and all the other gods in the Pantheon. I imagined
   the little wings on his temples were like propellers.
HYPNOS. You can think of me as a doctor if you'd rather, a doctor who
   doesn't wear a white coat.
LORENZ *(pensively)*. Hypnos with the little wings . . . He was gentle,
   and shy, a provider of beautiful dreams. Thanatos, his brother, held
   a guttering torch in his lowered hand. But Hypnos had a bunch of
   poppies, and in his hand he held the horn of sleep. He rushed through
   the night shaking it over the heads of the weary and anxious—over
   every living thing . . . *(Silence)*
HYPNOS. Why don't you go on?
LORENZ. What's the point?
HYPNOS. Sleep heals. Hypnos was a kind of doctor.
LORENZ. I don't want to hear any more about it. The only help I
   need is from Thanatos.
HYPNOS. You really are making a fool of yourself, Lorenz.
LORENZ. And what about you? What are you doing? Is this one of
   your beautiful dreams—that I'm dead yet can't die?
HYPNOS. No, Lorenz. It's your conscious state pursuing you into
   your dreams.

135

LORENZ. Do something about it then!

HYPNOS. I can't give you beautiful dreams, even if you do call me Hypnos. Dreams are the shadow side of reality.

LORENZ *(derisively)*. That's all I need! Interpretation of dreams! Hypnos the psycho-analyst . . .

HYPNOS. But I've told you, Hypnos was a doctor too, only not the white-coated sort.

LORENZ. A doctor who can't heal. Do you know what it's like to be incurably ill? *(Silence)* I'm sick and tired of being kept alive by the grace of respiratory tubes and infusion pumps. I'm sick and tired of being dead yet not being able to die. But last night I did die. I forgot everything, left everything behind me. I died. I really died. *(Pause)* Can't you understand that?

HYPNOS. Of course I can, Lorenz. It's a very understandable wish-dream. *(Silence)*

LORENZ. Can you help me to die? *(Silence)* Can you persuade the doctors not to be so conscientious?

HYPNOS. No.

LORENZ. Can you talk the nurses into not replacing the oxygen cylinder for the breathing apparatus?

HYPNOS. No, Lorenz.

LORENZ. What can you do then?

HYPNOS. I can have some effect on your dreams—your anxiety-dreams as well as your wish-dreams.

LORENZ. And what good will that do me?

HYPNOS. It might help you to feel clearer about things. Maybe even happier. *(Silence)*

LORENZ *(quietly)*. Last night my heart stopped beating. I saw myself lying motionless in bed. I stepped out of my own body and saw myself lying there motionless in bed . . .

Scene Two

Enter OTHILDE, LORENZ'S *wife, and the* NURSE.

OTHILDE. He is improving, isn't he, nurse?

NURSE. All things considered, Mrs Lorenz he is making good progress. He's in good hands.

OTHILDE. This is the fourth complication since he was admitted, the fourth complication— to say nothing of the cancer.

NURSE. You can't talk to him yet. Would you like to see him, though?

OTHILDE *(sobbing)*. Surely he wouldn't . . . He wouldn't do that to me . . .

NURSE. Our lives are in God's hands. The Lord has given and the Lord . . . *(Clears her throat)* We're doing all we can, Mrs Lorenz. As God's my witness.

OTHILDE. He will pull through, won't he, nurse? He's still a young
man. His heart's strong.
NURSE. The Lord will help. Would you like to see him now?
OTHILDE. He was never robust. But his heart's strong. He's always
boasted what a strong heart he's got. Forty-five is no age at all. At
forty-five you're still in your prime. He's always been a hard worker.
He's a glutton for work. Everything he's taken on he's done well at.
He's got a good job. His bosses think the world of him. He's a good
man. He's never smoked or taken to drink. His job and his family were
all he ever cared about. And now suddenly this . . . *(Sobs)* stomach,
lung, circulation . . . even his heart, strong as it is . . .
NURSE. I know, Mrs Lorenz. But let's try and be calm. And never say
die.
OTHILDE. How can he possibly pull through this, nurse?
NURSE. Keep calm, Mrs Lorenz. Inwardly calm.
OTHILDE. I can't go on any more. At night I hear voices. And my
daughter dreams about black . . . *(Sobs)*
NURSE. Do let's try to be calm, Mrs Lorenz.
OTHILDE. Black chrysanthemums.
NURSE. Nice and calm and never say die. *(Silence except for a quiet
sobbing)* There we are! It does you good to gather inner strength. And
I can tell you straight away, in the Intensive Care Unit no-one's
circulation breaks down. Everything is taken care of. If the blood
pressure drops, monitors give the alarm. If a patient stops breathing
the breathing apparatus takes over. Suction apparatus keeps the air-
passages clear. Any reduction in body-fluid is automatically topped-up.
Infusion pumps supply medication to the blood at regular intervals.
They are constantly reliable Samaritans. The rest is up to God. I always
say: trust in the Lord and Intensive Care. *(Pause)* Well, do you want
to see your husband now?
OTHILDE. She dreams about black chrysanthemums. My daughter
dreams about black chrysanthemums. *(She sobs)*

Exeunt NURSE *and* OTHILDE

LORENZ. Who are those two?
HYPNOS. You know them. Try to remember.
LORENZ. I've never seen them before.
HYPNOS. The one wearing the little cap comes to your bedside every
day and says: Well now, Mr Lorenz, how are we feeling today? This
annoys you. She still says it even if you're in a coma again. Though in
that case she talks to the machines you're connected to.
LORENZ. I can't remember.
HYPNOS. You don't **want to** remember.
LORENZ. I'm in a coma.
HYPNOS. That's no excuse for not remembering.
LORENZ. What's her name?
HYPNOS. The nurse?

LORENZ. The one in the little cap.

HYPNOS. If you like we'll call her Eve—the woman who gives life.

LORENZ *(laughs)*. Now you're making fun of me.

HYPNOS. At least you can still laugh.

LORENZ. And the other woman?

HYPNOS. Let's call her Othilde—the wife who fights for hearth and home . . .

LORENZ. What made you think up that name?

HYPNOS. She's your wife.

LORENZ. What do you mean?

HYPNOS. And let's call your daughter Blossom: that's what you used to call her—or Fleurette, that suits her better now she's started taking ballet lessons.

LORENZ. I don't have a daughter. Or a wife.

HYPNOS. Don't be childish. They come to visit you nearly every day. Take my word for it, your wife is standing by your bedside. And if your daughter hadn't had a ballet class, she'd have come, too.

LORENZ. You know a lot of stories. But I'm tired.

HYPNOS. You're sleeping now, Lorenz. That's all you can do.

LORENZ. I can die.

HYPNOS. Can you? *(Silence)* I know another story. Do you want to hear it?

LORENZ. What's it about?

HYPNOS. About living and not being able to die.

LORENZ. Did you make it up?

HYPNOS. It's a story you can read in any newspaper. *(Pause, then HYPNOS begins to tell his story)* There was this man whose stomach cancer was diagnosed very late. When the surgeon opened up the abdominal cavity he discovered extensive metastases in the liver and lower abdomen. The tumour was inoperable. But the surgeon didn't want to leave things as they were. He was afraid it would perforate the stomach and so—I'll give you three guesses—he removed it. The X-ray showed more metastases in the spine, and the intense pain this caused the patient meant he was continually taking pain-killers. About a fortnight after the operation a pulmonary embolism led to a circulatory collapse. But in another operation the surgeon managed to remove the embolism. When the patient regained consciousness he thanked the doctor for his skill and good intentions but in the same breath asked him—in the event of another collapse—to do nothing that would prolong his life, because the intense pain and his hopeless condition made it scarcely worth living any more. Shortly after the lung operation a heart infarction led to cardiac arrest. Against the patient's express wishes, stated when he was fully conscious, the resuscitation team at the clinic brought him back to life with complete success—from a technical point of view. During the following week his circulation came to a standstill on two more occasions; and both times he was resuscitated . . .

138

LORENZ *(suddenly as if wide awake)*. Who was resuscitated?
HYPNOS. The patient—his circulation, his respiration.
LORENZ. His corpse.
HYPNOS. If that's what you prefer.
LORENZ. His suffering.
HYPNOS. Yes, Lorenz.
LORENZ. His god-damned helplessness.
HYPNOS. At last you can see things as they are.
LORENZ. Everything he had gone through.
HYPNOS. The patient thanked the doctor for his good intentions but
    begged him all the more . . .
LORENZ *(interrupting)*. Why are you telling me **my** story?
HYPNOS. It's the same story for lots of people. *(Silence)*
LORENZ *(quietly)*. Everything came back to him—all the suffering he
    had been through . . . the harsh light, the practised flurry of activity,
    the ever-present resuscitation equipment, the remorseless way in which
    his bodily functions were forced to carry on, the monotony of one day
    after another, white on white, the whiteness of detergents, sterilised
    contact, aseptic friendliness. The whole rigmarole again from scratch . .
    Half-hearted enquiries from the professional Samaritans, the lowered
    voices, the averted eyes, an energetic note of jollity, the put-on
    cheerfulness of relatives—all the things which made him realise what a
    bad way he's in . . . A patient who is impatient to do something . . .
    With a fear no-one can treat . . . Tranquillizers prescribed for
    despair . . . No-one to hold his hand . . . No-one to help him die . . .
    (Silence) Can you understand what all that feels like? *(Footsteps
    approach)* Can you hear me? *(Footsteps louder)* Hypnos? Where are
    you?

Scene Three

SEVERIN. Hello, Mr Lorenz—are you awake? *(Pause)* I told you after
    the very first collapse, didn't I—cardiac arrest is by no means fatal.
    You're breathing again, your circulation is stable, your temperature's
    getting back to normal. We've been able to get the vital functions of
    your brain back into working order. *(Pause)* And that's what counts,
    Mr Lorenz. It all comes down to the brain-stem. Life itself depends
    on it. Take the case I've just come from—a very tricky business, brain
    injury following a road accident: no reaction in the pupils, hardly any
    pain reflex when we prick the nasal septum, falling body temperature
    and a virtually zero reading on the encephalogram; all the signs point
    to loss of breath for more than 3 minutes, and so presumably the man
    will never come to. But he goes on living—because we're able to get
    the vital functions of his brain-stem working again. Irreparably
    unconscious—but alive. Connected to tubes and cannulas, artificially
    fed, no control over his digestive processes—but alive; his brain is still

active, he can breathe, he has a pulse. Isn't that marvellous? 30 years ago in America a sailor was fished unconscious out of the water—he never regained consciousness but he only died very recently. Yes, Mr Lorenz, life is a miracle. But you're not merely alive, you're conscious as well. Medically speaking, that's more than you could reasonably expect from life. So don't you worry about these tiresome metastases. Your brain-stem is in fine shape. We can burn out or cut away the diseased parts of the body and if all else fails replace them with machines—but not the brain-stem, it all comes down to the brain-stem. No, no, don't say anything. You're still too weak. Everything's fine, Mr Lorenz. I'll give you an injection so you get a good rest. *(His voice getting more and more indistinct)* You don't need to worry about a thing. We'll take care of everything for you . . . everything for you . . .

Scene Four

HYPNOS *(laughing).*   Did he reassure you?
LORENZ *(surprised).*   Where did you go?
HYPNOS.   I didn't go anywhere.
LORENZ.   I shouted for you.
HYPNOS.   I heard. But there, where **you** were, I can't communicate with you.
LORENZ.   I must have been dreaming.
HYPNOS *(amused).*   On the contrary.
LORENZ.   A nightmare . . .
HYPNOS.   You'll just have to get used to the idea.
LORENZ.   What do you mean?
HYPNOS.   That sometimes you're awake.
LORENZ.   What do you mean?
HYPNOS.   You wake up, you look around, you talk to somebody . . .
LORENZ.   But I'm doing all that now.
HYPNOS.   Come on, don't be so naive. Even as a child you had to learn the difference between dreaming and waking. Later on you couldn't take dreams seriously. *(Sarcastically)* You were a man with both feet firmly on the ground.
LORENZ.   I don't know what you're talking about.
HYPNOS.   It made you furious to think you'd contracted an incurable disease. *(Silence)*
LORENZ.   Who was that man in the white coat?
HYPNOS.   You mean the consultant.
LORENZ *(after a pause).*   I used to know a man who had a cat. One day this cat was bitten to death by a dog. I saw the man fetch a saucer of milk and put it down in front of the cat. He waited for the cat to lap the milk. But the cat didn't move. He waited and waited, without moving a muscle, just as motionless as his cat. When he realised I was

watching him he threw stones at me. *(Pause)* I expect he's still
waiting.

HYPNOS. Why are you telling me this?

LORENZ. The man in the white coat reminds me of the man with
the cat.

HYPNOS. Does he look like the man with the cat?

LORENZ. He looks very serious, almost solemn.

HYPNOS. In that case let's call him Severin: the severe.

LORENZ. He seemed to be connected to a tube, just like me, though
he can move about freely.

HYPNOS. I expect you mean his stethoscope, it hangs out of his white
coat.

LORENZ. He played with it and kept on talking to me.

HYPNOS. He's very sociable. He likes talking to educated patients.

LORENZ. He was explaining to me what they have to do to save a
healthy head from a diseased body.

HYPNOS. His favourite subject. He's a surgeon. Total amputations
are his speciality.

LORENZ. Do you think he could operate on death?

HYPNOS. I daresay he thinks medicine has the right to do anything
it's capable of doing. So for him death is a spoilsport.

LORENZ *(after a pause)*. Operate on death—but with death out of
the way what's left of life? *(Silence)*

HYPNOS. I'll leave you on your own now. *(Amused)* The doctor said
you were to get some sleep.

LORENZ. Death is not a spoilsport. *(Silence)* As a clever man once said:
Death is simply the moment when dying stops.

HYPNOS *draws the screens round* LORENZ's *bed and then leaves.*

Scene Five

A courtroom. The NURSE, CHAPLAIN, FATHER, JUDGE *and* SEVERIN
are present.

JUDGE. The case before us is the entire medical history of Agnes K. The
defendant is accused of being afraid of surviving. Although lying in a
coma she is alleged to have stated loudly and clearly that she was dead.
(Clears his throat) Agnes K. is 20 years old. Her weight at the present
time is twenty kilos. In April of last year she was admitted to the
St Hedwig Clinic with serious irreparable injuries to the central nervous
system. However, the electro-encephalograph still registered weak,
intermittently recurring signals which indicated that one side of the
cerebrum had not completely stopped functioning. As the patient
was deeply unconscious her respiration, heart-beat, circulation and
metabolism were artificially kept going. Although handicapped in her
dealings with the outside world Agnes K. was a person not only capable

141

of living but in some respects even healthy. Is that correct, Dr Severin?

SEVERIN.   That is perfectly correct, your Honour.

JUDGE.   In accordance with a court decision the parents of the defendant were given permission to turn off the respirator which regularly pumped air into Agnes K's lungs through a tube inserted into her windpipe. Mr K.—did you turn off the respirator?

FATHER.   Yes, your Honour, we turned it off.

JUDGE.   As it transpired, Agnes K. was able to survive even without artificial respiration—by her own efforts. Though because Agnes K. was in a state of deep unconsciousness she still had to be fed artificially since she was of course in no position to feed herself. Nevertheless—despite this fortunate turn of events—Agnes K. is alleged to have made the statement mentioned at the outset. Nurse Eve—can you confirm this?

NURSE.   Yes, your Honour. I was present when Agnes K. claimed she was dead.

JUDGE.   Can you remember her exact words, nurse Eve?

NURSE.   Not her exact words but it was something like: I'm dead, let me die; I don't want to be a brain-stem vegetable.

JUDGE.   In other words she wanted to die even though she considered herself dead?

NURSE.   Yes, your Honour. That's how I understood it.

JUDGE.   How did you interpret this strange remark, nurse Eve?

NURSE.   Well, I think to myself: if a person wants to die she can't very well be dead.

JUDGE.   But Agnes K. did say she was dead. You heard that quite distinctly?

NURSE.   Yes, your Honour, I heard that quite distinctly.

JUDGE.   Thank you, nurse Eve. What seems to me incriminating here is the fact that simply by **making** this remark she herself contradicted her own assertion. Since when can the dead speak? The only matter that remains unclear is that curious expression: brain-stem vegetable. Dr Severin, can you offer any explanation of the defendant's statement that she didn't want to be a brain-stem vegetable?

SEVERIN.   There can only be one explanation, your Honour: the defendant thought nothing of belittling the vital functions of the brain-stem. She considered it humiliating **merely** to have a circulation and heart-beat provided for her—not to mention the care devoted to her metabolism. It wasn't enough for her to live quietly and contentedly in a coma.

JUDGE.   What is your opinion of this attitude, Dr Severin?

SEVERIN.   Words fail me, your Honour. This degree of ingratitude towards the almighty creator and his groundstaff, the doctors and nurses, is something I have never come across before in my entire medical career.

JUDGE.   Do you share this opinion, Reverend Father?

142

CHAPLAIN. No, your Honour, absolutely not. As a priest I too know a
little about the almighty creator, and as a chaplain in the St Hedwig's
Hospital a very great deal about mortally ill patients. I do not talk
in terms of the brain-stem, but in terms of the soul. May I elaborate?

JUDGE. Please do, Reverend Father.

CHAPLAIN. In my opinion the soul of Agnes K. was received by God
long ago. What is left is a living corpse which is not allowed to die.
On admission, Agnes K. weighed 55 kilos. In the meantime she has
wasted away to 20 kilos. Her emaciated body is so bent it has taken
on a foetal position. The girl's eyes are open but she stares blankly
into space. Only her eyelids function normally, moving twice a
minute. Her weak reactions to stimuli like lights or noise are
involuntary. Agnes K. is incapable of any kind of mental process. She
is like a child coming into the world with no brain. If she really did
make the claim which is the subject of this hearing then it was the
voice of God speaking through her. God does not merely ask us to
protect life, he also requires us to give it back to Him. It is cruel not
to do everything to help the disabled to live. But it is just as cruel
to prevent a dead person from dying . . .

JUDGE. I must point out, Reverend Father, that what you are now saying
is irrelevant to the case. The only point at issue here is the charge
against Agnes K.

CHAPLAIN. In that case I have nothing more to say.

JUDGE. Mr K.—are you also of the opinion that God spoke through your
daughter's mouth?

FATHER. Yes, your Honour. I do think that.

JUDGE. Do you think your daughter was afraid of surviving?

FATHER. No, your Honour, I don't think she can survive now.

JUDGE. So you consider her dead?

FATHER. Yes, your Honour, this endless vegetable-like existence isn't
life—not for a human being.

JUDGE. How much does your daughter mean to you, Mr K?

FATHER. She meant a very great deal to me, when she was alive. Now
I'd like to bury her.

JUDGE. How do you mean?

FATHER. I'm not thinking of Agnes when I say that. She'll rest in
God's hands even without a funeral. But it would be better for us,
for my wife and me. We'd feel more at peace. And anyway . . .

JUDGE. Go on, Mr K.!

FATHER. I don't know if you'll follow my meaning. I just thought,
maybe if another person was to take my daughter's place in the
clinic, well, perhaps they could be saved.

JUDGE. Thank you, Mr K.—I now call the witness Lorenz. *(The* NURSE
draws back the screens around the bed.) Mr Lorenz, you are in the
same Unit as the defendant. We are aware of the fact that the girl's
father has distressed you very greatly. You yourself have a daughter.

143

We also know that you have frequently sat at the girl's bedside and held her hand. Mr Lorenz, has the defendant ever spoken to you? *(Silence)* Perhaps just mumbled? *(Silence)* Whispered? *(Silence)* Moved her lips? *(Silence)* Did she indicate to you in any way whatever that she no longer wishes to live? *(Silence)* Mr Lorenz, did Agnes K. make the statement in question? *(Silence)* Can't you speak? *(Silence)* Did you get the impression that Agnes K. was afraid of life? *(The Court rises. We hear footsteps approaching.)* Are you feeling unwell, Mr Lorenz? *(The sound grows louder.)* Perhaps you'd take a look at him, Dr Severin. Your patient appears to be suffering from absent-mindedness. *(*SEVERIN *draws the screens.)*

Scene Six

The intensive care unit again. The NURSE *draws back the screens.*

NURSE. Well now, Mr Lorenz, how are we feeling? Did we sleep well? *(Silence)* I hear you haven't been eating again. That won't do, Mr Lorenz. We must get our strength back after all the excitement.

LORENZ. We've no appetite, nurse.

NURSE. And you're not shaved yet. I'll send you nurse Annegret.

LORENZ. We've decided to grow a beard.

NURSE. Mr Lorenz! What is your wife to think when she sees you looking so scruffy?

LORENZ. We're thinking of our Saviour. He had a beard.

NURSE. Now, open your mouth a minute, please . . . At least you've found your sense of humour again. Let's hope you get your appetite back, too. From now on you're to take these drops every two hours. Nurse Annegret will help you. *(Pause)* Are you in pain?

LORENZ. We're ill all over, nurse.

NURSE. But nothing specific?

LORENZ. Our bile, nurse, the black bile is causing us a lot of trouble.

NURSE. Nonsense, Mr Lorenz! According to the latest laboratory reports your bile is perfectly normal.

LORENZ. The black bile and the yellow bile are off balance. Blood and mucus are fighting it out.

NURSE. Mr Lorenz, stop this nonsense at once!

LORENZ. If the blend of body fluids isn't right . . . we go down to zero, nurse . . . The blend of body fluids must be right.

NURSE. Who's been telling you this nonsense?

LORENZ. Never heard of Dr Hippocrates?

NURSE *(amused).* I don't think your Dr Hippocrates has ever worked in an Intensive Care Unit. What would you say you're suffering from? Melancholia?

LORENZ. From the Intensive Care Unit.

NURSE. Oh yes, I've heard that before. I'll tell you what you're suffering from. I'd say it was impatience. We can't bear to wait till we start feeling better again. *(Silence)* Or is something getting you down? *(Silence)* Depression? *(Silence)* Tell me honestly now, Mr Lorenz, do you want to get something off your chest? Shall I send the chaplain?

LORENZ. Would you boil me some sage, nurse?

NURSE. Sage?

LORENZ. Swan's lung is supposed to help too, with saffron and olive oil.

NURSE. Mr Lorenz!

LORENZ. Maybe if you were to tickle the soles of my feet, if you put lice and ants on my skin, I could laugh again. Best of all, why not stick me in a tank full of live eels.

NURSE. Anything else you'd like? I can see you're feeling much better, Mr Lorenz . . . very much better . . . astonishingly better . . .

LORENZ. I'd like to talk to you, Hypnos. Are you there?

HYPNOS. I'm listening.

LORENZ. When I came here life was still fun . . . well, perhaps not fun, but something I was part of. I felt healthy. I didn't believe the doctors. I laughed at my illness . . . But when I didn't improve . . . Are you listening to me?

HYPNOS. I'm here, Lorenz.

LORENZ. When I didn't improve I was angry. I thought the doctors were bunglers, and the nurses could do nothing right for me. But because I needed someone who couldn't contradict me, I discovered God. I could shout at God without being given a sedative. I pleaded with Him: Why pick on me, why do you want to punish me? For being honest, hard-working and reliable? For taking care of myself all these years? For doing my level best to be a good husband and father? Other people live it up all the time and never even catch a cold. The bastards go on for ever. Where's the justice in that? *(After a pause)* Before, when I was arguing with God, these ideas didn't seem in the least childish. *(Silence)* You are listening, aren't you?

HYPNOS. What happened then?

LORENZ. I called God a hypocrite, a failure, a lousy father, who leaves his children in the lurch . . . And then I made a deal with Him. I said to Him: You're omnipotent—if you give me a few more years without pain and problems I'll do as many good works as I can fit in. I thought of going to Africa to work on development aid or to help out as a volunteer in a charitable institution. And naturally I was quite happy to be a model Christian and go to church regularly again. *(Pause)* Then I had my second operation. You can imagine what happened to me after that . . .

HYPNOS. We'll have to stop. You've got visitors. *(We hear footsteps approaching).*

LORENZ. I had hardly any problems with God any more, but plenty

145

with His embodiments on earth. The doctors lied to me to my face: with a bit of patience and faith in their skill I would definitely be back on my feet in no time. Every liquid the nurses poured into me had encouraging words spat into it. My wife still kept talking about the Mediterranean cruise we'd unsuspectingly booked before I was admitted to hospital. Can you imagine how I felt?

HYPNOS. You must wake up, Lorenz. You have visitors.

LORENZ *(getting quicker).* I wanted to be left in peace. Talkativeness was the last thing I needed. After all, I knew what a terrible state I was in, and I wanted to come to terms with it. *(Enter OTHILDE. She is carrying flowers. FLEURETTE is with her. OTHILDE gives FLEURETTE the flowers to hold.)* The thought of dying lost its terror for me. It depressed me a lot but didn't paralyse me. There was a touch of self-pity about it too—and a great deal of nostalgia . . . November feelings . . . *(Silence. OTHILDE exits left into washing-area. We hear her fill the vase for the flowers.)* Are you still there? *(Silence)* Hypnos? Where are you?

OTHILDE *returns with the vase.*

OTHILDE *(to FLEURETTE).* Put the flowers in the vase for him, darling. And draw the curtains a bit. I want him to see the sun shining.

FLEURETTE. But he's asleep, mummy.

OTHILDE. He's not asleep. His eyes are shut. But he's not asleep. *(To LORENZ)* You're not asleep, are you? *(Pause)* Can you hear me?

LORENZ. You don't need to whisper, Othilde.

OTHILDE. Can you understand me?

LORENZ. I'm awake.

FLEURETTE. He looks as if he's dead.

OTHILDE. It's true, isn't it—you can hear me?

LORENZ. I wasn't expecting you till later.

OTHILDE. We've brought you some tulips. They've no scent but they're nice bright colours. You're allowed tulips. Nurse Eve said so. *(Silence)* How do you feel?

LORENZ. I'm feeling better. Nurse Eve says I'm feeling better.

FLEURETTE. Are you feeling better? *(Silence)* Say something, daddy! Please say something!

LORENZ. You look very pretty, Fleurette.

FLEURETTE. Say something! Say you think I'm pretty.

OTHILDE. Nurse Eve tells me you won't eat. *(Silence)* But you've always been such a big eater. You said yourself: eating well keeps body and soul together.

LORENZ. I'd like to ask you something, Othilde: take me out of here.

OTHILDE. Surely you could make an effort to eat. Invalid food can't taste that bad.

LORENZ. **You** cook for me again, Othilde!

OTHILDE. Now promise me you'll really make an effort.

LORENZ. Get me out of here.

OTHILDE. Did you hear me? Promise! *(Silence)*
FLEURETTE. Please say something, daddy!
OTHILDE. Is it difficult for you to speak?
FLEURETTE. You haven't even looked at me.
OTHILDE. Shall I get you a glass of water?
FLEURETTE. I've changed my hair style, daddy.
OTHILDE. Do you want to sit upright? I can raise the bed-head.
LORENZ. Take me home, Othilde!
OTHILDE. Why don't you speak? Are you in pain?
LORENZ. Take me home. I want to be at home when I die.
OTHILDE. I've talked to the doctors. The doctors are very
   confident. They said it's up to you now. You musn't on any account
   give in. You have to convince yourself you're on the mend.
FLEURETTE. Mummy's right, you mustn't give up now.
OTHILDE. If all goes well, you could be back home in a couple of weeks.
   We can plan things, maybe a little trip. After all, you won't go back
   to work straight away. I've been wondering about Ischia. Don't worry,
   we'll have our cruise after all. Ischia in May: mild air, almond trees in
   blossom, thermal springs, a pretty little pensione by the sea . . .
   It would give you a new lease of life.
FLEURETTE. Mummy's right. You ought to go away somewhere.
   (Silence)
OTHILDE. You mustn't give in now, not now when things are on the up
   and up. You must think of us, too. You know how much we need you.
   How anxiously we're waiting for you . . . Every night before I go to
   sleep I turn down your bed. At mealtimes I always lay a place for
   you on the table . . . *(Begins to sob)* You mustn't leave us in the lurch.
   All these weeks we've been worried sick about you. You don't know
   what it's like . . . waiting and waiting, and always afraid you won't come
   back . . . *(She sobs)*
FLEURETTE. Say something, daddy! *(Silence, except for quiet sobbing)*
   You mustn't make it so hard for mummy.
OTHILDE *(calmer)*. At least they're going to put you into a room with two
   beds soon. Nurse Eve told me. That's a good sign in itself. And you won't
   be on your own any more . . .

Exeunt OTHILDE *and* FLEURETTE

HYPNOS. We were interrupted. *(Pause)* Why so pensive?
LORENZ. I'm tired.
HYPNOS. You're asleep, Lorenz.
LORENZ. I'm wide awake.
HYPNOS. That's not a contradiction.
LORENZ. You've sharpened my perceptions. But what for? It unsettles me.
HYPNOS. I gave you the chance to be clear about things.
LORENZ. I am aware of things, I'm aware of my family, I'm aware of the
   doctors and nurses, and do you know what's very clear to me? They're
   all terribly afraid of death.

HYPNOS. Of **your** death.

LORENZ. That's it, there's a connection.

HYPNOS. You're talking in riddles, Lorenz.

LORENZ. For you they're riddles. You're not mortal.

HYPNOS. Tell me the answer, then.

LORENZ. I don't know the answer.

HYPNOS. Then tell me what you do know.

LORENZ *(after a pause)*.   It was a long process for me too, losing my fear of death. And when I finally did lose it I was extremely clear-headed. I felt I had to get everything organised; cancel contracts and club memberships for instance, make advance payments, burn private notes, instruct my solicitor, and even work out my wife's pension claim and the education grant for my daughter. Dying, I thought to myself, is an organised retreat: arranging your estate, saying your goodbyes, and then finding your memories slowly fade away. There was only one thing I hadn't thought of: a dying man reminds his doctors and his family that they're mortal too. Do you know what I'm afraid of? That they won't allow me to die, because if they did they would have to admit they're not immortal.

HYPNOS. And you've only just realised that?

LORENZ. When death stops being a problem, other problems will disappear. But when you're prevented from dying, then you start asking questions. *(Pause)* Why is awareness of death something we shut out of our consciousness? Why is life prolonged instead of being made more human? What lengths will we not go to just to avoid admitting that we're mortal?

HYPNOS *(after a pause)*.   You want me to give you an answer?

LORENZ. No, Hypnos. To me you're a small winged god out of a school book. Your territory is dreams. Mortality is something mortals have to come to terms with . . . Give me a beautiful dream. Let me dream I'm dying at home. And someone is sitting next to me holding my hand—someone who's not afraid of death.

Scene Eight

Enter PAVEL *wheeled in on a bed. He is placed next to* LORENZ. NURSE *sets machines in order, then exits.*

PAVEL. Can you move? *(Silence)* Are you asleep?

LORENZ. I don't know.

PAVEL. Surely you must know wether you're asleep or not.

LORENZ *(after a pause)*.   I have to get used to my new surroundings first. *(Silence)*

PAVEL. Do you know where you are?

LORENZ. Up to now I've been in Intensive Care with the wide-awakes.

PAVEL. But always drowsy? *(Laughs)* Stuffed full of medication and

edifying sayings. Sedated and confident. Feeling ropey, but on a
recovery trip. *(Pause)* Come on, friend, let's have some sign of life
from you. Can't you infect me with your confidence? *(Pause)* Or
should I infect you with mine? Wonder who's got more?
In any case we ought to spend our time together—as enjoyably as
possible. *(Silence)* Can you move?

LORENZ.   Reasonably well.

PAVEL.   There's a fag-end on my bedside table. All you have to do
is light it and hold it to my lips, two or three puffs are all I need.
(LORENZ *lights a cigarette.* PAVEL *inhales the smoke and
slowly blows it out.*) Thanks, friend.

LORENZ.   My name's Lorenz.

PAVEL.   While you're about it you can scratch my shoulder. It's
itching like hell . . . further back . . . yes, there . . . It's always the
way—you crush your spinal cord and you itch all over . . .

LORENZ.   Better?

PAVEL.   Usually I get rid of it myself, by meditation. I think to myself:
an itch is something beautiful, heavenly, an itch is like an orgasm . . .
And then it goes away—like an orgasm. *(Silence)* Do **you** still
remember what it's like?

LORENZ.   An itch?

PAVEL.   An orgasm . . . A really good, healthy orgasm.

LORENZ *(after a pause).*   What happened to your spine?

PAVEL.   Not worth talking about . . . a little nose-dive into shallow water.
Woke up with a few scratches . . . *(Silence)* You can stub out the
fag-end now, but do it carefully . . . There are still a few puffs left
in it.

LORENZ.   Like there are in us. *(Silence)*

PAVEL.   And what about you?

LORENZ.   Hardly worth mentioning. Metastases right up to my chin
and a few extra complications.

PAVEL.   Not bad. How much longer do they give you?

LORENZ.   I don't give myself more than two months. But they'll know
how to get round that. Strictly speaking I've already died three times.

PAVEL.   Either way you can't complain. You won't survive me. You
lot from Cancer College are always better off. *(Silence)*

PAVEL.   My name's Paul. You can call me Pavel. The self-propellers
always call me Pavel.

LORENZ.   Self-propellers?

PAVEL.   All the crushed nerve cases who've been stuck on wheels.
Sometimes they roll in here and bring a breath of the big wide world
into my room. Some of them are far out. Do you know what one
of them told me? He said every sexual act is an act of death—and
vice versa. Not a bad idea, eh? *(Silence)* You just think about it. You
die and it's like an orgasm . . . a climax—and then relaxation. Gradually
your libidinal energy flows out of your body . . . slowly you step out
of yourself, cross a frontier, move into the unknown . . . Extend

your ego . . . Do you understand what I mean?

LORENZ. Why didn't they stick **you** on wheels?

PAVEL *(pensively)*. Sometimes at night when you can't sleep you do
start to wonder. The pain's bad and you feel you'd like to melt away,
just slowly fade out. And then you dream the door opens and in comes a
doctor, but not one of that lot that rule the roost here. He sits
on your bed and nods to you. From somewhere or other you can
hear music, Jimmi Hendrix singing 'The Wind Cries Mary' and the
doctor sticks a needle in a vein. You don't feel pain any more, just
happiness. You quickly fall asleep. An overdose of anaesthetic
Over and out. For ever. *(Silence)*

LORENZ. Pavel! Don't drive yourself crazy.

PAVEL. Do you know what it's really like? At night when I'm half
mad with pain I feel for the call button near my hand and call the
night-nurse to my bed. Pressing that button is the only thing I can
do for myself. The night-nurse gives me a sedative and goes away
again. And because the drug doesn't work I ring again and get
another sedative. And the third time I beg the night-nurse to give
me an overdose of morphine. Then she says I shouldn't make things
so difficult for her. And I say: the boot's on the other foot, she
shouldn't make things so difficult for **me**. And so you know what
happens then? She goes away again. *(Silence)* The next morning
the doctor comes and ticks me off for terrifying everybody. I try to
reason with him. I say: a grown man who is incurably ill must have
a legal right to a painless death if this is what he really wants. And
do you know what he says? Petition Parliament. I explain to him I'm
sick and tired of it all. No feeling in my arms and legs, my urethra
inflamed by the permanent catheter, my kidneys defective, stones
forming in my bladder, muscles deteriorating, fever and outbreaks
of sweat the whole time, constant pain. He knows all this. He knows
that the male nurse has to open my sphincter by hand to clear the
shit out. He knows that because of my crooked spine I can't even
sit in a wheelchair. He knows that bedsores cause ulceration, stinking
holes and rotting flesh. He knows better than anybody what it means
when the main nerve fibre in the fourth vertebra is crushed. But all he
can think of are the regulations. Killing on demand is illegal, he
says reproachfully. *(Pause)* And then he disappears. *(Silence)* All right,
killing on demand is illegal. But helping people to do it for themselves
isn't. He can't give me an injection himself, but he could leave a
syringe out near my bed. *(Pause)* Just a simple syringe. Nothing in it—
only air. Are you with me?

LORENZ. Take a drag. (LORENZ *lights the cigarette.* PAVEL *takes a
deep drag*)

PAVEL. The only question is: how does the air get into the bloodstream
if you can't move your hand? *(He laughs)* Nothing but problems, friend.
I tell you: Never do a nose-dive into shallow water.

NURSE *enters. Checks machines. Draws screens round both beds.*

Scene Nine

A courtroom.

JUDGE.   Now we have concluded the preliminary hearings against the
cancer patient L. there is nothing further to delay the main hearing. The
session is open. *(Clears his throat)* The charge against the cancer patient L
is that either at his own request or for as yet unexplained reasons, and
in any event by means of an injection from a syringe, he took the life
of the paraplegic P. The defendant has confessed. A reconstruction of
the events leading up to the act gives us the following scenario: in
circumstances yet to be clarified the defendant was able to procure
two hyperdermic-syringes, both of which were filled with air. With the
smaller syringe he stabbed the paraplegic P. several times in the region
of the pulse until he was certain he had hit a vein. Then he detached
the syringe from the point which remained stuck in the vein, put a larger
syringe on the needle and pressed. Dr Severin, when the incident
was reported to you, was P. already dead?
SEVERIN.   Yes, your Honour, there was nothing to be done. The air
introduced into the bloodstream led to an air embolism with fatal
results.
JUDGE.   The defendant maintains that he was acting on the express wishes
of the patient P. Nurse Eve, can you confirm that P. wanted to end his
life?
NURSE.   Yes, your Honour. He not only said so, he even made jokes about
it.
JUDGE.   What do you mean, he even made jokes about it?
NURSE.   For instance, he talked about having himself frozen by an
American funeral firm and existing as an icicle—that's the way he put
it—for as long as it took medical science to find a way to knit severed
spinal cord, with all its millions of nerve filaments, together again.
I couldn't convince him that American firms which specialise in
freeze-funerals will only freeze customers who have already departed
this life.
JUDGE.   Nurse Eve, did you take seriously the patient P's wish to die?
NURSE.   No, your Honour, not really and truly. He used to make
jokes about it.
JUDGE.   So really and truly you think he didn't want to die at all?
NURSE.   I don't know, your Honour. I work on the assumption that
such a thing isn't possible. It's against nature. It's not possible.
JUDGE.   Dr Severin, could it be said that the man killed by the defendant
was in a hopeless condition?
SEVERIN.   No, your Honour. For me the word 'hopeless' doesn't
exist, nor should it for a patient. So long as the vital functions of his

151

brain-stem are in order, there can be no question of a condition being hopeless.

JUDGE. You are, however, aware that the patient P. had a great many disorders: stones forming in the bladder, muscular atrophy, chronic inflammations, ulcers, not to mention his complete immobility— and all irreparable.

SEVERIN. I know, your Honour. May I make a personal statement on this matter?

JUDGE. Please do, doctor.

SEVERIN. In my opinion no sick person has the right to end his life simply beause he considers his condition hopeless and intolerable. And he has even less right to ask a doctor to break off treatment. A doctor's task is to serve life, nothing but life. His skill and the high standards of medical techniques ensure that life goes on. As a philosopher said: if we endorse the ends we endorse the means.

JUDGE. Is it true, doctor, that paraplegia sometimes also affects the breathing centre?

SEVERIN. Yes, that is true.

JUDGE. Was that a possibility the patient P. could reckon with?

SERVERIN. Yes, your Honour.

JUDGE. If one day this had actually happened, what would you have done?

SEVERIN. I would have attached him to the artificial respirator.

JUDGE. Even if he was fully conscious?

SEVERIN. Even if he was fully conscious.

JUDGE. For weeks and months on end?

SEVERIN. For weeks and months on end.

JUDGE. And suppose he were to develop pneumonia as well?

SEVERIN. I would have given him antibiotics.

JUDGE. You would not have let him die?

SEVERIN. No, your Honour. Never.

JUDGE. Dr Severin, you have known the defendant for a fairly long time. Considering him from a medical point of view, would you allow extenuating circumstances?

SEVERIN. No, your Honour.

JUDGE. After all we do know that even in his own case he flatly refuses medication that would prolong his life.

SEVERIN. Yes, your Honour. That is unfortunately the case.

JUDGE. But in your opinion he has no reason to do so?

SEVERIN. We managed to get a whole series of serious complications in the patient under control. Though it is true to say that the formation of metastases is very far advanced, there's no denying that.

JUDGE. And that doesn't alarm you?

SEVERIN. Not in the least, your Honour. As I've already said, the word 'hopeless' doesn't exist for me.

JUDGE. Could you give us the reasons for your optimism, doctor?

SEVERIN. We'd cut away the degenerated tissue and treat him with cobalt rays. In the first instance we'd get by with very conventional methods.

JUDGE. But surely there is a limit, doctor?

SEVERIN. Of course, your Honour.

JUDGE. And where does the limit lie?

SEVERIN. Figuratively speaking, at the exact point where the body stops and the head begins.

JUDGE. Do you mean: when the body can't go on any longer the head has to accept it too?

SEVERIN. On the contrary, your Honour. When the sick body is finished, the healthy head must be rescued from it.

JUDGE. What do you mean, doctor?

SEVERIN. Perfectly simple: radical amputation. We separate the body from the head.

JUDGE. You separate the body from the head?

SEVERIN. We would fix the head on a stand and connect it by tubes to machines which would take over the functions of heart, lungs and kidneys.

JUDGE. And this thing—this head could live?

SEVERIN. Absolutely, your Honour. It will even be able to speak. *(He draws back the screen round the bed.)*

JUDGE *(clears his throat).* What do you say to that, defendant? *(Silence)* Defendant! What do you say to that? *(Silence)* Do you actually realise how much medicine is capable of doing? *(Silence)* Did you bear this in mind when committing your act? *(Silence)* Defendant! Have you lost your tongue? *(Silence)* Would you mind examining him, Dr Severin. It seems to me your patient is not giving his full attention. (SEVERIN *does so, then closes the screens.*)

Scene Ten

LORENZ. Hypnos! Where am I?

HYPNOS. Surely you know.

LORENZ. Tell me where I am.

HYPNOS. Don't upset yourself!

LORENZ. Tell me, Hypnos!

HYPNOS. You're in the clinic.

LORENZ *(after a pause).* Am I in a hospital room?

HYPNOS. You're in an attractively furnished room with large windows and pictures on the wall. If you ask, the television set will be switched on for you.

LORENZ. Can I ring for the nurse?

HYPNOS. There's no need. She can hear you over the radiophone. You only have to call and she'll come to your bedside.

LORENZ. Am I lying in a bed? *(Silence)* Am I lying in bed, Hypnos?

HYPNOS. No, you're not lying in a bed.

153

LORENZ. Can I lie down at all?

HYPNOS. That's a question of perspective.

LORENZ. And I can't stand either. To stand you need legs. But I can dangle.

HYPNOS. You're dreaming.

LORENZ. Dangle on a stand at the eye-level of a man of average height who is standing upright on two sound legs.

HYPNOS. This is a dream, Lorenz.

LORENZ. At the eye-level of a man as tall as Dr Severin.

HYPNOS. Things are like this in dreams.

LORENZ. And below me, carefully clothed, pulse the heart-lung-machine and the artificial kidneys.

HYPNOS. In your dream, Lorenz. You're dreaming.

LORENZ. And what if I wake up? *(Silence)* I'll never wake up again.

HYPNOS. You will wake up.

LORENZ. And then the dream will be over?

HYPNOS. Definitely, Lorenz.

LORENZ. There are some dreams which go on even when you're awake. *(Silence)* Why don't you answer?

HYPNOS. I can hear footsteps. The doctor, the daily inspection.

LORENZ. I'll pretend to be dead.

HYPNOS. Don't forget, it's a dream.

LORENZ. I won't say a word. When the doctor talks I'll be as dumb as a statue.

HYPNOS. Rubbish, Lorenz. Make a joke of it. Laugh at him. Stick your tongue out at him.

LORENZ. Stay with me, Hypnos.

We hear footsteps approaching. DR SEVERIN *enters.*

SEVERIN. Well now, Mr Lorenz—still dumb? *(Silence)* I know you're capable of speech. Still, give yourself time. *(Silence)* Everything takes time. And now we have a great deal of that. *(Silence)* That's what you've gained, Mr Lorenz. You've gained time.

LORENZ. My name is not Lorenz.

SEVERIN *(delighted).* My God, Lorenz! You do want to speak. *(Silence)* I'm listening, Lorenz. *(Silence)* Talk, Mr Lorenz! *(Silence)* Come on now, talk!

LORENZ. Lorenz has died.

SEVERIN. Marvellous! Your voice is marvellous.

LORENZ. **My** name is Brainstem.

SEVERIN. I knew all along you'd be able to speak.

LORENZ. Glad to meet you, I'm Brainstem.

SEVERIN. I can understand you perfectly, Mr Lorenz.

LORENZ. Brainstem.

SEVERIN. But of course, my dear chap. Your brain-stem is working marvellously. How do you feel?

LORENZ. Where are your students, Doctor?

SEVERIN. My students?

LORENZ. The new recruits for the Brainstem Maintenance Crew.

SEVERIN. But my dear chap! Don't let's exaggerate.

LORENZ. Where are the press, and television?

SEVERIN. Now gently does it, Mr Lorenz. Demonstrations of
that kind are quite uncalled for. After all you do have a private
life—you may be without a body but you're not without dignity.
We're not going to sensationalize this. What do you take us for?

LORENZ. Doctor, a few headlines would bring some meaning into
my life.

SEVERIN. That is a subject you should discuss with the chaplain,
Mr Lorenz. And anyway: you're not the first bodiless head.
This form of survival is beginning to catch on. *(Laughs)* No, no,
friend, I'm afraid we can't make a celebrity of you here. But
surviving in peace and quiet, that we can guarantee.

LORENZ. How many volts does my peace and quiet need,
Doctor?

SEVERIN *(laughing)*. You'll have to ask the chaplain that. In the last
analysis, my friend, all life is nothing but accumulated energy.
But more about that another time. Is there anything else I can
do for you?

LORENZ. I've got stomach pains, Doctor.

SEVERIN. Now don't be silly. *(His voice moving away)* Where nothing
exists nothing can hurt. I'm very pleased with you. Chin up, old
chap! . . .

LORENZ *(calls)*. Doctor? For my lunch I want my nutritive solution
vanilla flavoured.

SEVERIN *leaves.*

HYPNOS *(laughs)*. Glad to meet you, I'm Brainstem. My mood today has
a voltage of one point five volts. Watch out you don't get a shock!

LORENZ. Let me dream something else, Hypnos.

HYPNOS. You've got stomach pains? I'll send the mechanics to have
a look at you.

LORENZ. Give me a better reason to laugh.

HYPNOS. Chin up, old chap! Or is there something else you can still
get up?

LORENZ. Did you hear me? I want a better reason to laugh.

HYPNOS. I'm not treading on your toes, my friend. I'm treading on
your tube.

LORENZ. I want a different dream . . . I want a different dream . . .

Blackout.

Scene Eleven

The lights go up to find LORENZ *in bed at home. The machines are all gone. Enter* OTHILDE.

OTHILDE. Lorenz! *(Silence)* Can you hear me, Lorenz? *(Silence)* You shouted in your sleep. *(Silence)*

LORENZ. I'll be out soon, Othilde. *(Pause)* It'll take some getting used to. If it's all right with you, we'll put my head on the window-seat in the oriel. Then I'll have a view of the street, it won't be so boring for me. *(Pause)* The heart-lung-machine and the artificial kidney we'll tuck away behind the flower-stand. They wouldn't be a very pretty sight for you. The rest we'll work out as we go along. *(Pause)* We'll have lots of time for one another, Othilde. I don't need much looking after. A little nutritive solution, that's all. Maybe in the evenings you could read me something—all the books I never got round to, a chapter a day. And now and again I'd like to listen to a record. You know what I like. *(Pause)* I don't need anything else. *(Pause)* Are you listening to me?

OTHILDE. You've had a bad dream. *(Silence)*

LORENZ. It will be lovely to be home again.

OTHILDE. You are home, Lorenz.

LORENZ. Lying in my own bed.

OTHILDE. You are lying in your own bed.

LORENZ. I've always wanted to die at home.

OTHILDE. You are at home, Lorenz. *(Silence)*

LORENZ. Is it true, Othilde?

OTHILDE. Yes, Lorenz. You're at home.

LORENZ. I'm lying in my own bed?

OTHILDE. Yes.

LORENZ. And you're near me?

OTHILDE. Yes, I'm near you.

LORENZ. And you're holding my hand?

OTHILDE. Yes, Lorenz.

LORENZ. And Fleurette?

OTHILDE. She's near you, too.

LORENZ. And it's all really true?

OTHILDE. Yes, it's really true. *(Silence)*

LORENZ. Thank you, Hypnos. Thank you for this last dream . . . *(Silence)*

Lights fade to black. End.

Home Work

(Heimarbeit)

a play in twenty episodes

by

Franz Xaver Kroetz

translated by Steve Gooch

Première: Kammerspiele Munich, April 3rd 1971 (with *Hartnäckig*).

The critical success of *Homework* in its first production in Munich established Kroetz overnight as a major force in the West German theatre. Like Harald Mueller and Fassbinder, Kroetz was concerned with the problems of the fringe groups of society, and in *Homework* his ear for lower-class Bavarian dialect and his sense of working-class behaviour are faultless. Ernst Wendt felt that it was Kroetz, not the writers at the famous Ohnsorg Theatre — the Hamburg 'popular' theatre — who offered the true play about German home life. 'Kroetz points towards hopelessness, to a totally destroyed language that can no longer perform its function — that can no longer even display the literary superiority of the author and does not want to.' (*Theater Heute* 1971 May p. 36). In this attitude to language, shared by Fassbinder and Harald Mueller, is the most apparent difference between the East and West German writer.

Yet Kroetz, until recently, was avowedly communist and the influence of the theory of alienation is strong in all his work. Men are alienated from work, husbands from wives, children from parents, people from themselves. Each form of alienation is focussed in the failure of communication, only uncomprehending violence emerging as a form of expression. The result, as Wendt says, is a world full of Woyzecks, and undoubtedly the Büchnerian episodic style has influenced Kroetz. So too have two English writers: Pinter in the language—Kroetz uses silences in very similar ways— and Bond in themes. As in *Saved, Homework* shows a baby being killed on stage, not stoned by hooligans but drowned by a man who will not accept the illegitimate offspring of his wife's affair with another man. The ease with which he gets away with the 'crime', the ease with which we as audience get used to his ease is the central point made, alienation now so deep-rooted in all our behaviour that murder becomes, as in Camus's *L'Etranger,* more an existential than a moral dilemma.

I wanted to try and break through a theatrical convention which is unrealistic—chatter. The most distinctive feature of my characters' behaviour is their silence; for them language doesn't function properly. They have no hope for the future. Their problems lie so far back in the past and are so advanced, they are longer in a position to express them verbally.

Characters

WILLY, the husband, 40
MARTHA, his wife, 35
MONICA, elder daughter, 10
URSEL, younger daughter, about 2

Place A house just outside a small town, with garden.

Dialect Cockney

Notes on the set

Use simple flats only. Set changes should be in full view of the audience.
Projection where needed. In principle very sparse. No 'decor'.

Notes on the part of Ursel

A small child can't act. It can only be there. There is no 'part', just the
stage direction when the child should be present. When she is present,
she may do more or less as and what she wants. She should be familiar
with the stage, that's all. She shouldn't behave as if new to it. Her
presence is all that's important, no details. Should this part be
impossible to cast for legal or other reasons, the suggestion would be to
leave it out completely, or replace her with an older child. This would,
however, necessitate changes.
The present alternative is for me, however, the ideal one.

Production note

Silence = an exceptionally long pause. The various indications of time-spans
should not be sold short.

Scene One

WILLY *is busy doing home work. He is filling seed-packets. A few hundredweight bags of seeds surround him.* WILLY *pours these seeds into the packets they will be sold in, using a small beaker as a measure. Having filled each packet, he sticks it down and places it in a carton.* WILLY *works quite regularly, above all not quickly, not hectically, not irregularly. He works with neatly defined, precise movements, which follow each other quickly but regularly. While working he looks up only very rarely.*
WILLY *walks with a distinct limp. He has had an accident, and has only recently been released from hospital. He is barely medium height, lean, around forty. He wears glasses for his work.*
MARTHA *is washing* URSEL, *their youngest, in an old-fashioned tub set up in the middle of the kitchen. She uses a rectangular sponge.* MARTHA *washes the child with fast, erratic movements, not very thoroughly, not very lovingly. The emphasis here is on the cursoriness, the speed.*
MONICA *is doing her school homework. She is writing an essay on 'Birds', spelling out aloud to herself as she goes. Now and again, between writing, she looks up.*
These movements should take as long as is necessary for the audience to perceive them as a 'tableau'. Distinct contrasts between the activities, above all between WILLY's *and* MARTHA's.
It takes three minutes for the first word to be spoken. Throughout the entire scene the radio is on, tuned to AFN.(1) *Music and announcements. The scene lasts 7–8 minutes.*

WILLY.   What we got fer tea?
MARTHA.   Yer'll 'ave to ask Monica.
WILLY.   Monica, what we got fer tea? (MONICA *doesn't hear*)
WILLY.   I said, what we got fer tea?
MONICA.   Spuds left over from dinner. They're still there. No more meat.
MARTHA.   Any eggs?
MONICA.   Eggs an' all. *(Long silence)*
MONICA *(spelling the words out loud to herself).*   Pinion is a poetic word fer the wing of a big bird.
WILLY.   So what we 'avin'?

_____

(1) AFN = American Forces Network, which plays much more hard-line rock and pop music than the Bavarian Third Programme and has a large young audience.

MARTHA. Fried egg an' potato. When I'm out cleanin', I can't be
botherin' about food. Thass up t' you two.
MONICA. An' what we gettin'?
MARTHA. Custard, if there's any milk.
MONICA. 'Ave a look, shall I?
WILLY. Sit still. Do yer 'omework. *(Long silence)*
MONICA. 'Ow d'yer spell rhythm?
WILLY. What?
MONICA. Rhythm.
WILLY. Tell 'er 'ow yer spell it.
MARTHA. I'm washin' Ursel.
WILLY. What yer wan' it fer?
MONICA. We 'ad it in singin' t'day. Y an' TH.
WILLY. Fings they learn 'em.
MONICA. An' 'ow d'yer spell . . .
MARTHA. Thass enough now. Do yer 'omework.
WILLY. Fings they learn 'em nowadays. We di'nt learn fings like that.
MARTHA. You do the washin'-up like I asked? (MONICA *doesn't hear*)
MARTHA. D'you wash up like I asked?
MONICA. Ages ago.
MARTHA *(after a pause)*. I don' wan' a 'ave t' wash up an' all when I
come 'ome.

MARTHA *has finished with* URSEL. *She passes her to* MONICA *in a
large towel.*

MARTHA. Take 'er then. Make sure she stays covered up. I'm gettin' tea.

Scene Two

MARTHA *in her underclothes. She is washing in the tub which* URSEL
had her bath in before. A sort of substitute for a wash-basin.
WILLY *is still at his work. From time to time he drinks from a large
cup.*
No radio now. Length of scene 5–6 minutes.
Long silence.

WILLY. Yer put on weight. *(Long silence)*
WILLY. Yer got fatter.
MARTHA. Soon lose it again.
WILLY. A proper paunch.
MARTHA. Where?
WILLY. A proper paunch.
MARTHA. Look the other way, yer won' see it.
WILLY. Don' get no exercise, do yer.
MARTH. Me, no exercise! *(Long silence)*
WILLY. When yer fink what baths cost. In new places they go with the

'ouse. Don' build 'ouses no more with no bath in. Goes with the 'ouse, like a lav.

MARTHA. I need the towel. 'Angin' on the oven.

WILLY *gets up and fetches* MARTHA *the towel. He stays standing next to her.*

WILLY. On yer belly an' yer chest yer put it on.

MARTHA. Soon lose it again. You'll see. (WILLY *goes back to his seat, goes on working.*)

MARTHA. Any coffee left?

WILLY. Should a said earlier.

MARTHA. You only drink it cos it's there.

WILLY. It's too late anyway. Go t' bed. I won' be long.

MARTHA. When I been cleanin', I'm tired. *(Pause)*

WILLY. Don' wan' a know, do yer.

MARTHA. When I been cleanin', I'm tired.

WILLY. Always got a ask in this marriage.

MARTHA. I'd like t' see you, if yer'd been cleanin' someone else's place all day.

WILLY. Jus' cos you go cleanin' once a week.

MARTHA. Twice a week.

WILLY. I'm stuck 'ere every day.

MARTHA. You can get tired too. Free country. If you 'ad a decent job, I wou'nt 'ave t' go cleanin'.

WILLY. This is nothin', I suppose.

MARTHA. Men's work don' belong in the 'ome

WILLY. 'Ow I earn money's my business. Got a get me strength back firs'.

MARTHA. If you 'adn't been drunk, yer wou'na fallen off yer scooter. If yer 'adn't fallen off yer scooter, yer wou'na 'ad t' go to 'ospital, yer wou'nt be limpin' now, an' yer wou'nt need t' get yer strength back.

WILLY. Can' do nothin' right, can I. If I stayed in bed an' said I was ill, you couldn't do nothin'.

MARTHA. Try it then. You ain' ill no more.

WILLY. Convalescin'. *(Long silence)*

WILLY. A quick 'un eh, jus' a quick 'un.

MARTHA. When yer're tired, yer don' even wan' a quick 'un.

WILLY. You don' even deserve askin'.

Scene Three

WILLY *comes into the bedroom. He puts on the light, undresses.* MARTHA *wakes up. Length of scene 3-4 minutes.*

MARTHA. D'you 'ave t' put the light on t' get into bed? Wakin' me up.

162

WILLY. I wan' a read the paper.

MARTHA. Yer can read yer paper t'morrer. People are sleepin'.

WILLY. If you wan' a sleep, sleep. When yer're really tired, yer can sleep anywhere. Light's not goin' a bother yer.

MARTHA. Jus' cos I say what I think fer once, 'e gets offended.

WILLY. Jus' a quick 'un then, an' I'll put the light out.

MARTHA. Like a kid.

WILLY. I don' need t' beg fer me conjugal rights, yer know. I can do without if thass yer attitude.

MARTHA. That case, 'ave some consideration an' put the light out.

WILLY. You got somethin' against love, you 'ave.

MARTHA. If I'm tired, I'm tired. It's got nothin' t' do with love.

WILLY. Easy t' say. Don' prove nothin'.

MARTHA. Can' see beyon' the en' a yer nose, thass your trouble.

Scene Four

WILLY and MARTHA working on their vegetable patch. WILLY passes top-soil through a sieve to sort out stones. MARTHA is planting strawberry shoots. Length of scene 7–8 minutes.

MARTHA. I reckoned yer'd find out sooner or later in any case. Bou' to. (Pause) It was ages ago away. Still, it's done now, so talkin's no more use neither.

WILLY. When?

MARTHA. Don' keep lookin' like that. Jus' cos I'm pregnant. November. Thass the truth. When you was in 'ospital, it was. (Long silence)

WILLY. Yer took advantage cos I was in 'ospital.

MARTHA. I definitely did not take advantage. Seein' I di'nt mean nothin' spiteful by it.

WILLY. You was so much in love, yer jus' 'ad to 'ave a kid.

MARTHA. I di'nt mean nothin' spiteful by it, cos I di'nt wan' it. to 'appen.

WILLY. An' me in 'ospital, not knowin' nothin'.

MARTHA. I already said I di'nt mean nothin' spiteful by it. I got taken advantage of, if anythin', cos I 'ad trust. An' I got none back fer it. I washed mesel' after but it di'nt do no good. P'raps cos I was on me belly when we done it. Makes yer get pregnant easier.

WILLY. We never done that.

MARTHA. 'E wanted it. You can do it with me an' all if yer like. I'd get rid of it anyway, if I knew someone 'oo'd do it fer a tenner, or free.

WILLY. 'Undred it costs. Thass all I needed, shellin' out an 'undred on some stranger's account.

163

MARTHA. Thass what I thought: we wou'nt do it. We need the money
fer other things, be a shame to waste it. *(Pause)* A child ain' a
disaster, yer know. Some people be only too 'appy t' get a kid. Give
God knows what fer one. *(Pause)* Now it's 'appened, there's no
point you bein' put out about it.
WILLY. Whass a kid t' me if I ain' the father.
MARTHA. Right. When it comes I'll 'ave it registered illegitimate.
Easiest thing then is adoption. Get it adopted by some American or a
black it's all the same.
WILLY. Long as yer find someone.
MARTHA. Put an ad in the paper. *(Long silence)*
WILLY. My mother got rid of three of 'ers with an ordinary knittin'-
needle. I got that from my father, thass what 'e always said.
MARTHA. 'Ow d'yer mean, with a knittin'-needle?
WILLY. With a knittin'-needle.
MARTHA. I could try that. I got a knittin'-needle. When the kids are
in bed.

Scene Five

Night. MARTHA *rummages in the drawer.* WILLY *is still working.*
Length of scene 5-6 minutes.

WILLY. What you lookin' for?
MARTHA. We got to try it out. Practice is better'n theory.

She takes a knitting-needle from the drawer. She sits down on the
sofa, pulls her skirt up over her thighs and drops her pants down over
her knees.

WILLY. You ought a disinfec' that firs', or you'll get an infection. *(He*
stands up goes over to MARTHA, *lights his cigarette-lighter and holds*
the end of the needle in the flame.) Right. Careful, it's 'ot.
MARTHA *(taking the needle from him)*. Get out of it, you don't 'ave t'
watch, do yer?
WILLY *(returning to his work)*. Poke it in right up the front. Where it
don't 'urt. Don' poke it where it 'urts, thass somethin' else. Yer got a
poke it in where the egg is.
MARTHA. Fat lot you know. The mouth a the womb's got a be
opened, then it'll come.
WILLY. I ain' a woman. You should know.
MARTHA. There's no feelin' there.
WILLY. Yer got a concentrate.
MARTHA. Can' feel nothin'.
WILLY. Yer're not right in, thass why. It's up the back, where yer can'
get normally.
MARTHA *(jerks suddenly, cries out)*. That weren't it. That 'urt.

164

(Pain again) I can' find a thing, it keeps on 'urtin'.

WILLY. Where it's soft, that ought a be it.

MARTHA. You keep talkin' all the time, you 'ave a go. P'raps you can do it better. *(She works. Pause)* I'm not stabbin' mysel' t' death on accoun' of a kid.

WILLY. You're scared. Thass what.

MARTHA. Come on then, you do it. I don' mind. I don't wan' a impose.

WILLY. I ain' got clean 'ands. Yer got a 'ave clean 'ands fer this sort a thing.

MARTHA. Mine weren't. *(Pause)* Somethin' there now. Sort of 'issin'. Nothin' else though.

WILLY. Thass got a be it.

MARTHA. Can' feel a thing now, an' it's goin' in further.

WILLY. Poke it in! Poke it!

MARTHA *does this. It takes a long time. Finally she pulls the needle out. Looks at it.*

MARTHA. Blood all over. Look.

WILLY *(going over to* MARTHA *and inspecting the needle carefully).* That was it, thass why. It'll come now. Careful.

MARTHA. I'll get a Dr Whites then. Stop it goin' everywhere.

Scene Six

WILLY *is chopping firewood in the shed. He chops several pieces at a time then stacks them on top of the others. Against the wall of the shed, the moped.*
MARTHA *comes in, dressed to go out, in advanced pregnancy, a small suitcase in her hand. Length of scene 5-6 minutes.*

MARTHA. Can I 'ave yer moped? I'm off now.

WILLY. An' leave it standin' outside the 'ospital all that time? Someone'll nick it, an' then it's gone fer good.

MARTHA. You can fetch it t'morrer. The baby'll be 'ere by then. You can 'ave a look at it.

WILLY. Thass one kid I ain't interested in.

MARTHA. If yer come, bring us a magazine, so I got somethin' t' read.

WILLY. Which one?

MARTHA. Woman or Woman's Own.

WILLY. They got them in the 'ospital. In the secon' class, up the corridor, on the table. You can pick one up yerself.

MARTHA. Bring us some oranges then, or some squash, so I got somethin' t' drink. I'll be 'ome in a week. If anyone asks after me, tell 'em I gone into 'ospital to 'ave it, an' I'll be 'ome in a week. Can I 'ave your moped?

165

WILLY. If you 'ad the kid at 'ome, yer wou'nt 'ave to go off special.

MARTHA. It's all on the National 'Ealth, so I'm makin' the most of it.

WILLY. They migh'nt pay it all, seein' it's not my kid.

MARTHA. They pay for everythin'. Nothin' in there about 'oo's the kid's got t' be. It's all on the National 'Ealth, like with Monica an' Ursel. Can I 'ave your moped?

WILLY. Put it in the yard where the doctors' cars are. Not outside or it'll get nicked.

MARTHA. I'll put it in there, up against the wall, so yer find it straight away. Get the key off me. If yer ask for me, they'll tell yer where I am. If they show yer the kid, look pleased. I don't wan' no talk in the 'ospital. Not with them nurses there. They'd 'old it against me.

WILLY. They won' be findin' nothin' out from me, cos I don' set no store by it.

MARTHA. Right. They don' need t' know, cos we don' set no store by it. None a their business. I'll 'ave it registered illegitimate, then there won' be no fuss with the adoption.

WILLY. If yer knew 'oo the father was, we'd at least get maintenance. Money like that's a boon, yer know.

MARTHA. Forget it. There ain' goin' a be no money in it. Thass a promise.

WILLY. Cos there's somethin' more be'ind it.

MARTHA. Right, there's somethin' more be'ind it. You ough' a know there's somethin' more be'ind it'. You were there, remember.

WILLY. Cos yer don' know 'oo the father is, thass why. It's well-known, that one.

MARTHA. I don' know 'oo the father is! You know everythin', a course, never believe a word yer're told.

WILLY. I'm goin' a chop the wood.

MARTHA *(goes to the moped, fixes her suitcase on the luggage rack).* Bring us some oranges.

WILLY. You ain' passed yer test.

MARTHA. I can drive all right. You know that. It's not the firs' time I driven. An' I ain' drunk like someone I could mention. I can drive.

WILLY. Everyone says that, then things get broken.

MARTHA. No chance. *(She drives off.)*

Scene Seven

MARTHA *is lying in hospital.* WILLY *is sitting by her bed. He wears a clean suit. He holds a bag in his hands. Length of scene 3-4 minutes.*

WILLY. There's yer oranges. Two poun'. Blood-oranges.

MARTHA. Put 'em on the cabinet. Nice 'ere, en it.

WILLY. Give us the moped key.

166

MARTHA. In the cabinet. The drawer. It's up against the front wall, like I said. *(Pause)* 'Ave yer seen the baby?
WILLY. No-one said nothin'.
MARTHA. It's a boy. Nice, but 'e's got two big lumps on 'is 'ead. Be nice otherwise.
WILLY. Where on 'is 'ead?
MARTHA. On 'is 'ead.
WILLY. Deformed.
MARTHA. There's nothin' else 'cept the lumps. Doctor reckons they'll go.
WILLY. If it's water on the brain, 'e'll die. They always die.
MARTHA. It's not water on the brain, jus' two lumps. Yer don' need t' look at 'im now specially. Yer'll see 'im at 'ome soon enough. I'll be 'ome Friday. The kid'll 'ave t' stay 'ere, probably. I'll be 'ome Friday, thass definite.
WILLY. I'll go then.
MARTHA. I'll be 'ome Friday.
WILLY. If 'e's got lumps on 'is 'ead, 'e's a cripple.
MARTHA. They grow out.
WILLY. I thought at the time it weren' right.

Scene Eight

Home again. MARTHA *is swaddling the baby.* WILLY *is at his work.*
MONICA *is washing up. Length of scene 4-5 minutes.*

WILLY. 'E's a cripple. No-one'll adopt 'im.
MARTHA. The lumps on 'is 'ead'll grow out, the doctor said so. You'll see. It often 'appens.
WILLY. Monica an' little Ursel turned out normal. What was its father like fer Christ's sake.
MONICA. We ain' got lumps on our 'eads.
WILLY. You never 'ad lumps on yer 'eads. Not like 'im. 'Is father must a 'ad lumps on 'is 'ead an' all.
MARTHA. No chance.
MONICA. What father?
MARTHA. Don' ask silly questions. Do the washin'-up, an' don' break nothin'.
WILLY. Every child 'as a father. An' the child takes after the father. Thass science.
MARTHA. Not in somethin' like this.
MONICA *(to* WILLY*)*. You ain' got lumps on yer 'ead. Nor 'as Mum.
WILLY. 'E's the only one with lumps.
MARTHA. We shou'na poked aroun' with that knittin'-needle, thass what I reckon.
WILLY. If yer didn' know 'ow, yer shou'na done it.

167

MARTHA.   Yer need to know that before, not after. It was your idea.
WILLY.   A suggestion a mine, a way out a the fix, thass all.
MONICA *(to* WILLY*).*   D'you poke Mum with a knittin'-needle?
MARTHA.   Don' stick yer nose in what yer don' understan'.
WILLY.   Just goes to show. Why yer wou'nt say 'oo the father was.
MONICA.   What father?
WILLY.   'Is. (MONICA *doesn't understand.)*
MARTHA.   Every child 'as a father. Thass obvious. 'Is father is 'is Dad.—
Now do the washin'-up.
WILLY.   My children ough' a know where they stan'. I ain' making' no
bad impression on my kids.

Scene Nine

MARTHA *and* WILLY *in their double bed.*[2] *It's dark. The baby's crying.
Length of scene 4-5 minutes.*

WILLY.   I'm not made a stone.
MARTHA.   No-one's sayin' yer should be.
WILLY.   You don' understan' nothin'.
MARTHA.   That case, shut up.
WILLY.   Did I say anythin'? *(Pause. The baby cries.)* My kids never
cried like that.
MARTHA.   Thass cos 'e's ill. Thass obvious.
WILLY.   'E cries all the time. It's not normal. *(Long silence)*
MARTHA.   You got it in fer that kid.
WILLY.   Yer can' 'ave it in fer a kid. It can' 'elp what it is.
MARTHA.   Right. All it is is a poor kid what's 'ere now an' that's that.
WILLY.   Yer can' 'ave it in fer a kid.
MARTHA.   Thass what I say an' all. *(Long silence)*
WILLY.   Can I come over t'night?
MARTHA.   Long as the baby don' upset yer again.
WILLY.   It's when 'e screams 'e upsets me. Thass normal.
MARTHA.   It's also normal t' scream if somethin's 'urtin' yer. Nothin'
yer can do about it. Don' listen. I don'. 'E screams, an' I don' listen.
You got no faith. Always lookin' on the dark side.
WILLY.   That kid puts me off.
MARTHA.   Don' listen.

(2)   The 'Ehebett'—'marriage-bed'—is a particularly German institution. It is a
double bed made up of two singles but so constructed that the singles
cannot stand on their own. This means it is very big—and encourages chaste
nights.

Scene Ten

WILLY *in Sunday best.* MONICA *and* URSEL *the same. They are playing on the floor.* MARTHA, *also dressed in Sunday best, pushes the pram in. Length of scene 4-5 minutes.*

MARTHA. If I 'ave t' tell you two not t' get dirty again, we're stayin' 'ome. *(The children get up from the floor.)*
WILLY. If 'e comes with us, I'm stayin' 'ome.
MARTHA. Yer're not startin' that again.
WILLY. 'E stays 'ome.
MARTHA. 'E needs 'is fresh air an' all. 'E's all pale.
WILLY. Put 'im out in the garden then.
MARTHA. 'E needs sunshine so 'is lumps grow out. The doctor said.
WILLY. Put 'im in the sunshine then. If 'e comes with us, I'm stayin' 'ome. People'll say, there's that family, they got an illegitimate child with lumps in that pram they're pushin'.
MARTHA. I ain' told no people.
WILLY. Me neither.
MARTHA. You must a told Monica. Kids talk, yer know.
MONICA. What did I say?
MARTHA. Nothin'.
WILLY. Monica ough' a know where she stands with 'im. *(Long silence)*
MARTHA. Supposin' it rains.
MONICA. Come on, let's go. Talk about it on the way.
MARTHA. It might rain.
WILLY. Put 'im by the open window, that'll do.
MARTHA. Only cos it's Sunday, mind. Day of rest. *(She opens the window, puts the pram by it. Then they go off.)*

Scene Eleven

The family in a beer-garden. MONICA *and* URSEL *aren't sitting at a table, they're playing. Length of scene 3-4 minutes.*

MARTHA. It's got cold.
WILLY. Gettin' late.
MARTHA. Monica, Ursel, come 'ere. Put yer coats on. It's cold, it's gettin' late. *(The children do this.)*
MARTHA. Let's go home. 'E's right by the window. If 'e's not covered up, 'e'll get cold an' be ill.
WILLY. I got a finish me beer firs'.
MARTHA. I di'nt say yer shou'nt finish yer beer firs'. *(Long silence)*
MARTHA. If you go on like this, Willy, you'll be sorry.
WILLY. Nothin's goin' a make me sorry, I tell yer.
MARTHA. You'll be sorry, Willy. You'll be so sorry, you'll rue the day.
WILLY. Jus' cos I wan' a finish me beer don' mean I'm goin' a be sorry.

169

Scene Twelve

Home again. WILLY *is sitting at his work.* MARTHA *is cleaning the floor. Daytime. Length of scene 4–5 minutes.*

MARTHA. I'm goin' off, Willy. I'm leavin' yer. *(Long silence)*
WILLY. Kids need a mother.
MARTHA. We all know that.
WILLY. Stay 'ere then. *(Long silence)*
MARTHA. I got my pride an' all, Willy. I'm not 'avin' you throw that kid in my face any more, like yer do. I don' 'ave t' stan' fer all that.
WILLY. 'Ave I said anythin'?
MARTHA. It's written all over yer, Willy.
WILLY. I mean, we can' 'ave 'im adopted, we're stuck with 'im.
MARTHA. That was the only time I'd been away from you. The only time I'd been with another man. You di'nt say a thing when I come back.
WILLY. Yer can forget a thing like that. Seein' as yer come back. Yer don' forget a kid though. Not when it's cryin' all the time.
MARTHA. It's not goin' a cry fer ever though. The doctor says it's in pain.
WILLY. It's marked, thass what.
MARTHA. If you're not goin' a accep' that child, I'm leavin'. I'm not avin' you humiliate me. I can do without that. That kid'll live longer'n I will. There'll be no en' to it.
WILLY. I wou'nt go away if I was you.

Scene Thirteen

WILLY *at his work.* MARTHA *comes in with a suitcase. She's got her coat on. Length of scene 5–6 minutes.*

MARTHA. There's ten quid in the cupboard. I took five fer mesel'. Clean clothes in the cupboard an' all. Everythin's been washed. I put clean sheets on the bed. Monica can do the dishes when she gets in from school.
WILLY. Yer're goin' then.
MARTHA. Everythin's clean an' there's money an' all.
WILLY. What about the kids?
MARTHA. I can' take 'em with me. You know that. My parents only got room fer one.
WILLY. They know yer're comin'?
MARTHA. I wrote. I'm sleepin' in their livin'-room.
WILLY. My kids can stay 'ere. Yer take 'im with yer.
MARTHA. I ain' takin' no-one with me. I can'.
WILLY. Leavin' me in the lurch.
MARTHA. I warned yer, but yer wou'nt listen. *(Long silence)*

170

WILLY. Yer son's ill. 'E's feverish.

MARTHA. It's a cold. It'll go away again. Call the doctor. Get some medicine. There's money in the cupboard. That'll 'elp.

WILLY. Give advice all right, can't yer.

MARTHA. Yer got Monica. She can cook an' clear up. You'll manage. I'm takin' yer moped. Yer can fetch it t'morrer. It'll be in the garden. I'll leave the keys in it. Don' come up, there's no point. *(She goes off.)*

Scene Fourteen

WILLY, MONICA *and* URSEL *at their evening meal. Length of scene 5–6 minutes.*

MONICA. When's Mum comin' back?

WILLY. 'Ave to ask 'er yerself! *(Long silence. They eat.)*

MONICA. When Mum wen' off las' time, she di'nt come back for ages.

WILLY. Three months, that was.

MONICA. She di'nt say nothin' yer forget t' tell me t' do?

WILLY. Yer got a wash up.

MONICA. I done that already. Whyn't she say why she's gone off? If I ever go off, I'll say when I'm comin' back.

WILLY. She don' wan' a know about us.

MONICA. What yer mean?

WILLY. Made 'is food, 'ave yer?

MONICA. In the pan[3]. I'll give it 'im now, or it'll go cold.

WILLY. Finish yours up firs'.

MONICA. I can cook all right, even without Mum, can' I? *(Pause)*. D'yer like it?

WILLY. Why shou'nt I?

MONICA. If I feed 'im, can I bring 'im in 'ere?

WILLY. Leave 'im in the bedroom. Better air in there, no noise.

MONICA. Cold though.

WILLY. It's not cold in bed. *(Pause)* Come on, finish up. Time for bed.

MONICA. I can' yet. I got a do the washin'-up.

WILLY. No, you do that tomorrow.

MONICA. It'll all go 'ard then, won' come off.

WILLY. Stay up then, but Ursel can clear off. I got work t'do.

---

[3] A 'Rein' is an Austrian dialect word for a flat saucepan, suitable for eggs, etc. Its use is almost exclusively confined to the mountain areas, including Bavaria.

Scene Fifteen

WILLY *is sitting on the sofa. He stares at an opened newspaper in front of him and masturbates. Late night. The radio is on. Finally the baby starts crying. Length of scene 2-3 minutes.*

MONICA *(off)*. Dad! *(Pause)* Dad, 'e's cryin'!
WILLY. Sleep, go t' sleep.
MONICA. Dad, 'e's cryin'!
WILLY. See whass wrong with 'im then. Cover 'im up or put 'is bonnet on. I'm workin'. I wan' a bit of peace.

Scene Sixteen

WILLY *sits at his work. The radio is on. The baby grizzles. Late night.*
MONICA *comes in in her nightshirt. Length of scene 6–7 minutes.*

MONICA. Dad, 'e's woken up. *(WILLY doesn't hear.)* 'E's cryin', Dad.
WILLY. Don' listen. Go t' sleep.
MONICA. P'raps 'e's come uncovered.
WILLY. 'E's covered. I covered 'im. Just now. Go t' sleep, 'e's ill. Don' go in there or you'll catch it. You'll get ill an' all. Get lumps on yer 'ead an' all. Anyone goes in there, they get ill.
MONICA. Whass 'e got?
WILLY. Somethin' very bad. 'E's marked. It's catchin'. *(Pause)* What yer want?
MONICA. I wan' a wee-wee.
WILLY. What yer standin' there for then? Go, then go back t' sleep. That water 'ot?
MONICA *(puts her finger in the pot to test it)*. Cold.
WILLY. Put it on the gas then.
MONICA. I done the washin' up.
WILLY. Do like I say then, an' clear off.
MONICA. If yer wan' some 'ot water, I'll put it on. *(She does this.)* Shall I make yer some coffee?
WILLY. Do yer wee-wee, then go t' bed again. Quick. T'morrow's another day. Yer got t' get up.

MONICA *goes. Long silence.* WILLY *works. Eventually* MONICA *comes back.*

MONICA. G'night.
WILLY. Sleep quick. Tight.

MONICA *goes. Long silence.* WILLY *works. Eventually he stands up, tests the water with his hand. Then he fetches the wash-tub from a small cupboard. He puts it on the dresser (as in Scenes 1 & 2). He pours hot water into the tub, then cold. He tests the temperature of the water several times. Then he goes. He comes back with the pram. The baby*

172

is grizzling. He takes it out of the pram (as far as possible the rest should be done so that the audience cannot see the baby, which is presumably a doll), lays it in the tub, washes it with a sponge, thoroughly and not incapably. Then he drowns the baby in the tub. He leaves the baby in the tub and dries his hands on the towel on the oven. Then he reaches into the tub again, takes the baby out, dries it off, lays the body back in the pram. Then he clears up: empties the tub, puts the sponge back, etc. Then he pushes the pram back into the bedroom. He comes back, washes his hands with soap under the tap and returns to his work.

Scene Seventeen

In a small allotment. WILLY and MARTHA sit at a table. A nice day. WILLY is very smartly dressed. Length of scene 3—4 minutes.

MARTHA.   Dad's got a give 'is allotment up in the autumn. The railways sent a letter. They're buildin' a cleanin' depot 'ere fer passenger-trains. *(Long silence)*
WILLY.   Martha, come back, yer son's dead.
MARTHA.   What makes you say that?
WILLY.   'E died, thass what. 'E's already buried. 'E got pneumonia, like I said.
MARTHA.   Poor thing.
WILLY.   Thass what I said. Come 'ome, eh. It was fate, thass all. We di'nt need t' get all worked up.
MARTHA.   No.
WILLY.   Come 'ome. The kids need you. Kids need a mother. An' I ain' feelin' too good mesel'.
MARTHA.   Yer don' look ill. ·
WILLY.   Can' go by that.
MARTHA.   It's nice 'ere. Peaceful.
WILLY.   We got a garden at 'ome.

Scene Eighteen

MARTHA and WILLY come on through the front garden. MARTHA is carrying her suitcase. MONICA and URSEL come on too. They have all brought their mother home together. The children remain somewhat in the background to begin with. MARTHA stops by a cross. Length of scene 3—4 minutes.

MARTHA.   Whass that?
WILLY.   A cross.
MARTHA.   That where the baby is? *(Long silence)*
WILLY.   I di'nt wan' no fuss.

173

MARTHA.   Easy death, was it?

WILLY.   I choked it.

MONICA *(comes up)*.   D'yer like the cross? I did it mesel'.

MARTHA.   Very nice, dear.

MONICA.   If the dog 'adn' already been dead, we'd a nursed it back to 'ealth. It was already dead though.

MARTHA.   The dog.

WILLY.   Dog got run over, front a the 'ouse. The kids found it. I said they could bury it there. Mongrel. Must a strayed off.

MONICA.   'E di'nt 'ave no master, cos no-one asked after 'im. Dad made the grave, an' I made the cross. I did the flowers an' all.

MARTHA.   Go indoors an' make some coffee. Dad's brought a cake. *(MONICA goes off.)*

MARTHA.   What if someone asks after 'im?

WILLY.   We give 'im to an American. Foster-parents. Only there's been no word from 'em. Must be back in America.

MARTHA.   No-one'll believe that.

WILLY.   I'm not stupid. I was jokin'. Really is a dog there. You can look if yer like.

MARTHA.   You got a nasty mind, Willy.

Scene Nineteen

MARTHA *and* WILLY *at the cemetery. Nicely dressed, as are the children. They stand by a grave. Temporary wooden cross of the usual kind before a grave is sunk. Length of scene 2–3 minutes.*

WILLY.   Thass it.

MARTHA.   Nice. A nice grave.

MONICA.   My cross at 'ome's nicer.

MARTHA.   Quiet. Yer're not s'pposed t' talk in a cemetery. Say a prayer. *(MONICA prays. WILLY and MARTHA slightly to one side.)*

MARTHA.   Did 'e 'ave an easy death?

WILLY.   I was bathin' 'im. Then 'e drowned. The police cam roun'. They 'ad an inquest. Lookin' after three kids is too much fer a man on 'is own. They understan' that. They reckon it was second degree manslaughter at worst. I got no previous convictions, so it won't be much.

MARTHA.   Thass all I need, me ol' man in prison.

WILLY.   'E drowned. I ain' got eyes in the back a me 'ead. *(MARTHA prays too.)*

WILLY.   Jus' died, like anyone else.

174

Scene Twenty

It is evening. Everyone is in the kitchen. MARTHA *is clearing the table.*
WILLY *is at his work.* MONICA *and* URSEL *are playing. Length of
scene 4—5 minutes.*

MARTHA. If you two don' get t' bed this minute, I'm goin' a get mad.
Little children belong in bed after seven o'clock.
MONICA. When you weren' 'ere, we never 'ad t' go till later.
MARTHA. Well I'm back now. Things are back t' normal.
WILLY. Do like yer mother says.
MARTHA. · If yer don' be'ave yerselves, I'll go away again.
MONICA. You goin' a do the cookin' again?
MARTHA. A course. Everythin's back t' normal again now.
MONICA. What we got t'morrow?
MARTHA. Pork an' veg. Look sharp now, get t' bed.
MONICA. G'night.
MARTHA. Go t' sleep quickly. T'morrer's another day. Yer got t' get
up. *(*MONICA *goes off with* URSEL. *Long silence.)*
MARTHA. I'll do the washin' t'morrer. It's all dirty. A real pile. It'll
be an 'ard day.
WILLY. Jus' as well yer come back. *(*MARTHA *pours fresh water into
the tub.)* You washin'?
MARTHA. Yeh. Cleanliness is nex' t' godliness. You could do with a
wash an' all. Yer're filthy.
WILLY. Any 'ot water left?
MARTHA. Put some on. *(She undresses to wash.)*
WILLY *(gets up from his work, goes over to the gas-stove and puts
water on. Goes over to* MARTHA*).* Ye're back again. *(Touches
her.)*
MARTHA. Wash yersel' firs'. Yer're dirty.

Blackout.

Neither Fish nor Fowl
(Nicht Fisch Nicht Fleisch)
by
Franz Xaver Kroetz
(Photographed by Ruth Walz)

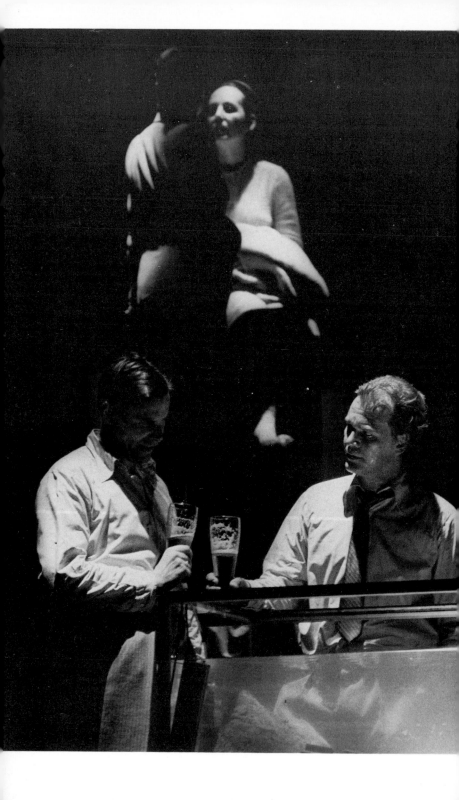

Flotsam

(Strandgut)

by

Harald Mueller

translated by Steve Gooch

Première: with *Stille Nacht (Silent Night)* Berlin, Schiller-Theater 1974.

Despite considerable critical interest and praise, Harald Mueller's plays have still to make their breakthrough. Commenting on his first pieces, *Grosser Wolf (Big Wolf)* and *Halbdeutsch (Half-German)* both of which were premiered at the Kammerspiele in Munich, Benjamin Henrichs wrote: 'Mueller, whose declared model is Pinter, has also taken over Pinteresque techniques. In both plays there is almost no sense of causality—Mueller's (as Pinter's) figures have no biography, no psychology, no sociology. But Mueller's settings are more shadowy. Not in bourgeois surroundings, the room or salon, but on the edges of civilised society are the plays enacted.' (*Theater Heute Sonderheft,* 1972). In *Flotsam* the setting is, however, more clearly 'normal'—the beach where the family outing is ending in disaster. The dialogue in all the plays carries most of the weight, displaying as well a clear debt to Pinter. Joachim Kaiser sensed its strengths and weaknesses having watched the premiere of *Big Wolf* and *Half-German:* 'Harald Mueller's not undangerous yet not unendangered strength is his relationship with spoken colloquial German.' Productions so far have not always caught the mood required, and perhaps they have suffered as well from the long shadow Pinter casts across them.

Henrichs is surely wrong, however, to suggest the characters have no sociology, for Mueller, like Kroetz, is very concerned with those groups in society that are emotionally alienated. Karl, whose emotional damage by industrial society is matched by his loss of two fingers in a machining accident. cannot accept the death of his daughter, does not grasp even his own inability truly to respond. Ruth, while apparently responding more openly, is side-tracked into rather enjoying the stir they cause, the photo that will appear in the local paper.

Given the influence that Pinter has had on the English theatre it would seem at least possible that Mueller's work could be more readily understood in this country than in his own. Our essentially easy relationship with our recent past means we are perhaps more inclined to see the seriousness in the drama of social isolation, the drama in which little happens. And in the way Mueller's dialogue tends towards the Beckettian rather than Pinteresque there is the potential for exploration of the relationship between Theatre of Cruelty and the drama of social alienation which Mueller sees as the way forward for theatre.

Characters
KARL
RUTH

182

Scene One

RUTH *and* KARL *on the beach.*

RUTH. Go in again.

KARL. No, there ain' no point.

RUTH. Karl, our child!

KARL. I wouldn't get past them breakers.

RUTH. There any sign of her?

KARL. No.

RUTH. Oh my God.

KARL. We get all the bad luck. *(Silence.)*

RUTH. But all that wood, Karl, the wood.

KARL. What?

RUTH. All that wood floatin' out there. Strips of it. Boards. Planks.
Beams. She's bound to have clung on to something.

KARL. There ain' no wood out there, Ruth.

RUTH. There is. All over the place.

KARL. Anyway, the kid ain' strong enough for that.

RUTH. Ain' strong enough? More like the opposite. Manu's exceptionally
strong. Abnormally so, for an eight-year-old. She carried her scooter.
Right to the top. All on her own. Right the way up. Right to the fourth
floor.

KARL. Ruth, take one of your pills.

RUTH. Karl, she carried it up the stairs. Honest, those really long stairs.
Single-handed up those stairs. That really heavy scooter. An' her only
just eight. A really heavy-duty one like that. All on her own. Right to
the sixth floor.

KARL. One tread at a time though. Take one.

RUTH. No!

KARL. An' slowly, very slowly.

RUTH. Her, slow! More like the opposite. Like a thing possessed, she was.
Shot up there like a thing possessed. Carryin' a heavy thing like that. That
scooter. A really heavy-duty one. Right to the eighth floor. An' so
pleased, she was. An' outa breath. An' laughin'. She laughed, Karl.

KARL. No, Ruth. One tread at a time.

RUTH. You just want to spoil everything for me.

KARL. An' to be honest, Ruth, we live on the second floor.

RUTH. You're really rotten, you know?

KARL. Open wide. Open! *(KARL gives RUTH her pills.)*

RUTH. Laughin', she was. An' so pleased.

Blackout.

Scene Two

RUTH *asleep.* KARL *is looking out to sea through binoculars. A helicopter circles overhead.*

RUTH. Karlie?

KARL. Yes, Ruth?

RUTH. How many pills you give me?

KARL. Four.

RUTH. Four?

KARL. Had to. You started ravin' like a lunatic.

RUTH. Even so. I been out long?

KARL. More'n three hours.

RUTH. Three whole hours? *(She looks around.)* What's been goin' on then?

KARL. Oh, no end a company. Death like this, you get famous fast. Only now it's turned nice again. Still a loada cloud there of course. Mind you, that's been there since this mornin'. When we come over the dunes from the camp site.

RUTH. Stop it. D'you find Manuela?

KARL. Not yet. Official version is she drowned, though.

RUTH. Then why haven't they pulled her out yet? Why not, Karl? Why on earth not?

KARL. Sheer incompetence. Totally useless. Call 'emselves lifeguards. They need guardin' 'emselves. Called the search off, just like that. No great success, apparently. Oughta try havin' a kid 'emselves. Then they'd know what it's like. Tearin' about in that soddin' boat. Like playboys, these geezers. You'd think they'd go in the water, wouldn't you. Well, you'd be very wrong. Didn't go in once. The only person in all the time was me. Them up in the helicopter I got nothin' against. I mean, they're makin' a reasonable effort. But this lot down here in the motor boat— leave things to them, an' they're left full stop. Official employees they are too. Me, I went in. On a totally voluntary basis.

RUTH. Karlie.

KARL. What?

RUTH. Don't. Please.

KARL. Don't what?

RUTH. Oh Karlie .... *(Silence.)* Come here. Hold me.

KARL. This is new.

RUTH. Silly ... *(KARL takes RUTH awkwardly in his arms.)* Karl, our child—

KARL. Careful Ruth, don't wanna crack up again.

RUTH. You're shiverin', you know.

KARL. Spent far too long in the water. All for nothin' too. Still, p'raps it's better this way.

RUTH. Karl!

KARL. Well, think how Manu must look by now—

RUTH. Oh my good God ... *(Silence.)*

KARL. You're all nice an' warm.

RUTH *goes to put his pullover on.*

RUTH. Here.
KARL. That wasn't what I meant.
RUTH. You'll catch your death.
KARL. Don't matter that much now, does it? *(Silence.* KARL *pulls on his cigarette, which has gone out.)* Bad roll. Proper boomerang. *(They both smile.)*
RUTH. Given your bad hand, it's ace.
KARL. What d'you mean by that?
RUTH. Two fingers out of action, that's all.
KARL. First chance I get, I'm takin' me senior cert.
RUTH. Really, Karlie?
KARL. Get away from the machines then. Higher up it's mostly brain work.
RUTH. Be nice . . .

Silence. KARL *tries to roll himself a fresh cigarette.* RUTH *does it for him and gets it started.*

KARL. New days, new ways.
RUTH. Left-handed boomerang.
KARL. The maestro is amazed. The company expresses its gratitude. *(Silence.* KARL *smokes.)*
KARL. Shall I rub your back in?
RUTH. Karlie, it's already done.
KARL. Ages ago though.
RUTH. Suit yourself.
KARL *(rubbing her in).* Caught the sun nice already.
RUTH. Even roun' the back?
KARL. 'Cept where your bikini comes.
RUTH. Can't help that.
KARL. You sure?
RUTH. Hands off. *(*KARL *obeys, but is irritated by it.)*
KARL. You come here, to relax for once. Finally do what you really want for once. A really nice holiday at last. Finally get something out of life—*(puts a cassette recorder with a pop tune on.)* Bloody sea. Totally fucked. A complete bloody balls-up. An' no mistake.

Both listen to the sentimental song.

RUTH. Well we're on our own again now. Like eight years ago.
KARL. Good as, yeh. Before Manu come. Just what we wanted. Fair to say, right? A joyous event, right?
RUTH. But Karl—
KARL. Really joyous. Weren't long ago she was diggin' in the sand. With her little spade.
RUTH. No, with her bucket.

185

KARL. With her bucket an' spade. *(Silence.)* They dragged someone out once. Boy of five. In some magazine. Went through the ice in the middle of winter. Been dead twenty minutes. Resuscitation worked, though. Happens sometimes.

RUTH. Karlie—

KARL. I'm only tellin' you what it said.

RUTH. Manu's been dead three hours. *(Silence.)* God, is there nothin' we can do?

KARL. Wait.

RUTH. Wait—

KARL. They're doin' a re-run. So the lifeguard blokes said. Can't get rid a nothin' round here.

RUTH. Karl!

KARL. Might take some time though. Have a tempo.

RUTH. What for?

KARL. The tears.

RUTH. I won't cry.

KARL. You won't?

RUTH. No.

KARL. Be better if you did.

RUTH. What?

KARL. Better havin' a good cry, get it over with.

RUTH. Karl, Karl, Karl, that's inhuman. You talk an' talk . . . Has it actually sunk in with you yet? Manu is no longer alive.

KARL. How come you reckon it's me that's crackin' up all of a sudden? Silent as the grave—you sayin' that's human?

RUTH. Please Karl—

KARL. We gotta stick together. Specially now. Like glue. I'll send you on that cure[1] after all this has blown over.

RUTH. All what?

KARL. You know, gettin' her home, the funeral, all that.

RUTH. No!

KARL. What's wrong?

RUTH. Karl, I'm still totally numbed by it all, an' you—

KARL *(referring to the tablets).* Delayed action.

RUTH. No, our terrible misfortune.

KARL. All right, our terrible misfortune—

RUTH. You never understand me. *(Silence.)* Is there really nothin' we can do?

KARL. Have a butchers. *(Offers her the binoculars.)*

RUTH. You'll be askin' me next to . . . *(A helicopter.)*

KARL. Still hard at it. Searchin'. Must be costin' a bomb.

---

[1] In the early 70s the average German would expect to go on a four week 'cure' to add to his annual holiday. This consists of a combination of medical checks and exercises and rather too much food in the majority of cases. Recent spending cuts have made this luxury much harder to get, but cities from Baden-Baden to towns like Bad Kreuznach still do very well out of the 'cure' industry.

RUTH. Stop it.

KARL. Petrol they've burned up already, run a Taunus six months.

RUTH. Stop it, will you!

KARL. Course, they're all specialists up there, ain't they. *(RUTH begins drumming on a bouy.)*

RUTH. Stop it, stop it, stop it, will you!

KARL. Costs a few bob.

RUTH. Stop it!

KARL. You havin' me on, or was all that supposed to mean something'? *(Silence.)* Was that supposed to mean something', Ruth? *(Silence.)* Just tell me if it meant anythin'!

RUTH. You're slow as horses, Karlie. As usual. Manu is dead! My daughter Manu! Dead! Dead! Dead! Dead! Dead!

Blackout.

Scene Three

KARL *shovels sand.* RUTH *paces up and down by the water. Gulls cry — first sporadically, then several together.*

KARL. Still no sign?

RUTH. Nothin'.

KARL. Had to have her hair cut, didn't you.

RUTH. It suited her a whole lot better, Karl.

KARL. An' now we can't see her. Body like that floats just under the surface. Just the head—

RUTH. Karl! *(Silence. Irritated, anxious)* No I mean, it really suited her better. An' above all, it strengthens the hair. It's scientifically proven. The more you cut kids' hair, the more its growth is stimulated. Gets stronger an' nicer-lookin' at the same time. The best time to start is really early on. You can definitely pick 'em out in the street later on—them who had it done in the cradle. They've got long, thick hair. Very strong. Doesn't break. Shines like silk. Doesn't break, so it improves our chances. I'm talkin' about **us** now, especially. There's definitely somethin' about hair. You lot fall for it time an' time again. Only Mum didn't know about that. Or she'd have had mine cut as well. Really short. Down to the roots. While I was still in the cradle. I might've had a few more chances then, too.

KARL. Really? *(Silence.)*

RUTH. Oh, God, I didn't mean it to sound like that.

KARL. Why not? Out with the truth, I say. Every time. Or what you think is the truth.

RUTH *(meaning the binoculars).* Where'd you get those things anyway?

KARL. Some reporter bloke. Lent me 'em just like that. Guess how many people there were here.

RUTH. How should I know?

187

KARL.   You can guess.

RUTH.   Twenty.

KARL.   Twenty! Sixty at least. At least. Maybe even a hundred.

RUTH.   Really?

KARL.   We certainly caused a stir.

RUTH.   I'd as soon done without. Stop that.

KARL.   What?

RUTH.   That shovellin'–drivin' me mad. Leave the sand where it is, can't you.

KARL.   You're gettin' touchy again. Starin' out to sea'll drive you even barmier. She'll be here when she gets here. *(KARL shovels.)*

RUTH.   Stop that shovellin'.

KARL.   Why, for Christ's sake!

RUTH.   Because I had to have my nerves seen to. An' I'm goin' to reach boilin' point any minute. *(KARL stops.)*

KARL.   Ain' I a sweetie?

RUTH.   What sort of reporter bloke was this anyway?

KARL.   Very nice man. Even took a photo of you for him.

RUTH.   For what paper?

KARL.   Local rag.

RUTH.   Oh I see . . .

KARL.   Went back to the caravan too.

RUTH.   What you do that for?

KARL.   Picture a Manu's bed.

RUTH.   Karl, how could you!

KARL.   In exchange for the binoculars.

RUTH.   My God–it wasn't even made.

KARL.   Typical.

RUTH.   I've only got one pair of hands.

KARL.   Yeh, two left 'uns. Mum'll have a fit when she hears that. *(Silence.)*

RUTH.   Sometimes I'd wake up in the night. And I'd see Manu in her little bed. Her little blond head and her tiny hands. Lyin' there peaceful next to me. Karl, she was somehow so . . . cute!

KARL.   Yeh well . . .

RUTH.   Wasn't she?

KARL.   Definitely. She was always somehow . . . Well, she was always a sweet little thing.

RUTH.   An' intelligent. Very intelligent.

KARL.   Oh she was always all there intelligence-wise.

RUTH.   Dad's pension. When they put it up. She worked it out in her head. Includin' back pay from January.

KARL.   Yeh well, we put a few bob behind her, didn't we. Them dance-shoes alone were more'n a pony.

RUTH.   She was really talented, Karl. A regular little talent for ballet, she had. *(She dances a few steps of the tarantella.)* Her tarantella was the tops. Oh my God, my child. Oh well . . *(KARL picks up the child's clothes.)* Karl what you doin' with her clothes?

KARL. Clearin' up.

RUTH. Leave them there please.

KARL. Just don't start believin' in the impossible, that's all.

RUTH. If I say Manu's things stay there, they stay there.

KARL. Why leave her togs lyin' around on the sand? They're all worth something.

RUTH. You oughta be ashamed, Karl. *(Silence.* KARL *photographs the clothes.)* That child shouldn't have been allowed in the water.

KARL. Course she shouldn't. *(He goes to photograph* RUTH. *Referring to her nose-guard.)* Take that thing off your nose.

RUTH. Why?

KARL. Because—it don't look normal now somehow.

RUTH. You think so?

KARL. Looks really stupid.

RUTH. Am I supposed to appear before you tomorrow with my nose all skinned? I can just see your face. I have an extremely sensitive complexion. If I lose skin, it takes weeks . . . D'you know what Manu asked me once? She was only just three too. Mummy, where do people go when they're dead? In the ground, I said. But they'd get sand in their eyes. But pet, you wouldn't notice it any more. Then I'd like to be dead, Mummy. Cos you're always rowin' with Daddy. So I'll keep my nose-guard if you don't mind. I need protection from the sun's harmful rays. Otherwise my nose'll peel off completely. Even with Piz Buin Après.

KARL. That's a pretty crummy thing to say. Just when we're waitin' for our little Dopeykins. Sand in your eyes when you're dead. The way kids talk. About dyin' too. They ain't old enough for it, are they. Come on, take that thing off your nose. For Manuela's sake, yeh?

RUTH. No. You an' your photo-bug.

KARL. All right then, don't. *(Silence.)*

RUTH. Thing is, she shouldn't have been allowed in the water.

KARL. Coulda been. With supervision.

RUTH. Come again?

KARL. What about a nice cool beer.

RUTH *turns the cassette recorder on and plays a pop tune provocatively loud.*

RUTH. You'll have to wait a bit longer. At least till the tide comes in again. *(She stretches out next to the recorder and closes her eyes.)*

KARL. Typical Gemini.

RUTH. What's that supposed to mean? *(Silence.)* So you're a coward with it too.

KARL. Only for the sake of a bit a peace.

RUTH. You had a sleep here this morning.

KARL. Did I say anything?

RUTH. The look on your face is all I need.

KARL. Not all the time.

RUTH. That endless boozin' last night.

KARL. No-one forced you to join in.

RUTH. I'm supposed to sleep while you rave it up. An' afterwards I'm allowed to wash the glasses up.

KARL. Didn't I put you lovingly to bed?

RUTH. Very lovingly. The poor kid was still completely confused at breakfast-time.

KARL. She was a good girl.

RUTH. A good girl! Why'd she run straight in the water then?

KARL. I ain' avin' nothin' laid at my doorstep.

RUTH. Me neither. *(Silence.)* There are other ways of makin' love, you know. Only tenderness with you—

KARL *(shouts)*. I can be tender!

RUTH. God almighty, what's goin' a become of us?

KARL. Ruth, all I did was mention Geminis. There's nothin' you can do about your sign. *(Silence.)*

RUTH. What sort of questions this journalist ask then?

KARL. How she got on in school.

RUTH. An' what did you tell him?

KARL. The unalloyed truth.

RUTH. Karl, the only reason she went down a class was cos I was under observation at the time.

KARL. You skive off sick an' I get the blame.

RUTH. Some skive that was. What a terrible business. Shots an' pills from mornin' till night. An' all them stupid questions. An' me job went for a burton. Helga Sikoreit standin' in. A scruff like her. At a food counter! Meanwhile the kid's left sittin' at home.

Silence. The recorder plays a sentimental tune. KARL puts his arms round RUTH.

KARL. Just don't let it get you down, that's all. Manu was really a hundred per cent all there. Those funny little poems of hers. Granma an' Granpa sit on the sofa; Granpa lets one fly, hits Granma in the eye.

RUTH. Karl!

KARL. This bloke took down everything she ever said. Every childish utterance. So she won't just go under. Not unhallowed an' unsung, I mean. *(Silence.)* Sun's really beatin' down now.

RUTH. I still ain' takin' my bikini off.

KARL. No-one said anythin' about your bikini.

RUTH. If anythin' we oughta get decently dressed.

KARL. You feelin' all right?

RUTH. A time for mournin'.

KARL. Mournin' Manu—

RUTH. That's right.

KARL. Black suit an' tie, eh?

RUTH. It's only proper. How was I lyin' when you took my picture for that reporter?

KARL. Why?

RUTH. Will people see I was asleep?

190

KARL. What if they do?

RUTH. All the mothers'll be up in arms, won't they.

KARL. I wouldn't mind your problems. *(He sees Manuela's clothes in the sand.)* That kid's as sloppy as you are. Why can't you teach her a bit a tidiness—

RUTH. Maybe you'd like to try it for a change?

KARL. Nothin' we can do about it now, Ruth.

RUTH. Clever boy.

KARL. I reckon you're definitely due for a cure.

RUTH. What d'you mean by that?

KARL. What I said.

RUTH. What about my job?

KARL. No-one's indispensable.

RUTH. In private life, yes, no-one's indispensable. But at my till . . . I can just see Helga Sikoreit, spots all over her face.

KARL. You don't rate her very high then?

RUTH. I'd like to see Buschke's face, that's all.

KARL. A lot of people live for their bosses an' nothin' else.

RUTH. An' there's others even let 'emselves get chopped to pieces for their job.

KARL. Highly hilarious.

RUTH. Yeh, highly hilarious. You did everythin', didn't you. Shut off the machine, informed the foreman, wiped the blood off your bench, an' only then did you pass out. Strictly accordin' to the rules. Highly hilarious.

KARL. Anyone there would've done the same.

RUTH. No, they'd have ripped the plug out.

KARL. In plain English made a right fuck-up. What d'you think a machine like that costs? Fifteen years I been in that place, graftin' an' sweatin'—

RUTH. So what?

KARL. You think I'm goin' a jeopardise all that?

RUTH. You'd still have your fingers though.

KARL. Women don't understand these things. You get used to everythin' in time.

RUTH. More's the pity.

KARL. When that 50 mark note went missin' you couldn't sleep two nights runnin'.

RUTH. Fifty marks is fifty marks. *(Silence.)* Why d'you have to torment me so?

KARL. Do what?

RUTH. Karl, I asked you a question.

KARL. A stupid question. *(Silence.)* You know, Ruth, some people are like lucky charms. They always seem to bring a good fortune. You know? They sort of radiate.

RUTH. Is that a fact?

KARL. Elfi Weber for example. She's always radiant. Brings Weber good luck all the time.

RUTH. Probably 'cos all she's interested in is the Fabiolas' miscarriages.

191

KARL. Even so. He lives in a sort of radiant glow. When you're with Elfi you feel amazin'ly good. Everyone. Includin' me. An' she only left school at fourteen, you know.

RUTH. So what?

KARL. Nothin'.

RUTH. You tryin' a tell me somethin'?

KARL. Only that you don't belong to the same breed.

RUTH. So?

KARL. Well Ruth, you know, you belong more to the kind who always balls things up for people. There's somethin' cheerless about 'em. You know? They make everythin' miserable. Never radiant. On account a bein' virtually eternal wet blankets. That's in spite a your 'O' levels, Ruth. *(Silence.)* Ruth?—What's the matter?—Speak to me. You dumb, or lost your voice or somethin'? You gotta say somethin'. Or you'll start ravin' again. I know the signs. You can't help it. Even if you don't like it. I'm bein' quite objective now. I'm only tryin' a get you back to normal. On account a you bein' such a dream of delight all the time. *(Silence.)* Now come on, open your mouth. Or it'll be too late. Hey, say somethin'—Ruth!—You gotta say somethin'! *(RUTH laughs. KARL hits her.)*

RUTH. D'you wanna bit a my potato salad?

KARL. Potato salad?

RUTH. Coupla sausages?

KARL. My flesh an' blood is bein' eaten by the fishes an' I'm supposed to stuff meself with potato salad?

RUTH. I thought you was tryin' a normalise me again. It's ages since we were all havin' breakfast together.

KARL. Potato salad is **out** till . . .

RUTH. When? *(Silence.)* When, Karl?

KARL. Till her mortal remains arrive.

RUTH. Mortal remains!

KARL. That does it.

RUTH. Don't touch me. *(Gulls cry.)* Oh the beasts! Those bloody beasts!

KARL. Ruth, what—

RUTH. Birds of prey, that's all they are.

KARL. Gulls?

RUTH. Look at 'em! Divin' at the water all the time. Pickin' the corpses' eyes out.

KARL. Not gulls.

RUTH *(throwing stones at them).* Yes, gulls.

KARL. Rubbish.

RUTH. They're just like vultures really. Crazed with hunger like that. Absolute vultures—really. Don't be fooled by their colourin'. Lookin' nearly like doves is just a dirty trick. Clear off, you! Soddin' things! Just clear off! Got one, Karl! I got it!

KARL. Musta pecked your eyes out already.

RUTH.   Nearly though. Nearly got his wing. That's where they feel it most. Oh, you filthy beasts! You rotten, filthy beasts!

RUTH *chases off, after the gulls.* KARL *rips a strip of Manuela's clothing off. He then buries his face in the rag.*

KARL.   Little Dopeykins with her soft little pink ears . . . What a bastard thing . . . A real bloody bastard . . . A complete an' total bloody bastard.

Blackout.

Scene Four

KARL *is writing something surreptitiously on the edge of a newspaper.*
RUTH *is reading a school exercise book.*

KARL.   Death like this changes everything.
RUTH.   What way?
KARL.   Spiritually, of course. No, really. Havin' been through it all spiritually, like. Livin' like you did before ain' on no more.
RUTH.   Oh Karlie—
KARL.   Anyway, it's only inner values got a future with me from now on.
RUTH.   You don't say.
KARL.   I do. Soon as we get back I'm buyin' a push-bike. I can do without a motor thank-you very much. Weber'll declare me insane on the spot of course. Let him, I don't care. An' no more TV either. Sooner enjoy me evenin's in peace. Somethin' to nibble, drop a wine—
RUTH.   Aha!
KARL.   Don't worry, it'll all be on me. Few old photos—
RUTH.   The ones you've taken here by the sea?
KARL.   Yeh.
RUTH.   Bit a music when Manu's in bed.
KARL.   Why not?
RUTH.   You really are a . . . *(Silence.)*
KARL.   We don't have to think about it all the time, you know. Do you?
RUTH.   Yes. *(Silence.)* What's that you're addin' up?
KARL.   It's private. Hope we're not in for somethin' over there. One drop an' I'm gone.
RUTH.   I ain't.
KARL.   What I meant was . . . *(Silence.)* You still dream numbers by the way?
RUTH.   Why d'you ask?
KARL.   Well, you know . . . the climate here. Bracin'. Just the job for your nerves.
RUTH.   You think so?
KARL.   Yeh. Better'n some old cure.
RUTH.   I've got used to the idea now.
KARL. , Really? Didn't take you long, did it.

193

RUTH. I'll just tell Buschke I'm completely overworked.

KARL. After three weeks holidays—

RUTH. You can look after the kid yourself for a change. *(Silence.)*

KARL. Tie a knot in your hankie. You've only got me now, remember.

RUTH. Just shows how much it's affected me. *(Silence. Pop music.)* Them an' their campers' party. Now of all times. In our darkest hour.

KARL. Better take a Tempo, eh.[2]

RUTH. Don't worry, I ain' goin' a crack up. I won't give you no bother.

KARL. You know what you can do. *(Whistles to the pop tune.)*

RUTH. D'you have to?

KARL. Still in me head from the firm's last do.

RUTH. I know all about what's in your head.

KARL. I bet. Bloody good party, that was.

RUTH. Cos Weber kept tryin' a touch me up?

KARL. Only as a joke.

RUTH. Some things are beyond a joke.

KARL. Ruth, the bosses stood us all a treat. Fun an' joy an' laughter. All on central office. Telegram from New York was all it took. Next year I get me cuckoo clock. Fifteen years service. *(Tries to pinch* RUTH*)* Then I'll be goin' cuckoo! Cuckoo, cuckoo!

RUTH. Stop that, please.

KARL. There's no-one for miles.

RUTH. What about the helicopter?

KARL. Every time I get enthusiastic about somethin', you start makin' difficulties. I was a bloody fool to think that kinda thing could make me happy.

RUTH. That's entirely up to you, chum. *(She reads the exercise book.)*

KARL. What's in there that's so bloody interesting?

RUTH. It's private, to me.

KARL. That case it ain't.

RUTH. Some notes Ruth done for an essay. 'Things I saw on the beach.'

KARL. So?

RUTH. Look around you.

KARL. See if she got it right.

RUTH *(reading).* Tin cans, plastic bags, steel cables, tar drums, coke bottles, paper plates, old shoes, sky—

KARL. What?

RUTH. Sky.

KARL. Where's it say that?

RUTH. There.

KARL. Never mind. *(Silence.)* Sky . . . *(Silence.)* Shame she ain't with us no more.

---

[2] Tempos—Tempotaschentücher—have a similar status to Kleenex tissues, i.e. the best known brand of paper handkerchief which is now so well established as to be a term in its own right.

RUTH. Oh my God, the child! *(Reaches for the binoculars, but* KARL *grabs them for himself.)*

KARL. I thought keepin' look-out was beneath you.

RUTH. 'An' what I saw when I closed my eyes.' On the other side.

KARL. Daft idea.

RUTH. That case I don't need to read on.

KARL. Please, please. *(*RUTH *tears the book up.)* You know, in some ways she got a rough deal with you.

RUTH. No way your idol Elfi would've sent her little Uschi to ballet classes.

KARL. Too true. It's sheer torture for them kids.

RUTH. If we're goin' a talk about who tortured her more, Karl—

KARL. Oh? What about when she crayonned on the wall? She only wanted to play. You don't lock someone in the cellar for that.

RUTH. An' who hit her so hard her nose bled? Who smashed her face?

KARL. She slammed the door, didn't she! Like a lunatic.

RUTH. Karl, you know it was the wind.

KARL *(shouts).* To err is human! On the other hand, you not takin' her to the optician—

RUTH. Why me all the time?

KARL. She kept fumblin' at things, didn't she?

RUTH. But why me?

KARL. Opticians are women's business. You gotta be able to see damn good if you're goin' in the open sea.

RUTH. I beg your pardon!

KARL. Yeh Ruth, that's how we destroy the things we love.

RUTH. You're knockin' on the wrong door, mate.

KARL. Well . . . somebody's got to be to blame! *(Starts to go.)*

RUTH. Karl, where you goin'?

KARL. No idea. In the water. Thought I'd just swim out a bit, one more time.

RUTH. There's no point.

KARL. I can't stand it here any more.

KARL *goes.* RUTH *reads what* KARL *has jotted on the edge of his newspaper, then notices the bow missing from Manuela's dress.*

RUTH. Dear God, help our Manu. Dear God, help our Manu. Help our Manu, dear God. Please, dear God, help our Manu. Help our Manu please, dear God. I . . . er . . . *(says what follows parrot fashion)* I carried her in my womb, bore her in pain, suckled her with these breasts. Dear God, why can't I feel sorrow? *(*KARL *comes back.* RUTH *poses.)* Dear God, help our Manu. *(*KARL *picks up the camera.)*

KARL. Ruth! *(*RUTH *turns. He snaps her in position, praying.)*

RUTH. Haven't you stored up enough memories already?

KARL. Blessed are those who suffer persecution, eh.

RUTH. Really, Karl! *(*KARL *puts the recorder on.)*

KARL. Just don't go on hopin', that's all. She's gone from us for good an'
that's that. An' you oughta say Manuela.
RUTH. What for?
KARL. So he knows who you mean an' don't get her mixed up.
RUTH. God don't get mixed up.
KARL. Oh? Why'd he let her snuff it then? A kid of eight . . . *(Silence.)*
RUTH *turns the recorder off.)* Might just as well chuck a few of these
woollies on his cross.
RUTH. Karl, please! That's blasphemy.
KARL. Well, it does no good prayin', does it.
RUTH. What **do** you believe in exactly?
KARL. Your backside.
RUTH. Karl! You oughta be ashamed! *(Pop music from the camp site.)*
KARL. Worse'n bloody animals.
RUTH. So what? Ain't much evidence of you mournin'.
KARL. You lost a screw or somethin'?
RUTH. I just been lookin' at your list of bills here. *(Picks up the paper.)*
The coffin'll come cheaper than you got here. We'll only need a little
one for Manu. *(Silence.)* Only feel half a man without a Taunus, do
you?
KARL. Ruth, that was only on account of your cure.
RUTH. That is a down payment on a Taunus!
KARL. Listen Ruth, everyone has his moment of weakness. Me included.
I ain' made a stone, you know. But life does go on, Ruth.
RUTH. Always the same stupid clichés.
KARL. It's just the way things are. Me tax refund'll be due soon, finally.
'Cept the fiddle-arses always take their time. Maybe it'll come through
the post for once. Lyin' there on the mat when we get home. What you
reckon? *(Silence.)*
RUTH *(ironic)*. Funeral costs are tax deductible.
KARL. Life goes on, don't it!
RUTH. Oh Karlie, how can anyone take you seriously?
KARL. An' what a life, eh . . . what a life. Pass me the feed-bag over.
RUTH. Get it yourself. *(KARL fetches the bag and takes a jar out of it.)*
KARL. So it's potato salad after all. *(Because of his injured hand KARL
can't unscrew the jar.)*
RUTH. Give us it here. *(She undoes the jar. KARL eats.)* What'd you do
with her little bow by the way?
KARL. What little bow?
RUTH. Off her dress.
KARL. Stashed it away.
RUTH. Why?—Karl, why? *(Silence. The helicopter approaches.)*
KARL. Won't leave off, them blokes. You wave too. There look, the
frogman's wavin' back. *(He photographs the helicopter.)*
RUTH. Why'd you stash her little bow away?
KARL. No idea.

196

RUTH. You must've had somethin' in mind.
KARL. For the Taunus. On the back window. For luck.
RUTH. For the Taunus—which you don't want to buy.
KARL. So what? Any more salad?
RUTH. Just hers.
KARL. Hm. *(Silence.)* Question is, d'you suffer much?
RUTH. I do.
KARL. Drownin'.
RUTH. You do think some horrible things sometimes.
KARL. No law against it. I reckon you pass out pretty quick.
RUTH. Please Karl—
KARL. That little boy, went through the ice. D'you know what he saw as he died, Ruth?—Well?—Somethin' really nice. Give you three guesses. *(Silence.)* Yeh well, you wouldn't get it anyway. I'll tell you: he saw fish.
RUTH. You don't say.
KARL. Fish. An' a lot a pretty stones. An' then a big, black man came.
RUTH. Approachin' oblivion.
KARL. I'm only tellin' you what he said. *(He jams Manuela's jar of salad under his arm and opens it awkwardly with his good hand.)* There y'are, see. Can be done.
RUTH. How can you do that to a child?
KARL. Why throw good food after her? *(He eats.)* You always make that kid out to be some kind of angel. Even Elfi's noticed that.
RUTH. Elfi?
KARL. She's got a sort of instinct.
RUTH. Point is, what sort. Anyway, what if I do?
KARL. Manu wasn't without her . . . you know . . .
RUTH. Oh God, really . . . !
KARL. That's right—God punishes the little sinners first.
RUTH. For Goodness sake, what crimes is the poor kid supposed to have committed?
KARL. Pullin' legs off beetles. One by one. Then burnin' 'em up with a match. *(He eats.)* Soon as we get home, I'm takin' me senior cert.
RUTH. Again?
KARL. This time it's serious.
RUTH. Serious—till somethin' trips you up—bloody washout.
KARL. You just say that one more time . . . !
RUTH. Karl, you been takin' that course for years.
KARL. This time it's for real though. Wanna bet? Afford a Taunus then, no trouble. *(KARL eats. Children come by from the right, singing.)* The other kids, off the camp site.
RUTH. They're goin' on their trip. *(Silence. The children singing.)* Karl, they're goin' on their trip!
KARL. I know, Ruth. *(Silence.)* So the grown-ups can have their fun. You bastards! *(He pokes around in the potato salad.)* What'd you put in here exactly?

197

RUTH. Gherkins, egg an' mayonnaise. Why?

KARL. 'S really vinegary, I can hardly stand it. 'S vergin' on herring salad.

RUTH. Pickled gherkins can be a bit vinegary sometimes, yes.

KARL. Vinegary maybe, but not that much.

RUTH. Jesus Christ, that's what it comes out like sometimes.

KARL. Not that bloody much though!

RUTH. You know, Karl, you make me sick sometimes. First you're even lickin' your fingers clean. Then suddenly you don't fancy it any more. *(Silence.)*

KARL. So what? If I don't fancy it any more, it means . . . I just don't like it any more. *(Silence.)* It's a hundred percent vinegar, that is!

RUTH. Karl!

KARL. Vinegar!

RUTH. The look on your face—

KARL. For a kid too. Call yourself a mother!

RUTH. Please, not in my bad ear.

KARL *(hitting her)*. A bloody mother! A bloody mother! A bloody mother! *(RUTH runs away. KARL weeps.)* Yeh well, water on the lungs. Soon run out of puff.

RUTH. Karl—I just wish the earth would swallow me up.

KARL. Another of your daft ideas.

A mood of something very fragile. Perhaps a gentle wind and a single gull.

RUTH. It's only got the thinnest of crusts . . .

KARL. You shouldn't believe everythin' in the papers. Come here.

RUTH. Why?

KARL. Don't just leave me standin' here like this. *(They come together.)*

RUTH. You've never hit me as hard as that before.

KARL. It's the climate here. Bracin'. *(He laughs.)*

RUTH. Karl, what's so funny?

KARL. Weber's always thinkin' up these awful sayings.

RUTH. Like what?

KARL. After meals a man should smoke; or should give his wife a poke.

RUTH. What you waitin' for then? Light one up.

KARL. Will you roll it for me again?

RUTH. No.

KARL begins rolling himself a cigarette. Blackout.

Scene Five

KARL *asleep.* RUTH *looking out to sea*

RUTH. Karl?—Karl!—Listen to me, Karl! God, how can you sleep
   like that at a time like this? *(She shakes him.)* Karl, Karl, Karl!
   (He wakes up.)
KARL. What?—Ruth, what's the matter?
RUTH. It's happenin'.
KARL. What is?
RUTH. Our child's comin' back.
KARL. Comin' back?
RUTH. Yes. Manu.
KARL. Manu? What about her?
RUTH. She's dead.
KARL. Dead?
RUTH. Drowned.
KARL. Don't muck about. *(Short pause.)* Oh, right . . . of course . . .
   so what?
RUTH. There's somethin' floatin' out there.

During what follows KARL *doesn't look out to sea.*

KARL. Where?
RUTH. Way out . . . to the right . . . it looks like a . . . child's head! . . .
   Go in again.
KARL. Might be somethin' completely different.
RUTH. Of course it might be somethin' completely different.
KARL. Keep calm. Let it come in first.
RUTH. God, if only I could swim!
KARL. No chance, not with a current like that. My guess is, the
   autumn tides are comin'. *(Turns on the cassette recorder. It plays.)*
RUTH. No-one else takes their holidays in September.
KARL. What's the matter now?
RUTH. Your holiday list was on the board for weeks. Why'd you
   wait so long to put yourself down?
KARL. I got my reasons.
RUTH. September makes a good impression.
KARL. Rubbish, what sort of impression?
RUTH. With the bosses upstairs. Everyone else wants the middle of
   summer.
KARL. You can drown in the middle of summer just as easy.
RUTH. Drown in a calm sea . . . ?
KARL. Wouldn't get far, dyin' that way in the mountains.
RUTH. D'you have to be so hurtful all the time?
KARL. I was the one wanted to go. But you, you had to go to the
   sea.
RUTH. You know mountain air's no good for me! *(KARL clutches
   RUTH to him.)*

199

KARL. We coulda been insanely happy there. Coulda waved to each other. From one lonely mountain-top to the other. Think what we've lost now, here on the beach. Ruth! Our entire happiness, that's all.

RUTH. You're always on about happiness. Have you any idea what that is?

KARL. If nothin' else, it's prescribed by law.

RUTH. Prescribed by law . . . ?

KARL. 'S right. Christmas bonus, child benefit, holiday pay, etcetera.

RUTH. Some happiness. Mind you, it's no surprise with the home you come from.

KARL. Just leave my home out of this, will you? I was happy as a sandboy there, in the old days. Every night. Regular.

RUTH. Every night pissed, you mean.

KARL. But happy as a lord. Till you come along with your fat belly. Product of one reckless night. Landed me in it nicely, didn't you.

RUTH. You don't care about Manuela any more, do you.

KARL. Who cares about her the most remains to be seen.

RUTH. Who half-raped who in the back of the Goggo then?

KARL. I didn't get the Goggo till sixty-seven.

RUTH. Must've been the BMW then.

KARL. That's right, throw that in my face.

RUTH. Completely different matter on a pillion, ain't it.

KARL. That's right. But only cos you were so dead set on marriage. Manu was sheer bloody blackmail. If only we'd done away with her.

RUTH. I tried. Wore meself to the bone over it. Pleaded with them like mad to do it. You think that moves 'em? They just roll their eyes in sympathy an' mutter on about protectin' innocent life. All it is is a bit a snot. 'Bring it into the world first, then we'll see.' See what? Soon as it's here, no-one lifts a finger. Might as well slit your wrists now. By the finish I was five months gone anyway. Missed the boat. *(Silence.)*

KARL. An' never said a dickybird to me.

RUTH. You wouldn't have had me then anyway.

KARL. Where've you put the Tempos?

RUTH. Here.

KARL. Well wipe them tears at long last, will you? *(Silence.)*

RUTH. Karl, she didn't get nothin' outa life at all.

KARL. She did.

RUTH. What then?

KARL. That joke of a ballet school of yours.

RUTH. And you? What did you give her, Karl?

KARL. Do what?

RUTH. What did you give her?

KARL. Ruth, I'm only a little man.

RUTH. What'd you say?

KARL. I'm only a little man.

RUTH. Too true. I wouldn't even have dreamt of marryin' a labourer in the old days. Now go on, swim out.

KARL. You know, a kid like that becomes a habit.

RUTH. I beg your pardon?

KARL. A bit, anyway.

RUTH. You are going to look for our ray of sunshine right now.

KARL. Easy said. Problem is, where?

RUTH. Take your time. I'll stay here. Even if it buckets down.

KARL. Ruth, a kid like that really is a habit.

RUTH *(vindictive).* Be careful with your gammy hand when you grab hold of her. Like a bloody claw, that is. Manu's got delicate skin. *(KARL goes. RUTH talks quietly to herself.)* Granma an' Granpa sit on the sofa; Granpa lets one fly, hits Granma in the eye. *(KARL comes back with a crate of empty pop bottles.)*

KARL. Your Manu.

RUTH. I see . . .

KARL. Worth a bit though. Five deutschmarks. West. On the bottles.

RUTH. Karl—

KARL. Yeh, that's it, I'm afraid.

RUTH. You didn't go in the water at all.

KARL. Tell me somethin' I don't know.

RUTH. Your trunks are dry as a bone.

KARL. What am I supposed to do—with my gammy hand?

RUTH. Coward! Coward! My husband is a coward!

KARL. So what?

RUTH. Havin' a father like you was a punishment. *(Silence.)*

KARL. Standin' there like that—

RUTH. Like what?

KARL. Really kinky.

RUTH. I can stand here if I like, can't I?

KARL. You're doin' it for a reason though.

RUTH. You're off your head.

KARL. I can see what I see.

RUTH. Don't you touch me!

KARL. You're all nice an' warm.

RUTH. Let go a me. *(Silence.)*

KARL. Well?

RUTH. I dunno Karlie; You've only ever been after one thing.

KARL. Not only that. Honest.

RUTH. The naked act.

KARL. No, I swear! I'd tell you, wouldn't I? *(KARL strokes RUTH.)*

RUTH. If there's no feelin' there, it don't happen for me. Somewhere out there she's—

KARL. There's hardly a trace a the birth on your belly.

RUTH. Eye-sockets like balloons—

KARL. A figure like—

RUTH. Silent. Cold. White.

KARL. You're goin' over the top again, you know.

RUTH. An' her little face, tossin' about, it'll be smashed by the breakers. No, I won't let my child be taken from me! Even in death she's gettin' a beatin'!

KARL. What's that mean—'even'?

RUTH. Well, look!

KARL. What's 'even' mean, Ruth?

RUTH. What d'you mean what's it mean?

KARL. Even in death. You said 'Even in death she's gettin' a beatin'.' D'you mean from me?

RUTH. I mean the breakers. Just look at 'em!

KARL. Fishin'-smack. So what?

RUTH. Karl, it'll run her over. Shout out! Shout! Can't you shout?

KARL. Too far away. Anyway, what? What am I supposed to shout?

RUTH. Hallo-oh! Have you seen a body? A little girl. Eight years old. Spit'n image a me.

KARL. You don't imagine they're lookin' this way, do you?

RUTH. I don't care: shout!

KARL. Too late. As luck would have it—

RUTH. Shout, Karl, shout! You must shout! God, what sort of man are you?

KARL. What's that mean? I'm quite normal.

RUTH. Shout, Karl. This is goin' to get to me in a minute.

KARL. Hallo-oh! Have you seen a body? *(Points meaningfully at* RUTH*)* Spit'n image of her? *(Quietly, to himself)* A little girl . . . just eight years old . . . Manu . . . Manu . . .

RUTH. My husban' howlin'. That makes me really very sad, Karl, you know? *(Silence.)*

KARL. I need you a hell of a lot.

RUTH. Pardon?

KARL. Help me.

RUTH. Why should I?

KARL. Our little Dopeykins with her soft little pink ears—

RUTH. But for her I'd still be like I was before.

KARL. What?

RUTH. Me nerves'd still be intact.

KARL. You can go on that cure. Honest.

RUTH. I can get it on the National Health.

KARL. You got that in writin'? *(KARL presses himself against* RUTH.*)*

RUTH. Now now—

KARL. Jus' let me snuggle up a bit. There was somethin' so precious about her, Ruth, somethin' so sweet—

RUTH. Whyn't you save yourself the trouble? *(Silence.)*

KARL. Just remember what you said at the altar.
RUTH. Any more orders, funny man? *(Silence.)*
KARL. Maybe I could put somethin' else on offer.
RUTH. You tryin' a bribe me by any chance?
KARL. Well, what good did it do, you prayin'? Them red shoes at
Ravel's. With the cork high heels. The ones you were always so keen on.
RUTH. God, you're a hard-hearted bastard.
KARL. D'you wanna go on mournin' for ever? Be a winter coat in it for
you an' all.
RUTH. But why now of all times?
KARL. You ain't against it in principle then? *(Short pause.)* With a fur
collar on, if you like.
RUTH. Since when could you shit money, Karl?
KARL. That's no great shakes on four hundred marks a week, take home.
RUTH. Did I just hear four hundred?
KARL. Overtime.
RUTH. That's precisely what does you in. What do I get out of you then?
(Silence.)
KARL. Well?
RUTH. Didn't I just hear somethin'?
KARL. Like what?
RUTH. A child callin'. *(Silence.)*
KARL. Ruth, don't make such a song an' dance. Ain't as if she was our
son an' heir.
RUTH. What if the helicopter comes back?
KARL. They can sail into the sunset for all I care.
RUTH. The risk'll cost you another pair a pumps.
KARL. Drive a fella to ruin, you could.

Blackout.

Scene Six

RUTH *and* KARL *looking out to sea.*

RUTH. It's gettin' dark.
KARL. Yeh, it is.
RUTH. What now?
KARL. No idea. *(Silence.)*
RUTH. The sea—
KARL. Yeh I know—
RUTH. Always makes me a bit sad.
KARL. There was somethin' so precious about her—
RUTH. I meant just the sea—on its own.
KARL. Oh?
RUTH. I get the feelin' it'll always sound like it does now. For ever an'
ever.

203

KARL.   What else is new?

RUTH.   I find it a comfort.

KARL.   Some comfort.

RUTH.   You either feel it or you don't.

KARL.   Daft. *(He gets dressed.)*

RUTH.   What's up?

KARL.   This cold wind's been blowin' for ever an' ever an' all.

RUTH.   I see, someone wants to go independent, does he.

KARL.   I'd just like to have a life of my own for once.

RUTH.   Oh Karlie—

KARL.   An' you can pack in the 'Oh Karlie' bit. You're turnin' out a right drag.

RUTH.   Would you mind bein' a bit more explicit?

KARL.   Right, the plain truth. *(Silence.)* The Webers are definitely gettin' ahead quicker'n us. Their mortgage is virtually paid off. It's only us take ages an' ages. Gettin' the Taunus an' the buildin' society thing. But then Elfi's contribution's different again. Not like my wife, weepin' an' moanin' all the time.

RUTH.   Go an' find yourself an Elfi then. You're so naive, Karl. You can feel completely independent now, can't you. Especially from Manu.

KARL.   Hark at her, with her 150 marks take home pay.

RUTH.   I got other opportunities too, you know. An' they've got a bit more in their bank account.

KARL.   Them wop dustmen, I suppose. Openin' a pizza in Rome, are you?

RUTH.   He's a dentist.

KARL.   Drill you all right, does he?

RUTH.   Yeh. An' his hands are especially nice. *(Silence.)* There's somethin' warm about him, human . . .

KARL.   I got somethin' warm an' human too. Could've saved yourself the effort.

RUTH.   I took Manu to him. What with all them sweets from Granma. She had several teeth going black already. You always have to drag things in the dirt—

KARL.   Rubbish. I didn't know. *(Silence.)* D'you remember, she was only six –

RUTH.   No!

KARL.   How come you don't remember all of a sudden? *(Silence.)*

RUTH.   You always come across so cold. I really hate you.

KARL.   I ain't standin' for that. Give me that ring.

RUTH.   I certainly will not.

KARL.   I paid for 'em both.

The children approach, singing, from the left.

RUTH.   They're comin' back now, from their trip. Karl, they're comin' back from the trip!

KARL.   I want my property. *(Silence.)*

RUTH. By the way, were you careful earlier?

KARL. Ruth, you really are the end. Askin' arsehole questions at a time like this.

RUTH. So you weren't.

KARL. State secret.

RUTH. Karl—

KARL. What if I wasn't?

RUTH. It could be serious.

KARL. Don't talk crap! *(Silence.)* For ever landin' me in the shit! An' always the the same shit! Gettin' yourself rammed over an' over. So I never actually get anythin' outa life. I want my freedom for once!

RUTH. Go on then, Karl, you've already hit me twice today. What are you waitin' for? Seein ' I enjoyed it so much, too.

KARL. You've had that coat an' them shoes now.

RUTH. But—

KARL. You got somethin' out of it, didn't you.

RUTH. Well . . .

KARL. Pick your stuff up. We're goin. *(RUTH goes on.)*

RUTH. Come on then.

KARL. We might've left somethin'. It's all worth somethin'.

RUTH. All worth somethin'. *(Silence. A seagull.)* I wouldn't mind 'avin' wings. An' then light an' carefree— *(She gestures as if flying.)*

KARL. Bloody vulture! *(Silence.)* Sometimes the truth's too much to bear. I've got the Tempos here.

RUTH. What for?

Final blackout.

 *Royal Scottish Academy of Music & Drama*

School of Drama

Diploma in Dramatic Art

A 3 year course in professional acting for stage TV and radio. This course is accredited by the National Council for Drama Training and the School of Drama is a member of the Conference of Drama Schools

Diploma in Speech and Drama

A 3 year course in educational and community drama. Discussions are now in progress with the Scottish Education Department and the University of Glasgow for this diploma to be validated by the university as a BA (Dramatic Studies). It is hoped that the first intake to this degree may be admitted in 1981

Technical Certificate

A 1 year course in technical aspects of theatre and TV

Entry to all courses is by interview, plus audition for the diploma courses, held in February, April, May and July each year

Prospectus giving detailed information is available from the Secretary, School of Drama, Royal Scottish Academy of Music & Drama, St George's Place, Glasgow G2 1BS. Tel 041-332 5294.

BIOGRAPHICAL NOTES
compiled by Julian Hilton

Rainer Werner Fassbinder b. 1946. Bad Wörishofen. Attended the acting
school at Munich 1964–66. Then worked at the Aktions theater (Action
Theatre) and Antiteater (Anti-theatre). 1969 awarded a bursary by the
jury of the Gerhart Hauptmann prize (with Harald Mueller) for his play
Katzelmacher (Cock Artist). The film version of the same work was
awarded the German Film Critics' prize and the television prize of the
German Academy of Performing Arts. Now West Germany's most prolific
film maker, his international break through came with *Angst Essen Seele
auf (Fear Eats the Soul)* and more recently with *Maria Braun*.

Friederike Roth b. 1948. Stuttgart. Studied Philosophy and Linguistics
in Stuttgart and then wrote a doctoral thesis on 'Aesthetic Theories in
the 20th Century'. Worked as an assistant at the university, then moved
to South German Radio. Her published work includes *Minimal Tales,*
1970, a collection of poems *Tollkirschenhochzeit (Deadly Nightshade
Marriage)* 1978, and *Schieres Glück (Pure Happiness)* a further collection
of poems, 1980.

Peter Turrini b. 1944, St. Margarethen, Lavanttal, mother Austrian, father
Italian. Passed his leaving exam at the Business college, Klagenfurt, 1963.
1963–1970 various jobs, metal worker, warehouseman, advertising slogan
writer. Drops out for a year to the island of Rhodes; returns to Austria
to write. Starts working as a barman to get an income, but soon able to
become a freelance writer. Lived since 1971 in Vienna; one of the most
performed modern playwrights, both for his own work and his versions
of the classics. Most successful of these is *Der tollste Tag*, (1972), a version
of *The Marriage of Figaro*.

Peter Hacks b. 1928. Breslau. Studied sociology, philosophy, modern
literature and theatre studies in Munich. Awarded doctorate in 1951 for
a thesis on theatre in the Biedermeier period (1815–1848). 1955, against
the trend, moves to East Germany. 1960–63 literary manager and drama
adviser (Dramaturg) at the Deutsches Theater, East Berlin. Since then a
freelance writer. His total of 20 or more original plays and reworkings of
the classics make him one of the most productive and one of the best
known of German writers. 1966 awarded the Lessing prize. His latest
play *Senecas Tod* opened in Berlin at the end of 1981.

Heiner Mueller b. 1929. Eppendorf, Saxony. After Peter Hacks, the most active and respected playwright in the German Democratic Republic. Career begins with socialist realist plays *Der Lohndrücker* (1956) and *Die Korrektur* (1957/58), both premiered in Berlin in 1958. After the official ban on *Der Bau* (1964)—still unperformed—moves towards versions of classics. Break-through in Munich with *Philoktet* (1964). Latest work *Der Auftrag* (1979), well reviewed in the West. Having worked closely with Hacks and Hartmut Lange (who left for the West) now taken a rather different line from Hacks.

Christoph Gahl was brought up in a Protestant vicarage after the Second World War. He studied drama, public relations and music in Hamburg and Berlin. While still a student he worked as a church organist and published numerous essays, reports and short stories in magazines and newspapers. After completing his studies he spent three years as a lecturer in sociology in a newly developed area of Bremen. Several of his publications and television films have also had international recognition. *Intensive Care* is his eighth radio play; he has also written a number of children's plays and short plays for radio. He now lives as a freelance writer in West Berlin, where for some time he was regional chairman of the Association of German Authors.

Franz Xaver Kroetz b. 25.2. 1946. Munich. Attended the acting school at Munich (as did Fassbinder). Continued education at the Max Rheinhardt seminar, Salzburg (together with Martin Sperr, author of *Hunting Scenes in Lower Bavaria*). Worked as an actor in the fringe theatres in Munich, amongst others in Fassbinder's Antiteater. Odd jobs as delivery driver, etc. 1970, awarded the Suhrkamp publishing house bursary (together with Alf Poss). 1975 awarded the 20,000DM Hannover prize for his play *Sterntaler*. Now seldom out of the repertoire.

Harald Mueller b. 18.5.1934, Memel. Worked as miner, docker, bell-hop, translator etc. 1957–60 acting school and study of German literature at Munich. Long stay in USA and Canada. 1962 starts to write. 1970 *Big Wolf* and *Half-German* premiered in Munich, 1972–74 Dramaturg at Schiller Theater Berlin. Translates Shaw. 1974 *Flotsam* and *Silent Night* premiered at Schiller Theater. 1969 shares the writing bursary with R.W. Fassbinder awarded by the jury of the Gerhart Hauptmann prize. 1969/70 awarded the Suhrkamp publishers writing bursary.

Das Ende einer Kunstperiode?

(The end of an artistic era?)

Modern German-language playwrights on their work and on the theatre.

Contents

Introduction

Franz Xaver Kroetz left the Communist Party shortly before the 1980 West German election. He had stood as a communist candidate several times and so his departure caused quite a stir. He had also spent some demonstrative periods working in East Germany which made his move something of a propaganda coup for the West. It is most unlikely that a writer of his standing in Great Britain would have caused so much fuss with his change of political affiliation, but the fact that Kroetz's politics are national news in Germany underlines how very much more political and politicised than Britain's is the German theatre. His change of affiliation is the most visible sign that we may now be witnessing the search for a new cultural base by the German writer, interfered, as such a search inevitably is, with a major political realignment. The cross-section of views we reproduce and analyse in this survey come from eleven working writers for the theatre, some like Peter Hacks with twenty-five years' experience, others like Friederike Roth with relatively little. To orientate these opinions historically within the 'modern classics' of German literature, however, we offer first some of the views expressed by Thomas Mann in his lecture at the Library of Congress, May 29th 1945. It is not just the date of his lecture which matters, but far more the formal acceptance by Mann of the collective responsibility of the German people for the events of 1933–45. The weight of this responsibility has been heavy on writers ever since. But now a younger generation is establishing itself with no need to feel any compulsion to atone for the past. The effect this may have on German culture is incalculable, but at last continuity is being sought with the literary tradition not discontinuity. If German culture abroad can now escape from the strait-jacket of needing to apologise, implicitly or explicitly, for the sins of the fathers, then it too may start to regain the international respect which it deserves.

In 1945 Mann, aged 70, had just taken American citizenship. He asks his audience: 'What dream-wave swept me from the remotest nook of Germany, where I was born, and where, after all, I belong, into this auditorium, on to this platform, to stand here as an American, speaking to Americans?' The imagery is revealing: Mann is like a private thought suddenly and unexpectedly made public by someone whose sub-conscious has just thrown him a googly. It is the imagery of Freud and of the Freudian slip; as the dominant pre-war thinker this influence of Freud is hardly surprising. Yet it is Marx who has held centre stage ever since— certainly until 1980. Is Freud—or perhaps more generally a new sense of the self—once again in the ascendant?

Mann saw in being an American being a 'citizen of the world.' But in 1945 this allowed him no freedom to ignore the key German question— that of war-guilt. 'For anyone who was born a German *does* have something in common with German destiny and German guilt.' That destiny is best caught in Goethe's Faust—'a man who stands at the dividing line between the Middle Ages and Humanism, a man of God who, out of a presumptuous urge for knowledge, surrenders to magic, to the Devil.' But, viewed from a different perspective, Faust is but mid-way between what for Mann are the founder and perfecter of the German language, Martin Luther and Friedrich Nietzsche. And the worrying question that then springs to his mind is that if the language was slowly maturing in the interval between the emergence of its two giants, what is the relationship between that and the growth of nationalism and National Socialism? The answer is a worrying inability of Germans to unite the concepts of liberty and social revolution: 'All the constricting and depressing qualities of German patriotic enthusiasm rest upon the fact that this unity was never achieved.'

The fruits of German culture come from 'inwardness': ' . . . a word that is most difficult to define: tenderness, depth of feeling, unworldly reverie, love of nature, purest sincerity of thought and conscience—in short, all the characteristics of high lyricism are mingled in it, and even today the world cannot forget what it owes the German inwardness: German metaphysics, German music, especially the miracle of the German Lied—a nationally unique and incomparable product—these are the fruits of German inwardness.' And, significantly for the mood of the 80s, Mann diagnoses in Romanticism what seems to be happening again: 'The Germans are the people of the romantic counter-revolution against the philosophical intellectualism and rationalism of enlightenment—a revolt of music against literature, of mysticism against clarity (. . .) It is pessimism of sincerity that stands on the side of everything existing, real, historical against both criticism and meliorism, in short on the side of power against the spirit, and it thinks very little of all rhetorical virtuousness and idealistic disguising of the world.' Mann sees psycho-analysis as a part of this romantic sincere pessimism.

Where Mann anticipates most clearly what was to follow in German literature comes at the end of the lecture: 'The tendency toward self-criticism, often to the point of self-disgust and self-execration, is thoroughly German . . . ' There has been much self-criticism since 1945: but perhaps the most hopeful aspect of the new mood in German culture is that it may start to put off its own burden of self-doubt and guilt.

Herbert Achternbusch

Herbert Achternbusch was born in Munich on November 23, 1938 (according to other sources 1939) and grew up in the little village of Mietraching in Eastern Bavaria. He attended the Art Academy in Nürnberg. A sculptor, painter, writer, film-maker, dramatist and self-exhibitor, he wrote of his life: 'born, grown up, educated, after some odd jobs I'm beating life about the head with attempts to write. I always wanted to experience something somehow.'

He made his debut as a writer with his volume of short stories *Hülle (Cover)* which was followed by a number of other works in prose, a radio play and two novels: *Der Tag wird kommen, (The Day Will Come)* 1973 and *Die Stunde des Todes (One Hour of Death)* 1975. His book *Land in Sicht (Land in Sight)* 1977 was more a collection of film texts than a novel.

All his works are concerned with his fight against depressingly banal surroundings: he attempts to break free from them in intellectual visions which border always on the fantastic and often on the catastrophic. For example, in one of his novels, he says: 'I'd rather be the most stupid of dogs and have my speech than have no speech and talk stupid.' In his book *Land in Sight* he bewails the fact that 'you are in a stilted culture in which you have to think so much because there's so little to live'. A critic said of him: 'to read Achternbusch means looking into a brain at work, which doesn't mean doing serious thinking but rather engaging in animal activity—sweating and dreaming.'

In 1975 he made his first strongly autobiographical feature film *Das Andechser Gefühl (The Andechs Feeling)*. In his second film, *Atlantik-schwimmer (Atlantic Swimmer)*, an almost surrealist work and very far removed from any classic Hollywood picture, he was author, director, producer and one of the main actors. The film was not distributed but was shown on German television. It was followed by *Der Bierkampf (The Beer Battle)* which provoked comparisons with the Munich comic Karl Valentin, which he rejected. He made *Servus Bayern* in 1977 which is in the nature of a farewell to his native Bavaria. In 1978 his first play *Ella* was produced in Stuttgart, and this was performed at the ICA, London, in 1981. In June 1977 he caused a sensation when, on being awarded the Petrarch-Prize, he burned the cheque for 20,000 DM. He is married to Gerda A., and has four children.

In response to questions about his hopes for the 80s put to him by the Munich *Süddeutsche Zeitung* at the end of 1979 Achternbusch replied in a manner not unfamiliar to those who know their way round Dadaism and early Modernism: 'I hope that I don't have to sit any longer in the station begging. A dog helps me with it. Not begging for money any more. For attention. For happpiness. That I don't go blind and can't see who is treading on my fingers. That my dog stays with me. That he doesn't die on me. (Dog = Art)'. Earlier, in 1971, he was rather more expansive about himself to Hella Schlumberger in the Munich *Abendzeitung*, accepting that it was indeed his self which dominated his attention: 'One must simply recognise how one lives oneself. In this respect the dominant factor is not writing but the nature of knowledge.' The remark was far from typical at the time, despite its affinities with the thoughts expressed by Mann in his lecture. Now, however, the importance of the self is growing again for many German writers.

Achternbusch is a rebel in the best traditions of romantic rebellion. He lived in a wood for a while and scavenged from rubbish dumps: 'You should see what they throw away'. Yet this act brought him only one knowledge 'That everything is shit'. Why then does he write? 'There's always this schizophrenia in me that I write and that I pretend not to write. That makes me a complete idiot. I can't accept the fact that I write without beating about the bush, can't accept that I appear in public, that I produce my wares.' The real dilemma of this situation, and one Achternbusch is by no means alone in feeling, is whether to engage in politics or not—whether even the act of living in a given society isn't *de facto* an act of complicity with it: 'You live like everyone else, you act like everyone else and the rest of what you do is merely trains of throught to wipe away the filth which you got all over you, throwing and being thrown at. So you live supporting the system but think endangering the system. That's the discrepancy.'

One important dimension to Achternbusch's work is its acutely Bavarian and organic nature—reflecting itself in a concern with natural forces and with nature as itself as complex and perversely logical as man-made society. In his sketch of his life something of the perverse logic of the organic cycle comes through: 'I had to come into the world in 1938, having already picked my parents. My mother was a sport-loving country beauty who felt at home only in the town; my father was very easy-going and liked to drink, he was very jokey. I had barely arrived in the world before falling victim to hospital, school and the like. I served my time and demanded time off. I wrote books until my bottom was sore; then I made films because I wanted to move about. My children are beginning from the beginning again. Grüss Gott.'

When asked of his other hopes for the 80s, Achternbusch said he wished 'Germany would no longer be afraid of anything except draughts. More than of the politician Strauss. More than of a war.'

Thomas Bernhard

Thomas Bernhard is one of the most successful of all modern writers in German. Since his debut in 1957 with *Auf der Erde und in der Hölle (On Earth and in Hell),* he has worked his way through the three classic genres, starting with poems, moving into the novel and such works as *Das Kalkwerk (The Chalk Mine)* 1970 and then into drama, where he has spent most of the last decade. The plays tend to be dense and linguistically complex dealing in questions of isolation, frustration, emotional and physical handicap and the specifically German handicap of history. The language of *Vor dem Ruhestand (On the Eve of Retirement)*—the 1979 play premièred at the Salzburg summer festival of that year—reflects these concerns:

7

Destroying nature
cutting down trees
cutting down those beautiful old trees
for the sake of a chemical plant
which produces nothing but poison
Profit-mongers everywhere
The world has never been so brutal
profit guides and governs everything
wherever there is still open land
you can be sure that industry will move in
But not here I told them
not here
not in front of my window
where nature is still untouched
I love our view.

Concern for both the emotional and the physical environment is growing rapidly in German-speaking states as a whole, reflected in the emergence of the Green Party, the Peace Movement and considerable television coverage for ecological and environmental abuse. This is clearly a theme of the future.

The question of the past also, quite naturally comes up on the eve of retirement, when the person retiring thinks both forward to the new life and back across the old one:

We were executing a mission
for the welfare of the German people
You are executing your mission
for the welfare of the German people he said
without ever taking his eyes off me
It was impossible to escape him
there was no other choice

There is no way to falsify history
it can be maligned for a long time
much can be hushed up distorted
but then one day it comes to light
shining in its truest colours
that's when the liars the falsifiers are gone
It usually takes decades

The devil must be exorcised by the devil

Shame who didn't know it

(with a glance at Himmler's picture on the bureau)

I lift up my glass
to this man
to this idea

The generation now retiring are, of course, caught on this threshold between past and present and there is a disconcerting similarity of rhetoric and problem—high unemployment, rising crime, social fragmentation—between 1980 and 1930.

A summary of Bernhard's main works shows how busy he has been in nearly a quarter century of literary effort:

Poetry: *Auf der Erde und in der Hölle (On Earth and in Hell)*, 1957. *In Hora Mortis*, 1958. *Unter dem Eisen des Mondes (Underneath the Iron of the Moon)*, 1958.

Prose: *Frost*, 1963. *Amras*, 1964. *Verstörung (Distraction)* 1967. *Prose*, 1967. *Das Kalkwerk, (The Chalk Mine)*, 1970, and a series of short stories and essays.

Plays: *Die Rosen der Einöde (The Roses of Solitude)*, Five Pieces for Ballet, Voices and Orchestra, 1959. *Der Berg (The Mountain)*, A Play for Puppets as Human Beings and Human Beings as Puppets, June 1970. *Ein Fest für Boris (A Celebration for Boris)*, 1970. *Der Ignorant und der Wahnsinnige (The Ignorant Man and the Madman)*, 1972. *Die Jagdgesellschaft (The Hunting Path)*, 1974. *Die Macht der Gewohnheit (The Force of Habit)* 1974. *Der Präsident (The President)*, 1975. *Die Berühmten (The Famous)* 1976. *Minetti*, 1976. *Immanuel Kant*, 1978. *Der Weltverbesserer (The Man Who Changes the World)*, 1979. *Vor dem Ruhestand (Eve of Retirement)*, 1979.

Literary Prizes: Bremen Literature prize, 1965. Austrian state prize for Literature 1967. Wildgans-Prize of the Austrian Industry, 1968. Georg Büchner Prize, 1970.

The dominant impression is that the handicaps under which many of the protagonists suffer are beyond healing, that human nature itself is beyond repair. Bernhard clearly feels this problem in his own self for his relationship with the theatre is curiously tense, on the one hand writing for it and on the other seemingly hating it.

Commenting on Bernhard, Helmut Olles wrote: 'not only the catastrophe of the family but also the catastrophe of each individual is unavoidable in Bernhard's work—products of a thoroughgoing hopelessness: Austria as compost heap, man as the worst symptom of the sickness of sick nature for whom there is no longer a cure—only recognition of the situation'. The mood is a combination of a Büchnerian acceptance of the inevitability of what happens as simply part of an organic and natural need and a Nietzschean artistic strategy of drawing energy for tragedy out of the very recognition that there is no hope, no cure.

In his speech on Bernhard's nomination for the Georg Büchner prize in 1970 Günter Blöcker points out in particular how existential need may be made plausible through linguistic need. This is a theme he shares with many of his contemporaries. Blöcker gives particular weight to Bernhard's statement of 1965: 'we hear, see and feel everything *because we wish to*, not *because Nature so ordains*, which makes our philosophies pointless and keeps our knowledge down at the laughable level of mankind.' Since it is we ourselves who will ourselves to perceive the real object of our attention must be ourselves.

Tankred Dorst

Tankred Dorst is prolific. He regards writing, by his own admission, as a way to himself, so let him speak for himself:

I was born in a village in the Thüringian Forest. The villagers were peasants or made toys in their homes or worked in the engineering factory. That belonged to my grandfather. I have a very strong impression of this grandfather, whom I never knew: he is sitting, a huge pale-skinned man in a bathtub in the garden, he is sitting in water warmed by the sun. He was in his own way a child of nature, a disciple, even, he believed deeply in keeping physical and mental health, and considered illness some kind of crime. In his black notebook he would write down maxims and rules that he himself followed scrupulously. As a child I remember writing them out myself— in the half-light of the large attic which smelt of camomile. His sons, including my father died of TB, an illness which was strictly taboo in the house for the whole of my childhood. I was thirteen when the War began, the Führer's speeches were broadcast to us in the physics lab. At that age I was smitten with a terrible adolescent death wish, I would run around in the damp meadows (now divided by the East German border) I wrote to the poet Lulu von Strauss and Torney, whom I worshipped, I felt I was the lonely outcast, I wanted to plunge from the heavens into the sea, to sacrifice myself, and the war arrived to give me that chance. I saw the end of the War in America: I remember how I got there. It was a case of having to. see New York and so there we were, creeping up from below decks where we'd spent many days and nights, up narrow corridors and iron stairways and suddenly there was the night above me and the city all round brilliantly lit up in the glow of peace and the ship glided slowly and silently into the middle of it all. A city that did not go dark at night, that was something outside the world I knew. During my years in prison I had read a lot, everything I could put my hands on: tracts from different sects, from Dostoievsky, I read Toller, Zweig, Werfel, Heine, hitherto unknown German literature to me and it was in this cramped life in the camp with all kinds of people, in the work in factories, on farms on the railways, that I really received my eduction. Once we had to dig under a house that stood in concrete supports and it was down there in semi darkness taking shifts with the others of digging and reading aloud that I got to know the book that was to be by far the most influence on me: Thomas Mann's *Magic Mountain,* two yellow paperback volumes which we had almost completely finished by the time we surfaced from beneath the house.
   When I was released I spent some time wondering what I would do without work, money or contacts. I did a bit of crossing the border, smuggling and black market work. In Wuppertal two actors asked me to write a cabaret so we could at least live, but I couldn't, I hadn't the imagination. I remember the currency reform, I remember the June night lying under the bushes behind the Hildebrandt Fountain in Munich, listening to shouting and noises from the station as people stormed onto the last trains to get home. Entrance exams in Münsterland. Studying in Münich until the mid-fifties. A fellow student who had lost his leg in the War, said he was too embarrassed to continue. The cripples disappeared from the lecture halls, the post-war years were at an end. I hadn't finished studying. I stayed in my cold room, covered myself with the carpet and couldn't imagine what I would do in my life. Then there appeared, first his stop half seen from the window below, a dramaturg; he came up and said: my project had been well received, could I write dialogue?

There was a competition for a play in project form. The Mannheim Theatre gave out themes, the current ones of that period: the refugee problem, the atomic bomb, racial conflict, none of which interested me. My experience had been different: contradictory and fragmented, and comic in a confused way. So the first play I wrote was a free adaptation of Tieck's *Gestiefeltem Kater (Puss-in-boots)* a piece that in a grotesque way brought all the artistic possibilities of the theatre into play and at the same time questioned their validity. It ended with a battle between the jailed author and the public over who should change: those who make theatre or those who watch it. There are no sure positions: everything is masks, caprice, make-believe and everything is play. I wrote them pretty quickly, one after the other, the latest one always written to beat out the predecessor that hadn't pleased me. I do believe many were not worth the effort, I was searching for reality, I wanted to write realistically and did not succeed. I knew too little or I shut myself out of what I did know. Not until *Toller* which appeared in 1968 but which I wrote 2 years earlier did I find a genuine reality and tried to some degree to transcribe it word for word into a play. I identified a lot with Toller, I wanted to criticise him by setting the overwhelming realities of that time and the political situation against his expressionistic, for me too generalised love of humanity. I wrote in search of real people, scenes, fragments of scenes, tableaux, dialogues—a whole pile which I organized into a disorderly review of the Munich Soviet Republic, which I knew little about when I started: I learnt as I wrote.

I have since then written almost exclusively for the theatre, sometimes working directly with a company; for Bochum, with Zadek, the Revue *Kleiner Mann was nun? (What Now Little Man?)* after Fallada; for Frankfurt, with Palitzsch, *Goncourt oder die Abschaffung des Todes (Goncourt or the Abolition of Death)* also with Chéreau in Milan and Villurbane: I prefer rehearsals to performances and during them I alter, add, shorten, change round my conception of what I have written, to suit the specific conditions of the theatres—and not without some pain. But a play is not something complete even if it is constructed with every gesture, step, look and silence between the dialogues in advance. So much arrives with the direction and so many people contribute to it before it becomes a theatrical performance. The author who writes for the theatre must protect himself, he can be submerged and suffer. But that he must always be arguing with the people of the theatre and that with his play he is directly confronted with the public, the enemy on this evening, during these 3 hours (he's not allowed any more time for this battle): that, I think, prevents him from losing himself into the esoteric or from petrifying in the 'Zeitferne' (time distance).

(From: *Deutsche Akademie für Sprache und Dichtung Jahrbuch 1978*, Heidelberg 1978)

Dorst's output may be measured in outline as follows:

Plays: *Geheimnisse der Marionette (Secrets of the Marionettes)* 1957, Munich.
Auf kleiner Bühne (On Small Stages) Puppet Show, 1959, Munich.
Die Kurve (The Curve) Farce, 1960, Lübeck.
Gesellschaft im Herbst (Society in Autumn) Comedy, 1960, Mannheim.
Freiheit für Clemens (Freedom for Clemens) Farce, 1960, Bielefeld.
Große Schmährede an der Stadtmauer (Great Diatribe at the City Wall) 1961, Lübeck.

Die Mohrin (The Negress) 1964, Frankfurt.
Der gestiefelte Kater oder Wie man das Spiel spielt (Puss-in-boots or How you Play the Game) Comedy, after Ludwig Tieck, 1964, Hamburg.
Der Richter von London (The Judge of London Comedy, after Dekker's *The Shoemaker's Holiday)* 1966, Essen.
Wittek geht um (Wittek gets Around) Comedy, 1967 Düsseldorf and Berne.
Toller 1968 Württemberg. Dir: Palitzsch
also   1970 Piccolo Teatro, Milan, Dir: Chéreau
          1973 Lyon Dir: Chéreau
          1974 TNP Paris, Dir: Chéreau
Dem Gegner den Daumen aufs Auge und das Knie auf die Brust (To Your Opponent a Thumb in the Eye and a Knee in the Chest) Political Revue on the Munich Soviet Republic 1969, Westfalischen Landestheater, Castrop-Rauxel.
Kleiner Mann, was nun? (Little man, what now?) 1972, Bochum, Dir: Zadek
Eiszeit (Ice-age) with Ursula Ehler 1973, Bochum, Dir: Zadek
Auf dem Chimborazo (On the Chimborazo) Comedy, with Ursula Ehler, 1975, Schosspark-Theater, Berlin
Goncourt oder die Abschaffung des Todes (Goncourt or the Abolition of Death) with Horst Laube, 1977, Frankfurt, Dir: Palitzsch.
Merlin oder Das wüste Land (Merlin or The Wasted Land) with Ursula Ehler, 1979.
Die Villa, 1980, Württemberg and Düsseldorf.
Translations: *Rameaus Neffe (Rameau's Nephew)* Diderot, 1963, Nuremberg.
Der Geizige (The Miser) Molière, 1967, Stuttgart, Dir: Zadek.
Der Pott (The Sliver Tassie) O'Casey, 1967, Wuppertal, Dir: Zadek.
Der eingebildete Kranke (The Hypochondriac) Molière, 1968, Kassel.
Libretti: *La Buffonata* Music: Killmayer, 1961, Heidelberg.
Yolimba oder Die Grenzen der Magie (Yolimba or The Limits of Magic) Music: Killmayer
Die Geschichte von Aucassin und Nicolette (The History of Aucassin and Nicolette) Music: Bialas, 1969, Munich.
Der gestiefelte Kater Music: Bialas, Schwetzing Dir: Rennert 1975
                                    Berlin, DDR Dir: Chundala 1978
Film & TV: *Die Kurve* 1961 Dir: Zadek
Rotmord (Red Murder) 1965, from Toller, with Peter Zadek.
Piggies 1969 Film with Zadek
Sand TV Film with Ursula Ehler. Dir: Palitzsch
Eiszeit TV Dir: Zadek
Mosch (Rubbish) 1980, TV and Cinema Film

Prose: *Die Münchener Raterepublik (The Munich Soviet Republic),* 1966.
Rotmord oder I was a German 'Ansehbuch', with Zadek and Gehrke.
Werkbuch über Tankred Dorst, Suhrkamp, 1974.
Dorothea Merz 'Fragmentary Novel' Suhrkamp 1976. Televised 1976, Dir: Beauvais,
Klaras Mutter (Klara's Mother) Suhrkamp, 1978. Televised 1978, Dir: Dorst.

Peter Hacks

Having been a student in Munich in the 50s—he wrote his doctorate on theatre in the period 1815–48, the Biedermeier—at Brecht's invitation Peter Hacks moved from the West to the East. Despite frequent difficulties with the authorities he has stayed in the East and represents a large number of similar thinkers, often misunderstood in the West, who criticise the East but with no intention of trying to import Western ideas as substitute. This stance of radical socialism—anti-totalitarian and democratic in ways not tolerated in either East or West—of course has recently had its most vigorous expression in Polish Solidarity. Russian keenness to suppress such movements stems from a fear that, once established, the tight-knit apparatus of the Communist Party could collapse: but to understand Hacks' position, we have to make a considerable political leap, towards a 'non-Western' socialist opposition.

Appended to the first printing of *Plundersweilern* in the West was a statement 'Warum ich für nichts kann' ('Why I can't help what I do'). Recently reprinted the play still has the same appendage and may therefore stand for Hacks' present aesthetic and cultural-political views.

I
Like all my rewrites of classic stories the work I did on *Plundersweilern* (based on a play of the same name by Goethe, written in 1778) arose out of a combination of an old liking for the original play, a flaw in it and a specific theatrical need. The process is always the same.
Someone—a theatre or a director or, like this time, a vagabond theatre group—asks me:
  But what shall we perform?
  I leaf through my brain and recommend:
  This and that.
  —What is that?
  —Ah, a play, a great play!
The relevant person goes away, reads and returns:
  But you can't perform that, really.
  —If I tell you.
  —If I tell you . . .
Then I go away and read. Then I have to write.

II

I wanted, I promise on my reputation as an honest man, simply to add the missing third act.

Then I felt the need for more fun, I mean more seriousness;
I changed here and cut there until in my hands little of Goethe's funny story was left.

In its place arose, rather surprisingly, something that Goethe at the outset had intended to do.

The first version of *Plundersweilern* shows the ridiculous struggle of a bureaucratised enlightenment with down-at-heel sensibility. Mine is, in fact, about just the same thing. It shows the stupid misunderstandings which arise between the grosser and the finer flatheads.

That is just as true for Haman's quarrel with Mordechai as the Schoolmaster's with the Principal. It is true of the loutish scenes between the town-crier and the silhouette-cutter, between the Costermonger and the Policeman, between the respectable town women and the little tramp. It concerns in particular—and here it accords most happily with the original dramatic conception of the play—the relationship between the people and the theatre.

It may well be that I have already written about this material, but which is the funnier?

III

My references are checkable. If I was able with *Helena* and *Polly* to build on the fact that the aesthetic magistrates of this most hypocritical of centuries without exception would be impudent enough to praise me without even the most cursory of glances at the original, here it is equally likely that one or other of them will have an inherited edition of Goethe in their otherwise scanty library . . .

—Enough, good. Then tell us, what else should we do?

—Hrosvith von Gandersheim.

—But they aren't plays.

—Ah, what a talent, what a dramatic talent!

The stage works: a brief survey 1955–1975:

Eröffnung des indischen Zeitalters (Opening the Indian Age) 1954,
(premiered 17 March 1955 Kammerspiele, Munich)

Das Volksbuch vom Herzog Ernst (The Folk-book of Duke Ernst) 1955,
(premiered 21 May 1967, Mannheimer Nationaltheater)

Die Schlacht bei Lobositz (The Battle at Lobositz) 1955–56,
(premiered 1 Dec 1956 Deutsches Theater, Berlin)

Der Müller von Sanssouci (The Miller of Sanssouci) 1958,
(premiered 15 March 1958 Deutsches Theater, Berlin).

Die Sorgen und die Macht (The Worries and the Power) First Version 1958,
(premiered Spring 1959, Deutsches Theater), Second Version 1960
(premiered 15 May 1960 Theater der Bergarbeiter, Senftenberg)
Third Version 1962 (premiered Oct 1962, Deutsches Theater, Berlin)

Polly oder die Bataille am Bluewater Creek (Polly or the Skirmish at Bluewater Creek) 1963 (after John Gay) (premiered 19 June 1965, Halle)

Moritz Tassow 1965 (premiered 5 Oct 1965 Volksbühne, Berlin)

Margarete in Aix 1966 (premiered 23 Sept 1969, Basel)

Amphitryon 1968 (premiered 17 Feb 1968, Göttingen)

Omphale 1970 (premiered 7 March 1970, Frankfurt am Main)

Adam und Eva 1973
Das Jahrmarktsfest zu Plundersweilern (Market day at Plundersweilern)
1973 (Premiered 1975, Berlin)
Rosie träumt (Rosie Dreams) 1974 (Premiered Berlin 1975)
Prizes:
Lessing Prize, 1956; German Critics' Prize, 1971.

Franz Xaver Kroetz

Like many other modern German writers, Kroetz began by adapting
classics or using motifs as the starting point for his own work. His first
play *Romeo and Julia 66* (1966) was in this mould as were *Julius Caesar*
and *Oblamov* (both 1968). In 1970 he broke through with three plays
Heimarbeit (Homework), Hartnäckig (Stubborn) and *Männersache (Men's
Business)*. Since then his output has been regular and successful, both
in West Germany and abroad. Though Kroetz has now left the Communist
Party, his drama still is seen as part of a wider, and more important
political struggle against oppression, capitalism, alienation and inarti-
culacy. To understand his plays, his political views need at least to be
taken into account. Kroetz has written thirty or more plays which have
been performed in fifty countries. In Sweden he is the most successfully
performed foreign writer. Among his best known plays are *Wildwechsel
(Rutting Time)*, 1968, *Stallerhof* 1972, *Das Nest (The Nest)*, 1976,
Mensch Meier (Tom Fool) 1977. His play *Der stramme Max (Strapping
Max)* 1979, was first performed at the Ruhrfestspiele in Recklinghausen.

He has just finished his latest play about the introduction of modern
technology in the printing industry called *Nicht Fisch Nicht Fleisch
(Neither Fish Nor Fowl)* 1980, which deals with the varied effects this
has on the work and lives of two workers and their families. All his
plays are about 'ordinary' people, small farmers, industrial workers,
and their families. Kroetz brings their 'normal' life in everyday situations
to the stage, revealing how life—despite all kind of illusions—is determined
by the basic class struggle between capital and labour. He is not interested
in 'individual' problems.

After leaving the CP he gave an interview to the *Neue Arbeiter Presse*
explaining his present position. Living closely with a particular community
is most important to him, as it is to Achternbusch and Bernhard. He is
suspicious of artificial meetings with 'workers' in order to get material
for his plays, and much prefers the knowledge he has to stem from
genuine relationships which grow out of his belonging to a community.
Talking of *Mensch Meier* he said:

What interested me most in *Mensch Meier* was a man who was not yet 'broken'
completely but who had been 'broken' through the alienation of labour; how he
transfers this helplessness in its final stage onto this family, and how—dialectics
on a small scale—those trampled upon hit back—his wife and son decide to leave
this mad man.

That process interests me, not out of compassion for certain sections of the working-class who have to engage in alienating labour; I don't even feel the need to show the urgent problems of industrial society, although there are many.

I always write about relatively marginal problems and I like writing about them—these are subjects which fascinate me. They have to fascinate me just as much as they have to inspire me artistically.

My plays are absolutely fictitious; I am not at all interested in how somebody else feels about something—I couldn't care less—I have to feel it myself.

Of course, the processes of work are important—so I don't want to make any mistakes. I was in Goteborg and they told me: 'We were at Volvos—it's exactly how you portrayed it.' That must be right—one shouldn't write about proletarians when one hasn't got knowledge about fundamental things like that. But more important—everything which has to do with thinking, feeling and doing in a play must be fictitious. That's the difference between playwriting and reporting.

Not surprisingly, Kroetz is more concerned with contemporary issues than with history, although there are distinct echoes of the problems before and during the Third Reich in the modern world he portrays. The key, however, is 'confrontation' especially the confrontation engendered by historical forces—such as capital and labour—in conflict.

His reasons for leaving the CP were perhaps more cumulative than dramatic and sudden, but one factor stands out:

What I've done—and that's what a party member shouldn't be doing—was to forget about the party and think to myself: what do you really want, where are you going? Do you want to be loyal to the party or what? And then I took my decision: I will vote for the SPD in the autumn and to a certain extent I also want the people who have listened to me until now (that sounds a bit bigheaded), well, I want them to know that too.

The 'autumn' he refers to is that of 1980 when Helmut Schmidt led the Social Democrat-Liberal coalition back to power against Franz Josef Strauss and the Christian Democrat alliance. What Kroetz underlines, however, is how hard it is to write to a particular political programme without, sooner or later, wishing to explore its limits in ways the politicians don't like. Hacks has the same problem.

Kroetz talks forcefully of the specific problems the writer faces:

As committed writers we do not put ourselves at the centre of attention, but instead portray the working people, the weak, the fringe groups of society. We write for those who cannot afford a court writer. Literature, especially committed literature, should not be treated as a sub-division of publicity work, not even when the bourgeoisie pays the leading article writers a high fee.

In literature I always prefer the artist who talks not about eternity but about unemployment, which I hope won't last forever. I believe that the dialectic between content and form moves so radically that one can in general, say that there can emerge no new form from old content, and that pure form in itself is never revolutionary.

On the other hand, new revolutionary content cannot be poured into old formal pipes. New revolutionary thoughts are not art. They lack an adequate radical aesthetic.

We realists especially should accept form as the radical reality, and not just as mediation. Today I feel more in a crisis of form than a crisis of content. In many of my fellow writers' texts I detect similar difficulties. Our traditional methods of presentation in our works often fail to move reality forward in a complex way. The world processes have become more complicated as well. We can only move with them when we have at our disposal adequately complex methods of presentation.

We need a radical form. There is not only socialist realism, but also a socialist aesthetic. And 'meaning well' is still the opposite of art. He who, in the heat of the fight, however hot it may be, throws away the form in order to fight better, throws away a part of his weapon. Art without teeth is no art. Art without form is no art either. But if art—and committed literature should be, must be, art—if art is the most real, painful and human expression of longing for harmony, never mind how bloody the subject may be (like Picasso's *Guernica),* then art has to be in a fighting position.

This sense of needing a 'fighting position' characterises not only Kroetz's stance but also that of many of his contemporaries, not least for those in the West because of the relatively easy life many of them are allowed by West Germany's capitalist success, a success which all too easily dulls the radical political will.

Kroetz works in the theatre because it is so immediate: but he is also acutely aware of the degree of isolation in which writers, even for the theatre, tend to live. How to reconcile this isolation with political commitment remains a great problem:

When I came to understand that again I had consciously taken a stand with the working class, out of which I had wanted to write myself, I committed myself strongly and I stood up for it strongly, because I realised that my profession has the tendency to isolate you; it is the professional disease of all writers. I had the feeling that I was writing myself away from others; I had got to ward against it so that I would not become homeless. I mistrusted writing totally. I also wanted to leave out my little Ego, the writing Ego, which you cannot influence with short-term experiences and recognitions, even if they are very deep. I only wanted to be politically active. That was wrong for myself, but it was a productive mistake; what remained was that I made bigger demands on my writing.

I have said a lot before about the subjective Ego of the writer. But the objective Ego, which is the situation of the writer in society, is especially endangered; he has none of the securities which the trade union movement has fought for and gained over the years, the decades of struggle. That objective Ego, from which the writer himself closes his eyes, must be the starting point to integrate himself with the fighting part of society. If he recognises the interconnections he will not be alone. If he feels afflicted he must take up the fight on the side of the working class.

Horst Laube

Like Hacks, on whom he has written, Laube is both critic and playwright, a combination Anglo-Saxons tend to find difficult to accept. He studied philosophy at Marburg and Vienna and then became literary editor of newspapers in Essen and Wuppertal. From 1968–72 he was the senior 'Dramaturg' (literary manager and adviser) at the Wuppertal theatre, followed by a spell as dramaturg in Frankfurt, 1972–77. His first play *Der Dauerklavierspieler (The Non-stop Pianist)* was performed at the Schauspielhaus in Frankfurt, under the direction of Luc Bondy. He then collaborated with Tankred Dorst on a second play *Goncourt oder die Abschaffung des Todes (Goncourt or the Abolition of Death)* which was first performed at the same theatre in 1977, under the direction of Peter Palitzsch. *Der erste Tag des Friedens (The First Day of Peace)* was written in 1978, and in 1980 came *Endlich Koch (At Last Koch)*. As well as this dramatic output, Laube has written several novels, books on the theatre and radio-plays.

In *The First Day of Peace* Laube's concern is with the psycho-pathology of the nuclear family in its normal state—understanding by 'normal' something psychotically flawed. The family, led by the father, is in revolt against a world that seems to the father to be destroying him: 'It's like this. They want to force me to get a check-up. To see if I'm fit to work.' The logic of his obsession leads him to see the whole of his environment as set against him. Laube summarizes:

Jakob Nachthage's fear of the world outside has built itself into a mad system. A process that takes place in the head here turns into a movement of resistance whose strategy determines the whole life and behaviour of the Nachthage family: emergency training for the coming liberation, the first day of peace.

The structures of petit-bourgeois family relationships seem to be made to suit this defensive strategy. The members of the family adapt themselves to the plan with the utmost ease. None of them needs change his 'normal' role in this hermetic system; the mother whose fate is that of her husband's, the son, who is no longer a child of revolt but rather a youth with a desire to conform and who identifies thankfully with a strong system; the daughter, whose oedipal relationship with her father indicates she would like to take over her mother's place; and finally, the father, Jakob, who shores up his existence with the Bible—all behave as a normal family might. But all are caught in an emotional and sociological no-man's land.

Commenting on the première of the play in Düsseldorf, Lukas Rüsch wrote:

Laube develops a dramatic technique that contradicts any simple notion of causality, which he calls the 'dramaturgy of experimental methodology'. With this term he links himself with Heiner Mueller's conception of theatre as a 'laboratory of social fantasy'. As in the laboratory—so argues Laube—the theatre's business is to use certain elements of reality to set up experiments. The constellation of the elements in relation to one another, the methodology of the experiment, stand in this process for the context of the laboratory, or likewise of the theatre, but not for reality as such. The experiment has succeeded if it stimulates the social fantasy of the audience with all its wishes and dreams.

Günther Rühle sees a continuity between Laube's novels and plays: 'His subjects are the fixations of the human psyche on experiences, wishes and imagined goals that determine a whole life-span.' The way he sees reality is also his reason for excluding the dramatic from his plays, which

18

one can hardly call 'drama' any more, but rather scenic snap-shots. 'The central experience, according to Laube 'of several playwrights in West and East Germany is that of history seemingly stopped in its tracks, depoliticised, administered and lacking in imagination. The dramatist, traditionally dependent on large-scale conflicts, where possible, and recognisable movements, sees no movement, sees above all stasis, historical landscapes cast in concrete. How should he react with his plays against this evil whose roots nestle in the depths of German history?'

Writing on Hacks, Laube singles out this feeling of being caught in the crossfire of two forces neither of which one admires as Hacks's major dilemma. But what he says is pertinent in more general terms:

His theatre should, by rights, convey that energy to its audience which comes from the creative dialectic between task and solution. But Hacks makes things more difficult for himself. Between the camp of the poet and the camp of his products lies a no-man's-land that, or so it seems, is getting bigger. This land is getting darker. Is this so because the movement of this period, such as there is, is slowing down? As a result, the point at which the flawed world and the anticipation of Utopia of form as realisable possibility (the point can only be the consensus of Author and Audience) dissolve. It is certain that his theatre at present lacks both the wrong and the right kind of applause, lacks both the wrong and the right kind of resistance. Apparently one may not yet wake the sleeping dogs of the classics without being eaten by them.

And besides, one who is a poet and not just engineer to his themes and images, runs the risk more openly of sharing their fate. Peter Hacks—or at least so it seems from here —is participating himself in a movement whose direction is timelessness. Hard to say if he wants this or not.

The tendency which Laube sees in Hacks seems to be quite widespread, towards a more aesthetic and perhaps more élitist and private view of theatre than in the past twenty years, where theatre has been a forum of public debate. Private life is more emphasised and public issues given less weight. The question Laube poses, as to whether authors want this shift to happen, may perhaps be answered with a provisional yes; but it is also certain that the growing concern for private experiences is not intended as a snub to more political concerns. Rather the interest has switched to the effects of political decisions where previously they had focussed on the cause— and the causers.

Heiner Mueller

Heiner Mueller first came to attention in the West as a result of difficulties he had with the East German authorities over his play *Die Umsiedlerin oder das Leben auf dem Lande (The Resettled Woman or Life in the Country)* 1961. This was performed on the stage of the East Berlin University of Economics where it met with official disapproval. In *Der Lohndrücker (The Wage Cutter)*, 1956, set in 1948/49 just as the East began to rebuild, Mueller considered how the hopes for a radically new sort of socialist state generated the enthusiasm and energy needed for rebuilding. *Die Korrektur (The Correction)* 1957-8, takes place eight years later on a large building-site. The enthusiasm has gone and the problems remain, the same sort of problems as Hacks was tackling at the same time in *The Power and the Worries.* The workers are caught between knowing that the old system of labour contracted to an entrepreneur is dead but not yet able to come to terms with the notion of property as commonly owned, labour as for the general good. The villain, if only by implication, of this failure is the Party, not ideologically but in practice, since it is a failure of practical education which has caused the failure of energy.

By 1969 the dream of a Utopia, which still underpins Mueller's plays well into the 1960s seemed, according to Henning Rischbieter to have gone—from Hacks and Hartmut Lange as well. In their place came— so Rischbieter in 1974—a mixture of thought-games, escapism and rather complex visions of 'reality.' Mueller comes out into the open in 1975 in a discussion in which he took part on the issue of translating Shakespeare: 'An author who knows his business won't want to know much more about his plays when he has finished them.' Polemically, he agrees with Brecht that 'What makes art works last is their mistakes. As long as something has mistakes it is alive'. On the act of writing he is less laconic: 'As author I would say this: When you start to write you have the need to make something that is perfect. And the longer you do this the more you notice those passages where you have failed. And then I have the increasing feeling I should leave them as they are, even when I know that there is something not working.' Most significantly, however, and despite the difficulties he faced, Mueller stands behind the concept on which the East German state is based, for that concept makes his role as artist much clearer and socially more relevant: talking of the 'increasing difficulty of theatre people, at least in the West, of finding a social purpose for their work' he reckons that the West views 'work as increasingly an aim in itself'.

Like Hacks, with whom he once worked closely, Mueller turned away from the dangerous present to the past in his play *Herakles 5,* but in one respect there is no change. This is the vision of the world as battle-ground. Werner Brettschneider summarises as follows: ' The dramatist who experiences the world as a battle cannot rid his consciousness or his language of the conception of a coming apocalypse.' It was in fact with another 'classical' piece, *Philoktet* that Mueller broke through in the West, a play that began its highly successful run in Munich in July 1968. It was the mixture of Mueller's dense and imagistic language and his remarkable sense of controlled tension which were singled out for praise, and in *The Mission* he shows he has, if anything got even better in both respects.

Uwe Schweikert, in discussion with Mueller, has caught Mueller's concerns particularly well: 'Heiner Mueller, who has always refused to play the part of the oppressed intellectual has increasingly become,

through his work, the most decisive and sharpest critic of the perversion of socialism, of the "petrifaction of a hope". But he has nevertheless not withdrawn his basic assent to a view that still sees in socialism the only possible way of bringing into being the realm of possibilities (. . .) If one surveys the Production-plays, those plays drawn from and about the construction of socialism, so one can see from *The Wage Cutter* (1956) to the dramatisation of the revolutionary novel *Cement* by Fedor Gladkow, completed in 1972, an increasing differentiation of plot, of action, an increasingly penetrative analysis of the contradictions of the processes of history. In the same way, the aesthetic targets Mueller sets himself get more demanding: the large-scale form demands a language in which poetic prose and Shakespearian rhythms alternate and complement each other, a form of montage in which increasing numbers of different components of the most varied origins— particularly those which come from the liberation of ancient greek history and mythology—are made into a fully-synthesised totality.'
Not surprisingly, Mueller sees in the myths a series of models of human— and therefore class—conflict.

The key to Mueller's language lies in his sense of image, and his poem of the subject elucidates his attitude:

> Images mean everything in the beginning. Are lasting. Spacious.
> But the dreams trickle away, become form and disappointment.
> Even the sky can no longer retain an image. The cloud, from the plane
> Seen as a vapour that interrups the view.
> The crane now only
> A bird.
> Even communism, the closing image, that always refreshed
> Because, washed with blood, again and again, everyday life
> Repays with small change, unexciting, with sweat
> Blind
> Ruins, the great poems, like bodies, long loved and
> Now no longer needed, on the road of the squandering
> Limiting genre
> Between the lines crying
> Happy at bones of the stone carrier
> For the beautiful means the possible end of the terror.

The feeling much of Mueller's work engenders in its audience is of being present with what feels like an imagistic sub-text as the text itself, inviting one to construct the main text for oneself. To achieve this the audience must work hard, and it was by no means disadvantageous that the première of *The Mission* in East Berlin was to an audience of 40 with a cast of 5, giving a ratio of 1:8 (actor:audience) of a kind generous enough to make the reconstruction of the more complex images that much easier.

In 1979 Mueller was awarded the prize of the city of Mülheim, but he did not attend the prize-giving. In a letter he explained why, then going on to give some views on theatre, especially theatre in the West:

The subject matter of modern drama is the Already or Still, a question of political standards, of the reduced man. On the reduction of man many of the best brains and giant industries are hard at work. Consumerism is the training of the masses in this process, each product a weapon, each supermarket a training camp. That elucidates the need for art as a means to make reality impossible, The weight of the masses, a precondition of capitalism, in socialism is a corrective to politics, the blindness of experience the proof of its authenticity. (. . .) My solidarity is with Franz Xaver Kroetz and his heroic attempt to claim communism as the centre of your world which has nothing but a political vacuum as its present centre, although my experience would suggest that it is more the vacuum than communism which is likely to succeed.

Mueller's enthusiasm for Kroetz is now perhaps a little tempered.

Maria Reinhard

Maria Reinhard is one of a number of women now writing for the theatre (Friederike Roth is another) and whose perceptions and style cause considerable upheavals in what till very recently has been a very male-dominated world. She studied theatre and sociology in Munich and at the same time worked at various student and fringe (Keller) theatres. In 1969 she became an assistant at the Kammerspiele in Munich and in 1971 moved to the Schauspielhaus in Hamburg where she directed her first play in an established theatre. In 1975 she left Hamburg to work freelance and in 1978 she started to write for the theatre.

Maria Reinhard's fringe experience led to her joining a group to set up a community theatre company TIK (Theater in der Kreide—Theatre in the Chalk) in Neuperlach near Munich. Like community theatre groups in England, this company tackles contemporary issues, and baby battering is the subject of her *Schlag auf Schlag (Blow on Blow)*. The play is based on the report of an actual case of Veronika M, 37, a housewife charged with the maltreatment of Angelika, 6. Reinhard summarizes:

Veronika M. relates how it happened. She describes her childhood and youth, which she spent in numerous institutions, how beatings affected her relations to other people, how flight became the only possible means of survival. She talks of her marriage, its collapse, the endless search for a secure, peaceful existence; of her five children, two of whom were precipitously put into care when their mother had to go away; of the long fight to get them back, of the shock, which her daughter Angelika was unable to cope with.

Veronika M. describes the ever-tightening chains of mistrust and authority. We learn of her love for the child, her desire to keep her, her helplessness in the face of her own behaviour, her 'losing control', the second removal of her child into a home and the renewed fight to get her out.

During the long separation the child grew distant from her and under the pressure of the situation she loses any chances of getting through to the severely disturbed Angelika. In her life beatings had been the way she had learnt things and she adopts the same way of 'helping' herself and her child. She turns for support to all the available people, but the vicious circle of authority moves too rapidly for her to break through it on her own. Her maltreatment of the child becomes so serious that outsiders finally intervene and the case is reported. Veronika M's child is finally taken away from her and sent permanently into an institutionalized existence.

Veronica M. will not, however, give up. She tries to learn from the experience, she wants to change. She describes her efforts to bring up her other children without hitting them. She draws on all her vitality and deep belief in humanity, but she is aware that the others, that is society, must also change.

The problem Reinhard tackles is much like Laube's in *The First Day of Peace* an 'everyday' occurrence like baby-battering which we are used to seeing from the outside—and condemning the mother—but which needs to be seen from the inside as well. This requires of the playwright the documentary neutrality of the good journalistic report, and in her article on the source for Reinhard's play—Karlheinz Knuth's radio presentation of the specific case-study—Hedwig Rohde points to the factors which Reinhard found so important in achieving this objectivity:

There is one type of offence to which the naive listener responds with particular sympathy for the victim, for it is very hard to plead for a fair hearing for the guilty party: that is the maltreatment of helpless children. Karlheinz Knuth's 'original sound' report is, as far as I know, the first attempt to present such a case of a parent 'overstepping permissible punishment' without taking any emotional position, with no other commentary save that of the social workers, police, prosecutors, court doctors and children's home personnel. The effect is all the more shattering as none of them talks about events which normally induce high feelings in newspaper readers, except in a purely factual way (sometimes alarmingly as official 'experts' and sometimes humanely concerned behind their professional impartiality).

The level of emotion is set by the 'inhuman' mother herself in the author's sober, tight, concise and very modern direction. Knuth shows the 'Example of Veronika M.' the mother with problems, and not the 'Case of Martina M.' the maltreated child. He has discovered a classic example of a woman who embodies typical socio-psychological tensions and who must awaken sympathy in even the most uncritical of listeners. This Veronika M. is one of those mothers who have been damaged by the well-known world of social-workers and courts, who loves her child and fights to keep it, although she knows what she has done to it and may do again as soon as she 'loses control', because in the pressure of the situation she no longer knows how to behave towards her. It is hard for Frau M. to be articulate, but the will to be so is burningly obvious. She begins talking in Berlin dialect of her own childhood memories, and every sound is genuine: 'Well, I don't really know about it any more, but I do know that my father got in somehow and my parents started fighting and my mother was crying—and— *(hesitating)*—I don't know, something happened, anyway my father got me by the leg and bashed me against the cupboard. And then my mother got between us and—well I can't remember that far back. Well, and then I was back in the home, and then sometimes, in between I was, I was at my grandmother's.' Veronika M. wanted to spare her own children the Home. There are five—Martina was the only difficult one. What happened to her, as the proesecutor said, was typical of 'cases of moderate severity'. Nevertheless charges were made because the five-year-old was found to have shown signs of maltreatment and to have been tied to her bed while her mother was 'at work'. The matter took its own course and several times Martina, to whom she still clung, but who she found just too much on top of the other children, was officially taken away without notice; for two years Veronika M. could not discover the address of the Foster home.

We now come to the child's double tragedy: barely adjusted to her foster-mother, Martina has to go back home again—the two mothers confused in her mind, Martina is now more obstinate and less approachable than ever and 'rescue' by the helpful foster-parents is merely a matter of time: eventually, changed, and also disfigured by a terrible blow across the face, Martina becomes malicious and cannot be left alone with the foster-parents' own children. Final solution: the feared Home, which means six homes and clinics in the space of a year. And so Martina becomes one of those immediately recognisable children who suffer most clearly from Hospitalitis. The programme gives the facts and leaves nothing out. All the participants have obviously done their best to avoid sensational scandal of any kind or suggestion of negligence on the part of the social workers.

But the voice of the mother constantly reminds one of the helplessness of society in the face of such misery: 'I don't know what would've happened, if my sister-in-law hadn't reported me. Either I would've stopped hitting her, or just let everything carry on as it was. But what would've happened then? I know I wouldn't have stayed a human being. Or, but . . . if that had got worse . . . I just don't know, I can't say. I'm really sorry. I'd really like her back again, but I'm not sorry for myself, it's for the little one . . . . I just can't bear to think about it . . . But I really didn't want to give her away, I really wanted to keep her. How I'm supposed to do that, I just don't know...'

There are few more potent examples of what Heiner Mueller talks of in his letter to Mühlheim than this type of case and its concern with both sides of the problem and with the image of the state as a whole in which such problems are on the increase confirms the trend towards more private and personal concerns in German drama. At the same time, the fact that Reinhard's generation can feel no guilt about the Third Reich (other than by association) means that it is possible for her to write a concentrated statement about the present without having to reach back into the past. It is a most encouraging sign, despite the nature of the subject matter of the play.

Friederike Roth

Like Maria Reinhard, Friederike Roth belongs to the new generation of German writers to whom the past is not a personal encumbrance. Her work is orientated towards problems of self-hood and identity, but she has a strong sense of the potential of language for image-generation, and her deliberate use of unorthodox semantic and linguistic patterning— derived perhaps from her days as a linguistic student—give her work a strikingly edgy quality. Marion Fiedler assessed Roth's work in 1978, before she wrote *Klavierspiele (piano-play):*

Her list of published works is still small, but what we already have from this author is definitely outside the norm of contemporary writing. Superficial social criticisms are just as hard to find in her work as autobiographically influenced variations on the usual clichés about sex-roles. Roth denies her readers, and herself, simplistic answers, wallowings in emotion, any sense of 'destinies'. She is not concerned with Identification (between the reader and the author, or her characters), but rather, on a different level, with Identity. This consciously strange aspect is most obviously seen in the short stories, *Ordnungsträume, (Dreams of Order)*. Perhaps one should add, she is really concerned with identities in the plural; for the identities of real people, like the schoolteacher Pfaff and Fräulein Schulze, who is always rejecting his propsals, are treated in the same way as those of things or thoughts, such as the idealised love between those two characters, or the tortoise which Pfaff keeps in his bath and which evokes in him dreams of a possible order in the chaos of thought. Roth insists that identities cannot be captured once and for all, and certainly not through verbose descriptions of their external appearances, but rather through examining their contradictions: a philosophical or a poetic principle?

It is surely both, for it is about exploring all possibilities, about an illuminating probing of connections and relations which can sometimes be traced as a continuous arc spanning early to middle age. 'Ausdenkbar also fast alles' (So almost everything is conceivable)—this sentence from the text may be applied in general to Roth as it describes the fundamental basis of her writing.

Whether it is the poems, which occasionally read like the recitation of ancient spells, or the prose-work, Roth rejects instant categorising. Poetry is having fun with thoughts, playing with them, leading to no definitive closed system of interpretation; there is at the same time an associative logic made up of perceptions and quotations, which can suddenly display a great liveliness, produce a life of their own (in *Ordnungsträume,* for example they are organised by a poetical-logical annotation apparatus of asterisks and ciphers) all newly thought out by this philosophical observer who can meaningfully combine extracts from Brehms' *Zoology* with quotations from Hegel, and in doing so does not forget to watch the people around her, how they 'ihre Wohnzimmergeheimnisse vergolden' (gild their living-room secrets). For 'wer am Tug mit nichts als dem Leben davonkommt/zeichnet zur Nachtzeit sich aus' (whoever manages to get through the day alive, may feel by nightfall they have really achieved something).

In her dialect plays for radio, we may also see Roth the realist who painstakingly investigates the pressures of everyday petit-bourgeois life: the fetishes of work, cleanliness and order, for example, peculiar to Swabia, where she comes from herself. . .

Friederike Roth considers she was lucky in her education, lucky because her father let her study what she wanted and did not demand to know its usefulness for a career. She wanted to study philosophy and linguistics and she did—two penniless arts by the standards of bourgeois rationale. A tentative speculation: independence of thought, has, as a basis for literary indepdenence, something to do with the possibility of leading an independent life, financially and personally. This basic condition is seldom found in the position of women, because it is still not provided for in our society's socialisation of the female's role.

Writers like Roth symbolize the hope that women's literature in the 80's will not remain stuck to the feminist wailing-wall. The women's movement has certainly given many women the courage to write, but much of what comes out of it never goes beyond the portrayal of their own individual desolate position as women in a patriarchal society. With Friederike Roth it is clear that she will contribute greatly to overcoming such 'female speechlessness'.

The assessment is a good one, if a shade optimistic: for the problems Roth has faced with *Piano-play* are considerable, the Hamburg premiere being dogged by tensions and disagreements which resulted in the first director leaving the show, a second being drafted in and a production that was a travesty of the text. Roth, like Mueller and Schuetz, sees poetry as a weapon in a struggle:

I think that it is literature, and especially poetry, that should make a stand against the all-too-smooth, the all-too-easily digestible and comprehensible in the production-consumption cycle. Of course poems should be read, but I don't write with any concern for marketability.

Roth is not agressively provocative, but the subjects she touches inevitably arouse strong feelings, as did *Piano-play:*

The play, apart from having its own 'action' is also about the differences of reality and unreality, a play in which uncertainty in a world of feeling takes precedence over a smooth clear-cut understanding, full of compromises. But it is also a play about a woman who has long-since given up finding emancipation through working, because she finds anything but self-realization in her everyday career—a problem which is very widespread. A job organised under the present system of production-relations can only in the rarest cases offer any possibility of self-realisation.

Men think that by giving women jobs they give them emancipation. This is not so; if fact, the very act of giving brings with it its new form of enslavement. What women need is, paradoxically not to feel emancipated for as long as emancipation is conscious rather than unconscious as a state of mind it is flawed, restrictive.

Roth was justifiably disappointed at the way the play was done in Hamburg, but as a challenging and original writer she will have to live with the fact that it will take audiences, let alone actors, a while to catch up with her. Elisabeth Henrichs, in a sensitive interview, asked Roth about her feelings on the Hamburg debacle and about her attitudes to art. Roth has a remarkable memory: 'I can still remember years later almost word for word what someone said; but I have no memory for visual detail.' She began writing as a student, as an extension in a way of studying. Then the desire to be 'synthetic' not 'analytic' took over. From a phase of concrete poetry she learned 'precision' and one of the hallmarks of her language is its spareness and economy.

One of the themes of *Piano-play* is getting old: 'I realized that there were two types of being old; particularly for women: the resigned old-age and the fighting old-age. Surprisingly enough I have known more fighting old women that fighting old men.'

What interests Roth about this, as about the whole of the 'action' of her play is not its exceptional, exotic nature as 'theatre' but its commonplace nature as 'reality', a concern much like Laube's and Reinhard's. Roth must, however, be aware that the mere act of theatrical representation renders to some extent exotic what may in reality be

26

thoroughly mundane. But she is right to protest at the excesses of director's and dramaturg's theatre—a German vice—and right, too, to see in this another of those paradoxes that the world of the theatre is in fact among the most conservative of all.

Stefan Schuetz

Peter Hacks and Heiner Mueller are now well-established: Stefan Schuetz, born in 1944, is rapidly becoming so and Mueller holds him in high regard. In the programme to the première of Schuetz's play *Weder der Teufel los, noch stille (Neither One Hell of a Row, nor Silence)* at the Hans-Otto-Theater, Potsdam, 1975 Mueller wrote:

The first piece I read by him was a dramatic satire, which came out of something rather private, a slight, which he felt too deeply not to write a satire—the result, a literary bomb dropped on a theatre. The disproportionate nature of the reaction, as it seemed from a bourgois point of view, distinguishes him as a playwright. Kleist is the German model for that.

Since then Stefan Schütz has written half a dozen plays. His gifts occasionally make him go beyond what is at present possible in the theatre. That means: his plays should be played, because they extend the domain of the possible. The first reason why a society that is building Socialism, allows itself the luxury of drama, is the possibility of such an extension. Theatre, as a utopia, remains alive only so long as it constantly renews itself. Repertory theatre is a self-contradiction, with which we still must live. What strikes one first of all in Schütz's texts, is the theatrical nature, in the best sense of the word, of his imagination. He is too much of an actor and too strongly marked by life in East Germany to write for his desk drawer. Every new play is a new greedy snatch at living theatre. The quality of the often intoxicatingly beautiful language lies in the fact that he does not colour out printed pictures but draws dynamic curves, which suggest new aspects to the reality of his characters and to what happens on stage. The basic form of the movement is the spiral and not the circle. That is rooted in history, with a creative attitude to history. When he collides with something, the reason is, that he wants to get up and out. A society which is orientated towards production instead of the wear and tear of productivity, does not find it easy to deal with drama, which whether comic or tragic, lives on sharp contradictions. In the particular way that Stefan Schutz deals with the contradictions of our age—contradictions which he experiences painfully and deeply—the need becomes increasingly apparent for a balance of forces, for a state of the world that no longer needs drama, except as a free play of forces. Hans Henny Jahnn has prefaced one of his late plays with the sentence: *Love has gradually become our property.* Here and now the accent is on gradually and not on property.

Schuetz's eruptive language, his taut and aggressive poetry are his dominant characteristic. This comes across as much in the way he describes what it is like to write as in the writing itself. Typical is the statement in 1978 of what the difficulties were in writing a play:

1

Our time is a rag of blood and phrases. The gulf between art and society is an abyss. Every word, every sentence, every figure of speech, every action on the stage, is consumed like drying one's hands. The wretched nature of fashion and conservatism are the ingrained scourges, which deal our world of illusion those sweet festering lash wounds, which lie somewhere between contentment and vomiting. But I ask, what use is that to the victims: the South American Indian, those who starve in India, the blacks in the USA, the women of the world? To write in these parts of the world only makes sense, if one tears habitual practices, conformism, out of one's own head if one hurls body and brain against the social order, so as to remind the few who still have an ear for words, and also the many who have been drilled to be deaf, of the need to question things.

The form of the impulse may vary from case to case, and one must always overcome oneself, but the logic of the struggle in art knows no compromises. To the uttermost, for only then does a spark of interest arise in the public, and even when it rejects one must be ready to break one's own chains.

For art is always an opposition to what is. It must be either destructive for oneself and society, or else productive for both (revolution). Only time brings to light the character of art. What is needed in any country, is the fight against intellectual mediocrity, the subjection of minds, which subject themselves and whose reality is a world of illusion, born of economic compulsion and the misery of history. The daydream has become a nightmare.

2

Everyword that one writes down, freezes in the same moment. The ego-machine presses on with the slaughter of words out of hope and, ruthlessly, out of conviction and doubt and believes in resurrection and knowledge of the anatomy of life, whose sounds one uses unspeakably.

What is frozen can be copied. On the humpback squats the art of time and the past, and sweetish blood spurts out of this monster which demands, threatens and whips you into copying him in spurting out dramatic writing and speech, form and content. Using what has been, relying on what has been digested: fear and pleasure have already found their perfect masks and words. Consumption of means. Addiction to laurels. And insight into the aesthetics of past art. Powerlessness kills. For the machine is the result of the experience of other machines and the process can no longer be reversed. Only that which one quickly forgets, hunger and the whipped, possess uncontrolled gestures and words. The degree of ordinariness is measureless. The fire in this world makes every sentence I write a farce. Consumption of art as storage systems.
The only hope that matters is that liberations take place which destroy the satiated machines and there are once more human beings permitted to exist, whose machine reflexes are now just perceptions which one once had to endure. The painlessness of habits. One must not trust one's eyes and ears anymore. The cement streets and the houses have faces. The machines can still weep, they cannot laugh anymore.
A play, made out of a single scream, that would be honest.

The dangers of this sort of position are self-evident. Schuetz tends to find it hard to vary the intensity of his work and constant density of image can be tiring to listen to. Yet there is no doubting the linguistic power he controls nor the remarkable energy of his structures. Christoph Müller found summarising his works somewhat difficult:

The feeling of pain at the mistaken course of the history of mankind, particularly at points of dissolution in the (class) struggle, shows itself clearly in pre-Christian, greek, roman, medieval, reformation, revolutionary, and modern subject matter. His heroes are Antiope, Theseus, Odysseus, Seneca, Ablard, Heloise, Shakespeare's Richard III, Kleist's Michael Kohlhaas, saw-mill workers in the Soviet Union during the construction of Socialism, revolutionary artists and blustering, long-haired youths—but the peep-hole of freedom which they seek their author never lets them see, they are all disappointed idealists who come to a sticky end.

It is the range that strikes one and the emphasis on those periods in history when radical change is called for but frustrated. And the conclusion is inescapable that Schuetz sees in these past phases of suppressed tension a model for the state of the world now. His very sense of creativity as like volcanic eruptions shows how creativity is a form of release, both for him personally and for societies in general— artists are therefore seen as vents to social tension. The artist must provoke reaction for the very reason that his task is to let off society's steam. The theory is curiously Aristotelian, redolent of catharsis.

Plays: *Gloster* (1970) based on Shakespeare's *Richard III*
       Mayakovsky (1971) performed at the New Half Moon, London 1980
       Seneca (1971)
       Odysseus Heimkehr (1972) *(The Return of Odysseus)*
       Fabrik im Walde (1973) *(The Factory in the Wood)*
       Die Amazonen (1974) *(The Amazons)*
       Heloisa und Abaelard (1975)
       Kohlhaas (1975) based on the novelle by Heinrich von Kleist
       Der Hahn (1977) *(The Cock)*
       Stasch (1977)
       Sappa (1980)
       Die Schweine (1980)

Peter Turrini

Peter Turrini is of mixed Austrian and Italian ancestry, perhaps one reason why his feel for the German language is different from most other German-language writers. He came to writing after training in business so it is not surprising to find consumerism as one of his concerns, as in *Josef and Maria* which is set in a department store. But Turrini is also concerned with waste, not just the litter of the consumer society—though he sets *Rozznjogd (Rat Hunt)* on a litter-dump—but the way in which society wastes its own most precious resource, people and their memories. He comments:

The belongings of people who have died are often left out on our city streets. These remnants of life's possessions are taken off, put into storage, mixed up with others' possessions and all individual identity is lost. The memories and feelings of these people manifested in school reports, letters from army days, documents and papers, gradually turn from day to day into wastepaper, into rubbish. I have felt for some time now that when I come across such things I want to know more about the lives of these people or indeed to imagine these lives, to try and rescue them from total oblivion. It is not a case of wanting to write a play 'about' people. I want to absorb, to take on their story, their past, their memories. It is my task as a playwright to disentangle and systematize these stories and to bring the old people into a dramatic situation.

Just such a situation is *Josef and Maria,* a montage of memory and present feelings of rejection. Turrini, like Dario Fo, is committed to reaching with his plays the 90% of the population that never goes inside a theatre:

I have to divide my work into official and unofficial activity. Apart from writing poems, plays, films a large part of my work consists of giving readings, having contact with youth groups and alternative circles—to be continually in touch with what one might call 'the second culture'. It is a very important and very creative part of my work because I am learning from people. I am of course preventing myself from being more productive in the literary sense.

His reply, given in an interview to the *Arbeiterzeitung* (Workers' Paper) explains why *Josef und Maria* was his first play for seven years. The reasons he came back to theatre after such a gap are slightly different:

These are things you do for emotional reasons, from desire, and I'm someone who has an unrestrainedly passionate relationship with the theatre. That's how *Josef und Maria*—came about. Second reason: film gives an author only a limited freedom—you write the text—the director comes along with a very strong visual interpretation; then the cameraman's on top of that. In the theatre people are more cautious.

Turrini's political commitment to the left is strong, but he has also written admiringly about Bruno Kreisky, Austrian Chancellor: 'he has impressed me as a man who seems to be one of the last people to feel a real passion for politics. He can unify talking and thinking, he can improvise, he lives with passion. Quite simply he impresses me.' This admiration has caused a good deal of controversy, Turrini being accused of moving from his previously much harder line stance. Like Kroetz he is distancing himself from his former political affiliations, but again like Kroetz, his actual pattern of beliefs has not shifted. Two concerns stand out:

If I'm going to criticise the Social Democrats then I must first distance myself from the Right. My criticism is the disappointment of a friend who can no longer bear the path his friend has chosen.
  It's extraordinary that so much militant and critical potential in the party leads to so little courage. The Social Democrats like any other party are not homogenous. Working in a section, as I do, one sees a great deal of critical and militant potential amongst the old and the young. And it's all covered over with a red cloth, suffocated.
  The second point of my critique is more dramatic. It is a terrible mistake to

always present the contradictions between economies and ecology as irresolvable:
a little pollution a little growth. I would much rather we owned up to our
helplessness in the face of this situation and openly discussed changes. As soon
as we admit these are things we can't just leave to the politicians: the sooner
we have broader, more comprehensive, more democratic debate and struggle,
the sooner we'll find solutions.

It's just the same on the question of inequality. You can't cover up the fact
that a few people in a social democratic country are earning disproportionately
too much and others disproportionately too little, because one day the cake to
be cut up is going to get too small.

Whether or not 1980/81 signals the end of an artistic era in general, there
is no doubt the date marks a turning point for Turrini. Writing on
Turrini, Elfriede Jelinek suggests certain types of imagery to express
his energy and his rage against the semi-detached bourgeoisie:

Sometimes in this land of ours the ground trembles from the tread of strange
monserts, who crawl out of the earth, drag themselves slowly onto the surface and
only then loose a great jet of flame from their nostrils. Then they heave themselves
off with an energetic purposeful stride, crushing a few semi-detached houses, front
gardens with neat rose-beds, upholstered fittings and fireside chairs. This damage
rarely satisfies them and they set to work by telephone. They wait by it and if
anyone requests their intervention in a co-operative youth club, in the case of
anti-fascists sentenced after a battle with Young Nazis, or in any attempted
suppression of freedom of expression, then they will do so immediately. Such
a creature is Peter Turrini. He is normally the first to be called on.

Yet Turrini is not quite an Austrian version of Stefan Schuetz,
for Turrini has learned more about varying the pace and intensity
of his work, more too about economic lyricism. Not that this lyricism
is not directed at the same targets as the plays:

In his best poems Turrini gives voice to what suffocates and constricts us. Already
almost discouraged, but with concentrated energy, he throws himself against
the hoarding which says 'Bill Posters will Be Prosecuted', against it again and
again and against those others where smart men walk miles for cigarettes and
exquisitely beautiful women drink mineral water endlessly and look so
insubstantial; he throws himself against them in order to finally rip them down,
because behind them his destroyed childhood and his mother are waiting for
him and he wants to experience them again but this time much more beautifully!

I fear that there is nothing behind them but another debris-strewn building
site.

The Works
Television Films:
Die Alpensaga (The Alpine Saga) 1974-79 written with Wilhelm Pevny.
Six part television series. ORG-ZDF-SRG
Der Bauer und der Millionär (The Peasant and the Millionaire) 1975,
with Wilhelm Pevny. ORF-ZDF
Josef und Maria 1980 ORF.
Published works:
Erlbnisse in der Mundhöhle (Experiences in the Oral Cavity) Novel 1972
(pub. Rohwolt)

Rozznjogd (Rat Hunt)	Three plays, published
Sauschlachten (Sowslaughtering)	1973,
Der Tollste Tag (The Most Fantastic Day)	Edition Lenz.

Der Dorfschullehrer (The Village Schoolmaster) 1975, with Wilhelm
Pevny, Edition Roetzer.
Die Wirtin (The Landlady) 1978 Edition of Plays, Souffleurkastenreihe.
Turrini Lesebuch (A Turrini Reader) 1978 Omnibus Volume Europa
Verlag.
Die Alpensaga (The Alpine Saga) 1980 Filmscript Residenz-Verlag.
Josef und Maria 1980 Frischfleisch und Löwenmaul Verlag.
Ein paar Schritten zurück (A Few Steps Backwards) 1980 Poems.
Autoren Edition.

There is much to suggest that the early 1980s, like the early 1830s,
represent a turning point or even an end in a period of German-language
culture. In the West the move to the right, the end of the economic
miracle years and the problems of unemployment and racial tension
make the socio-political climate less temperate by far than it was in the
70s. At the same time, events in Poland and the cold propaganda war
between Washington and Moscow make generosity about each other's
attitudes harder to sustain. In *Das Treffen in Telgte (Meeting in Telgte)*
1979, Günter Grass, sensing this change in progress, implies that once
again it is only the artists who can carry the burden of German unity,
now that disunity is as good as formally recognised. If this is to be so,
the authors whose views we have surveyed will be among those responsible for the unity.

Julian Hilton